Temagami's Tangled Wild

The Nature | History | Society series is devoted to the publication of high-quality scholarship in environmental history and allied fields. Its broad compass is signalled by its title: *nature* because it takes the natural world seriously; *history* because it aims to foster work that has temporal depth; and *society* because its essential concern is with the interface between nature and society, broadly conceived. The series is avowedly interdisciplinary and is open to the work of anthropologists, ecologists, historians, geographers, literary scholars, political scientists, sociologists, and others whose interests resonate with its mandate. It offers a timely outlet for lively, innovative, and well-written work on the interaction of people and nature through time in North America.

General Editor: Graeme Wynn, University of British Columbia

NATURE | HISTORY | SOCIETY

Temagami's Tangled Wild

Race, Gender, and the Making of Canadian Nature

JOCELYN THORPE

FOREWORD BY GRAEME WYNN

UBC Press • Vancouver • Toronto

21 20 19 18 17 16 15 14 13 12   5 4 3 2 1

Printed in Canada on FSC-certified ancient-forest-free paper
(100 percent post-consumer recycled) that is processed chlorine- and acid-free.

Library and Archives Canada Cataloguing in Publication

Thorpe, Jocelyn
Temagami's tangled wild : race, gender, and the making of Canadian nature /
Jocelyn Thorpe.

(Nature, history, society, ISSN 1713-6687)
Includes bibliographical references and index.
Issued also in electronic format.
ISBN 978-0-7748-2200-8

1. Temagami, Lake, Region (Ont.) – Race relations – History. 2. Nature – Social aspects – Ontario – Temagami, Lake, Region. 3. Land use – Ontario – Temagami, Lake, Region – History. 4. Temagami First Nation – History. 5. Social ecology. I. Title. II. Series: Nature, history, society

HD319.O5T56 2012   333.309713'147   C2011-906188-0

Canadä

UBC Press gratefully acknowledges the financial support for our publishing program of the Government of Canada (through the Canada Book Fund), the Canada Council for the Arts, and the British Columbia Arts Council.

This book has been published with the help of a grant from the Canadian Federation for the Humanities and Social Sciences, through the Aid to Scholarly Publications Program, using funds provided by the Social Sciences and Humanities Research Council of Canada, and with the help of the K.D. Srivastava Fund.

UBC Press
The University of British Columbia
2029 West Mall
Vancouver, BC V6T 1Z2
www.ubcpress.ca

Contents

Illustrations

Nature and Nation in a "Little Known District amid the Wilds of Canada"

BY GRAEME WYNN

Some thirty years ago, after reflecting critically and historically on such concepts as culture, society, individual, and class, the novelist, critic, and cultural studies scholar Raymond Williams famously suggested that "nature" might be the most complex word in the English language.[1] Despite the nominal continuity of its use through many centuries, the term is richly freighted with intricate and quite diverse meanings. Does "nature" refer to the "essential constitution of the world" or to the inherent and immutable laws that govern (or describe) its physical processes? Is it "red in tooth and claw" or an "extraordinary interlocking system of mutual advantage"? Do references to "nature" include or exclude people? What of the common idea that "nature" betokens the "essence," the "ultimate, irreducible character or quality of something," as in the "nature of things," the "nature of existence," or in the way that we explain human characteristics or athletic gifts as "natural"? Little wonder that the American cultural historian Leo Marx concluded, toward the end of a career devoted to studying such matters, that "the word nature is a notorious semantic and metaphysical trap."[2] The lean and "proper" definitions found in dictionaries provide neither escape nor intellectual comfort for those alert to these contradictions and fascinated, as Williams was, by the ways in which the shifting and contrasting connotations of certain words expressed "radically different and often at first unnoticed changes in experience and history."[3]

Much ink has been spent, since Williams wrote, pondering the nature of Nature (so to speak). Indeed, the Australian environmental historian George Seddon used this very phrase in 1991 as the title of a lively essay devoted to understanding how various meanings have been ascribed to nature. After exploring some of the antonyms to "Nature" and "natural" – including Supernatural, unnatural, human, and artificial – Seddon concluded that the contrasts between human and "not-man" and natural and unnatural underwrote "most current discourse using the word 'Nature'" and that the use of "unnatural" often carries "specifically moral overtones." To illustrate the latter claim, he recalled the once common assertion that "sodomy is an unnatural practice" to remind his readers that although "not many people use that expression today [this] does not mean that the concept of the 'unnatural' has disappeared, but rather that its range of application has changed. Some will now say, for example, that celibacy is unnatural, or that it is not natural for a young girl to lock herself away in her room reading books all day, or whatever." The larger point, of course, is that the societal consensus about what is natural and unnatural changes through time and that "our concept of Nature is a cultural product."[4]

Postmodern and post-structuralist scholarship has made similar claims, more formally and more strongly, in describing nature as a social construction or insisting, more tendentiously, that it is solely a product of discourse. As the geographer David Demeritt noted a decade or so ago, much writing in this vein "has challenged the apparent self-evidence and ontological fixity of nature," to the point of insisting that unmediated knowledge of the material world is impossible.[5] These are complicated matters. Following the philosopher Ian Hacking, Demeritt has usefully sought to categorize and clarify the various forms of constructionism by distinguishing between two broad types – social construction-as-refutation (which usually evinces strong political commitments) and the "more metaphysically inclined" sense of social construction-as-philosophical-critique. The latter is further subdivided, according to the primary intellectual wellsprings from which differing approaches derive, into phenomenological and discursive constructionisms, approaches associated with the reflexive stance of those interested in the sociology of scientific knowledge, and ideas of embodied practice as reflected, for example, in actor-network theory. The intricacies of these distinctions are of little concern here, except to note, as Demeritt does, that "construction-as-refutation" generally maintains the "conventional distinctions between culture/nature, subject/object, and representation/reality" upon which divisions between true and false conceptions of nature rest, whereas "construction-as-philosophical-critique" generally challenges these dualisms. Beyond this, all these approaches share a commitment to the notion that things are not what they are generally taken to be and insist that "what we had once accepted as self-evidently pre-ordained and inevitable is in fact contingent and might conceivably be remade in some other way, if only we would try."[6]

Similar impulses have affected the ways in which scholars have come, in recent years, to think about many things, from race, gender, and class through wilderness to the nation. These and more have come, increasingly, to be understood as made rather than given, as ultimately malleable products of history and relationships, rather than as preordained immutable entities. Contingency and power, it is now widely acknowledged, shape knowledge claims and the ways in which the world and its constituent parts are comprehended. In the end, of course, it may be true, as Ian Hacking has pointed out, that all constructionist arguments "dwell in the dichotomy between appearance and reality set up by Plato, and given a definitive form by Kant."[7] And it may thus appear that contemporary discussions are prefigured to some degree in earlier works. Indeed, Hacking has gone so far as to suggest that although "social constructionists bask in the sun they call postmodernism, they are really very old-fashioned."[8] But scholarly agendas, emphases, and purposes shift, for they, too, are constructed, and it is unwise to draw too direct a line between past and present, or to posit continuities where there may be ruptures.

Consider by way of example the shifting reception of E.P. Thompson's 1963 book *The Making of the English Working Class*.[9] Emphasizing agency in its title, this landmark work offered an intricate, robustly empirical account of "out-workers, artisans, and factory workers" constructing, in ways that were clearly historically and geographically contingent, "a consciousness of their own interests as opposed to the interests of those who sought to dominate them."[10] It argued that class was not a structure or a category but something that "happens (and can be shown to have happened) in human relationships." In this view, the English working class was forged through a complex dialectical relationship between experience and consciousness; it was created by men and women living in particular circumstances, coping with a certain "ensemble of social relations" and interpreting (and acting within) their specific situations on the basis of their inherited culture and expectations. It was the result of "an active process, which owes as much to agency as to conditioning."[11]

Hailed as a tour de force of historical scholarship and serving as an inspiration to a long generation of social historians, the book spawned considerable debate in the 1960s and 1970s for its rejection of the base-superstructure model of Marxist thinking, which Thompson described elsewhere as reducing "human consciousness to a form of erratic, involuntary response to steel-mills and brickyards, which are in a spontaneous process of looming and becoming."[12] A quarter century or so after its publication, however, the fundamental arguments of *The Making* were found wanting for other reasons. Although Thompson's central claim – that culture was as important as economic activity in shaping people's lives – may have contributed to the rise of discourse theory, Gareth Stedman Jones and Joan Wallach Scott drew inspiration from "the linguistic turn" and post-structuralist theory to offer sharp critiques of Thompson's work. Elevating discourse above agency and experience, they made "cultural dynamics" the driving force of class formation. For Jones, it was the radical discourse of Chartism, derived from Thomas Paine and the idea of natural rights, not the harsh experience of economic exploitation and political oppression, that "determined the form taken by the democratic movement."[13] By Scott's account, both experience and agency are "actuated in discourse," and class is a discursive field with "multiple and contested meanings." In her view, Thompson marginalized the feminine by locating the roots of class formation "in labour exploitation and rationalist radical politics" and failing to treat class construction as contingent on shifting meanings of gender.[14]

All of this discussion of social constructionism, and of the ways in which scholars have sought to understand the lives of poor English "stockingers" and "'obsolete' hand-loom weavers," might seem to have carried us a long way from considerations of nature and nation, and even further from the wilds of Temagami, which are the declared subjects of the significant, provocative book that you hold in your hand.[15] Not so. With this work, Jocelyn Thorpe follows along the trail opened, in earlier part, by Gareth Stedman Jones and Joan Wallach Scott, turning to discourse analysis and asking us to rethink the ways in which we interpret the world by constructing such categories as wilderness, race, gender, class, nation, homeland, forest, park, and tourist attraction. Trained in English literature and equity studies, women's studies, and environmental studies, Thorpe brings the perspectives of post-colonial theory and social nature scholarship to her inquiry, and thus brings social constructionism to bear as both refutation and philosophical critique. She employs Michel Foucault's genealogical method to shape *Temagami's Tangled Wild* as "a history of the present" intended to question contemporary convictions about this place and to demonstrate how knowledge and power have joined to yield particular, and by no means unimpeachable or self-evident, ideas ("subjects and truths") about the territory and those associated with it. At the same time, she challenges "the fiction of a culture-free nature" to insist that "nature and society are everywhere implicated in one another" (14, 13).

With this book, then, Thorpe aims, as she writes on page 5 of her Introduction, to have us "examine again the ground we thought we knew" – and that ground ranges from the storied indigenous territory of n'Daki Menan, through the region later known as Temagami, Ontario, to the larger invention we call Canada.

These commitments differentiate Thorpe's work from most other writing about Temagami, of which there has been a significant amount because the area has long been valued – in different ways by different groups who have often disagreed over how it might be used. From Thorpe's perspective, even the most thorough of attempts to see the contested past of Temagami as a series of struggles between competing interests fails to account for the making of this place as "a site of Canadian nature" and falls short of explaining the asymmetries of power that made the region available to some people and denied it to others. In her view, such approaches are not only wanting, they are dangerous because they tend to reinforce the status quo. Continuing to address contemporary and enduring conflicts in Temagami through compromise, by balancing the competing claims of diverse interests, "risks reproducing colonial and nationalist relationships of power and inequality" (29).

Thorpe is not the first, on the larger canvas of Canadian scholarship, to develop such a perspective. She acknowledges the methodological and substantive parallels between Bruce Braun's account of the historical and contemporary processes that produced the British Columbia rainforest as a site of nature and her own interpretation of Temagami, noting that environmental activists not only drew attention to destructive logging practices in both places but that these protests "also helped to mask contemporary Aboriginal claims to land, thus making the forest appear unproblematically a part of the Canadian wilderness" (16-17). There are echoes, too, in this account of Temagami, of Braun and Joel Wainwright's discussion of the BC rainforest as a discursive construction, which concludes that "struggles over nature, land, and meaning are simultaneously struggles over identity and rights" – of indigenous peoples, the state, corporate interests, forestry workers, and others.[16] For all that, Thorpe moves analysis of these matters in new directions as she examines persistent portrayals of the Temagami region as both a wild territory and a space encompassing iconic Canadian characteristics to expose "the processes of colonization upon which a racialized and gendered Canadian nation rests" (24).

Through the successive chapters of this book, it is clear that Thorpe has a message to convey and an important purpose to her argument. By recounting how the indigenous homeland of n'Daki Menan was reconfigured

as a forest reserve and part of the Canadian wilderness, through the imposition of powerful colonial (and, to those with power, seemingly obvious)
ways of thinking about, describing, and organizing the world, she hopes
to better equip readers of this short but impassioned book to "tackle the
complex questions and demands that result from the history of colonialism, exclusionary nationalism, and environmental exploitation." More
than this, she would aspire to bring non-Aboriginal Canadians to "support
rather than impede or remain silent about Aboriginal struggles for self-
determination" (129).

Because these aims are not universally embraced, and because the ideas
of several of the scholars from whom Thorpe draws theoretical insight
remain relatively unfamiliar to many, some may carp at the way in which
she explicates the arguments underpinning her advocacy. There are precedents to hand. As ideas about the construction of nature have come to
prominence, critics have noted a certain ambiguity in much writing about
the hybridity of nature and culture; some discussions of socio-nature, for
example, couple strong idealist claims that things can be known only
through words and concepts with assertions of the materiality of the world.
Others have suggested that those who are critical of the ways in which
people living in different circumstances framed their understandings of
the world might be a little more reflexive about the rhetoric and the contexts of their own accounts.[17]

There are shades, in such claims, of the criticisms leveled at Gareth
Stedman Jones and Joan Wallach Scott for their unsympathetic assessments
of *The Making of the English Working Class,* which drew fire for constructing,
as Marc Steinberg had it, "a neostructuralism of discourse in which language is invested with imperial ascendancy, and actors have diminished
agency," and for assuming that "experience has no reality outside of its
signification."[18] Reflecting upon these tendencies and the linguistic turn
in historical scholarship more generally, Marxist historian Bryan Palmer
argued that something important was "lost in the assimilation of agency
and structure, culture and materiality," and that Thompson's claims had
been "all too easily incorporated into an emerging orthodoxy," in which
"the cultural became the material; the ideological became the real."[19]

But much has also been lost in the adversarial tone of intellectual debate
over these issues, and this is worth bearing in mind in thinking about
Temagami's Tangled Wild. Here it is important to recognize that although
Thorpe draws upon Foucault's theory of discourse in her analysis, she also
insists that "this book maps stories" (6). This is significant. Although the
formal term "discourse," as it has come to be understood in the humanities

and social sciences, bears some similarities with the everyday concept of "story," they are not equivalent and there is important interpretive space between them.

"Discourses" have been defined in various ways, but for followers of Foucault the term generally implies "systems of thoughts composed of ideas, attitudes, courses of action, beliefs and practices that systematically construct the subjects and the worlds of which they speak."[20] Although Foucault noted that discourse "contains the power to say something other than what it actually says, and thus to embrace a plurality of meanings," some insist that discourses set "the limits of acceptable speech" and define what can be said about a topic.[21] By more self-conscious definition, discourses are specific, heterogeneous, regulated, embedded, and situated "representations and practices through which meanings are produced, identities constituted, social relations established and political and ethical outcomes made more or less possible." To put this slightly differently, discourses "shape the contours of the taken-for-granted world, naturalizing and universalizing a particular subject formation and view of the world."[22]

Stories also help people to make sense of their world and of their places in it, and they have been shared in every culture as a means of entertainment, education, and cultural preservation, and in order to instill moral values. Typically, stories are accounts of events (actual or imagined) in words, images, and sounds; they include plot, characters, and narrative point of view, and their narration is often marked by improvisation or embellishment. Much has been written on the differences and relations between stories and discourse (in the formal sense outlined above), but one recurrent distinction, worth attention here, can be expressed quite simply: the story is what is told, but discourse shapes the way in which it is told.

Although Thorpe pays little explicit attention, in the pages that follow, to this difference between "what" and "how," to this distinction between mapping stories and identifying the systems of thought that constitute a prevailing discourse, her treatment of Temagami works between these poles to open space for further reflection upon the ways in which people make sense of their places in the world, and indeed their very being, even as it "demonstrates that wilderness and nations are made" and challenges us "to tackle the complex questions and demands that result from the history of colonialism, exclusionary nationalism, and environmental exploitation that brought us here in the first place" (129).

One way of thinking about these things actually returns us to Gareth Stedman Jones' discussion of English radicalism, in which he sees discourse less as a naturalizing, universalizing force than as a construct mediating between experience and consciousness. On this view, which is not incompatible with materialist theories of language and history, discourse does not so much construct the objects of our knowledge as it marks "the process through which actors create propositional or evaluative accounts of the relations between themselves, other actors and situations, and larger social processes."[23] In other words, discourses help people understand, or create meaning in, the world by tying "actors and contexts" together "historically and reciprocally." Forged in the course of everyday activities through social routines and engagements with the material world, they are shaped by networks and reflect people's collective efforts to make sense of their experiences. They may be ideological and hegemonic, but they are invariably "tied to particular social and institutional contexts," and each exists in severalty with others. Individuals exercise agency by adopting or adapting what they take to be the most intelligible, plausible, and comprehensible of these different discourses to structure their view of their situation.[24]

Another is suggested by J. Edward Chamberlin in his remarkable book *If This Is Your Land, Where Are Your Stories?* which offers a luminous reflection on the ways in which stories give meaning and value to the places we call home, and to much else in the world besides.[25] Taking his cue, and his title, from a question posed to government officials in British Columbia by a Gitksan elder, Chamberlin ranges widely to show how stories hold us together and keep us apart. Challenging questions lie at the very heart of these reflections – *"Where do we belong?"* and *"How should we live?"* foremost among them – and it is Chamberlin's singular accomplishment to show that even as people confront these existential mysteries, as almost all do, they readily settle for easy answers framed and passed on in "stories" of many diverse forms, "from creation stories to constitutions, from southern epics and northern sagas to native American tales and African praise songs, and from nursery rhymes and national anthems to myths and mathematics." For the most part, these stories draw from two basic forms – one describing "stages and sequences, causes and effects," the other telling "how things and events fulfil an overall purpose and design." But most "shuttle between" these archetypes, and – it is important to recognize – almost all of them bring "imagination and reality together in moments of what we might call faith" so that they are "ceremonies of belief as much as they are chronicles of events."[26]

On this view, Chamberlin's stories are rather akin to Jones' discourses, in that they articulate what groups and individuals take to be the most intelligible, plausible, and comprehensible account of their particular circumstances. But precisely because these accounts exist in severalty – because different groups invoke different stories to guide their actions and explain their place in the world – they work to produce multiple forms of *"Us"* (we who subscribe to this particular version) and *"Them"* (who don't). So, too, the varying constructions of, or stories about, Temagami to which Thorpe draws our attention in the pages that follow – the indigenous inhabitants' view of their homeland n'Daki Menan, the foresters' vision of the territory as a timber reserve, the recreationists' conception of it as an empty land of woods and water, the legal professions' assumption that truth is arbitrated rather than produced by law – worked to separate, divide, and entrench asymmetries of power and entitlement among groups and individuals.

Need it be ever thus? Stories of the sort we have been considering here – creation stories to constitutions and myths to mathematics – are powerful and enduring. Shaped by history, embedded in tradition, compelling to those who believe in them, and dear to hearts and minds, they are neither easily forgotten nor readily cast aside. Yet surely, one hopes, the answer is no – although the future is unlikely to turn out that way unless we learn to see things anew and act accordingly. Injustices produced by time and chance, by "colonialism, exclusionary nationalism, and environmental exploitation," or by other circumstances, will not be resolved by continuing insistence on the particular virtue or unassailable "rightness" of any single discourse or foundational story (129). Distinctions between "Them" and "Us" are inevitable, inescapable corollaries of our ways of being in the world. Moving forward requires a commitment to tolerance and understanding, a capacity to see things from multiple perspectives and a willingness to embrace and respond to the consequences of difference. This will require serious, careful, and thoughtful attention to the stories of others and the ability to marvel at what is new and strange. To develop inclusive, mutually respectful, and more equitable communities, we need, Ted Chamberlin and Jocelyn Thorpe insist, to avoid the monocular vision that ultimately translates religion into dogma, myth into ideology, and community into conflict, and to find the common ground of wonder that lies at the heart of all our stories.

Notes

1 The most complex word claim appears in Raymond Williams' *Keywords* (London: Collins, 1976), but the larger discussion of these matters, on which much of this paragraph rests, is Raymond Williams, "Ideas of Nature," in Raymond Williams, *Problems in Materialism and Culture: Selected Essays* (London: Verso, 1980), 67-85.

2 Leo Marx, "The Idea of Nature in America," *Daedalus* 137,2 (Spring 2008): 9.

3 Williams, "Ideas of Nature," 68.

4 George Seddon, "The Nature of Nature," *Westerly* 4 (1991): 7-14, republished as "The Nature of Nature," in George Seddon, *Landprints: Reflections on Place and Landscape* (Cambridge: Cambridge University Press, 1997), 9.

5 David Demeritt, "What Is the 'Social Construction of Nature'? A Typology and Sympathetic Critique," *Progress in Human Geography* 26,6 (2002): 768. See also Noel Castree and Bruce Braun, "The Construction of Nature and the Nature of Construction: Analytical and Political Tools for Building Survivable Futures," in *Remaking Reality: Nature at the Millennium,* ed. Bruce Braun and Noel Castree (New York: Routledge, 1998), 3-42; Noel Castree and Bruce Braun, eds., *Social Nature: Theory, Practice and Politics* (Oxford: Blackwell, 2001); D. Demeritt, "The Construction of Global Warming and the Politics of Science," *Annals of the Association of American Geographers* 91 (2001): 307-37; D. Demeritt, "The Statistical Enframing of Nature's Limits: Forest Conservation in the Progressive Era United States," *Environment and Planning D: Society and Space* 19 (2001): 431-59; and J.D. Proctor, "The Social Construction of Nature: Relativist Accusations, Pragmatist and Critical Realist Responses," *Annals of the Association of American Geographers* 88 (1998): 352-76. In the conclusion of "What Is the 'Social Construction of Nature'?" 786, Demeritt notes that "the 'social construction of nature' is used in so many ways that it is not always clear what is meant by the term. Some use it in a nominalist vein to denaturalize 'nature' as always conceptually and discursively mediated, others in a more literal, ontologically idealist way to suggest that natural phenomena are literally built by people, while yet others use the construction metaphor to explore the ways that the matter of nature is realized discursively or through networks of practical engagements with heterogeneous other beings."

6 Ibid., 776; and Ian Hacking, *The Social Construction of What?* (Cambridge, MA: Harvard University Press, 1999).

7 Hacking, *Social Construction of What?* 49.

8 Ibid.

9 E.P. Thompson, *The Making of the English Working Class* (New York: Victor Gollancz, 1963).

10 Marc W. Steinberg, "The Re-Making of the English Working Class?" *Theory and Society* 20,2 (April 1991): 174.

11 Thompson, *The Making,* 9; the phrase "ensemble of social relations" is widely attributed to Karl Marx in his *Theses on Feuerbach* (6th Thesis); see *Marx/Engels Internet Archive,* available at: http://www.marxists.org/archive/marx/works/1845/theses/theses.htm (accessed 9 November 2011).

12 E.P. Thompson, "Socialist Humanism: An Epistle to the Philistines," *The New Reasoner: A Quarterly Journal of Socialist Humanism* 1 (Summer 1957): 113-14.

13 Gareth Stedman Jones, *Languages of Class: Studies in English Working Class History, 1832-1982* (Cambridge: Cambridge University Press, 1983), 126.

14 Joan Wallach Scott, "Women in *The Making of the English Working Class*," in Joan Wallach Scott, *Gender and the Politics of History* (New York: Columbia University Press, 1988), 68-90; and discussed in Steinberg, "The Re-Making," 179-80.

15 "Stockingers" and hand-loom weavers from Thompson, *The Making*, 12.

16 Bruce Braun, *The Intemperate Rainforest: Nature, Culture, and Power on Canada's West Coast* (Minneapolis: University of Minnesota Press, 2002); Bruce Braun and Joel Wainwright, "Nature, Poststructuralism, and Politics," in Castree and Braun, *Social Nature*, 59.

17 See, for example, Demeritt, "What Is the 'Social Construction of Nature'?" 785.

18 Steinberg, "The Re-Making," 182-83.

19 Bryan D. Palmer, *Descent into Discourse: The Reification of Language and the Writing of Social History* (Philadelphia: Temple University Press, 1990), 210. See also B.D. Palmer, *The Making of E.P. Thompson: Marxism, Humanism and History* (Toronto: New Hogtown Press, 1981).

20 As defined, for example, in Iara Lessa, "Discursive Struggles within Social Welfare: Restaging Teen Motherhood," *British Journal of Social Work* 36,2 (2006): 283-98, quote on 285 (and see also 286: "through discourses, realities are constructed, made factual and justified, bringing about effects").

21 M. Foucault, *The Archaeology of Knowledge*, trans. A.M. Sheridan Smith (London and New York: Routledge, 2002), 134. I am indebted to Matt Dyce for this point and for his careful reading of and insightful comments on a draft of this essay.

22 Derek Gregory et al., eds., *Dictionary of Human Geography*, 5th ed. (Oxford: Wiley-Blackwell, 2009), 166-67.

23 Steinberg, "The Re-Making," 187.

24 This discussion depends substantially upon arguments outlined in ibid., especially 187-91.

25 J. Edward Chamberlin, *If This Is Your Land, Where Are Your Stories? Finding Common Ground* (Toronto: Alfred A. Knopf, 2003). Ted Chamberlin's characteristically gracious reflections on this foreword arrived too late to affect its substance, but, as so often, his words led me to consider horizons beyond the limits of my current vision.

26 Ibid., 210, 2-3.

Acknowledgments

When I began this endeavour, I had no idea how much work it would be for the people around me. I am sure that many of them had no idea either. But when they figured it out, they neither stopped talking to me nor suggested I choose another path. Instead, they walked this one with me, for which I am more grateful than I can express, but I will do my best to try.

Members of the Teme-Augama Anishnabai welcomed me onto their territory, gave me a place to stay, put me to work, allowed me to sit in on meetings, let me access records, taught me about their history on n'Daki Menan, and shared with me food, laughter, and stories. I will never forget this generosity; nor will I forget that stories are much bigger than books. I am particularly indebted to Victoria Grant, who took me on as a student and as a friend, and whose wisdom about life's complexities has very much informed my thinking and writing. I owe thanks as well to Chief Alex Paul, Chief John McKenzie, and the Joint Council for making me feel welcome and for allowing me to observe council and negotiation meetings. Great thanks also to Florence Becker, Deb Charyna, Holly and John Charyna, Leanna Farr, Doug Friday, Monty George, Fabian Grant, Joe Katt, Mary Katt, Peter McKenzie, Marie Paul, and Betty Ann Turner for sharing their perspectives and stories. I also appreciate the insights offered by the First Nation's negotiator, Ian Johnson, and lawyer, Alan Pratt.

Anders Sandberg, Cate Mortimer-Sandilands, and Ena Dua at York University guided my thinking and my writing, and provided the perfect balance of support and criticism that allowed the work and me to grow.

At later stages, Graeme Wynn, Dayna Scott, Ilan Kapoor, and two anonymous reviewers provided invaluable comments and suggestions that resulted in a clearer (and much shorter!) text. Colleagues and friends at York University, the University of British Columbia, and Memorial University of Newfoundland have not only forced me to think harder and better, but have also made the moves from Toronto to Vancouver to St. John's a lot more fun and a lot less lonely than I could have imagined. I would like to acknowledge in particular Jill Allison, Natalie Beausoleil, Sonja Boon, Pablo Bose, Kate Bride, Joan Butler, Hart Caplan, Michel Ducharme, Bruce Erickson, Leesa Fawcett, Sean Kheraj, Tina Loo, Leslie Paris, Paige Raibmon, Stephanie Rutherford, John Sandlos, Katherine Side, and Yolanda Wiersma.

All of this moving around makes me think about what it means to be at home. From my new vantage point at the eastern edge of Newfoundland, I see home as where my people are. Sometimes the fact that they are so scattered makes me feel scattered as well, but it also reminds me of the importance of family, of friendship, and of finding home in new places. Deborah McPhail and our daughter, Willa, have made this process easier. They have come with me, and they are my home. My parents, Wendy and John Thorpe, have encouraged my sisters and me to be brave and kind, to do our best, and to follow the paths of our lives, even when those paths have resulted in having daughters and granddaughters living far away on opposite sides of the continent. My faraway sisters, Hilary and Dinah Thorpe, are never more than a phone call away. Thank you to them, to our parents, and to my other people who make home home, wherever that is: Dawn, Judi, and Quinn Burgess Dalley; Libby Dawson; Cindy, Anne, and Kate Fleming Holmes; Gillian, Paul, Emma, Maggie, and Rebecca Hilchey Street; Sarah Lamon; Zoë Newman and Sapphire Newman-Fogel; Tyler and Hazel Peet; Wendolyn Schlamp; J.J., Angela, and Clayton Sheppard Donnelly; and Julie Sinden.

Randy Schmidt and Anna Eberhard Friedlander have proved patient as well as excellent editors for a first-timer like me, and I am grateful for their kindness and for their guidance. I acknowledge the financial support for this project from the Social Sciences and Humanities Research Council of Canada, the Ontario Graduate Scholarship, York University, and Memorial University. Adriel Weaver came through with court documents and support at a crucial moment. Numerous archivists and librarians laboured hard to track down files. Mariko Obokata worked wonders on my endnotes and bibliography, and Rajiv Rawat is the cartographer of the maps that accompany this text. Thank you to all of them.

Temagami's Tangled Wild

Welcome to n'Daki Menan
(Our Land)

On Highway 11, about an hour's drive north of North Bay, Ontario, a new sign marks the entrance to an ancient territory: "Welcome to N'Daki Menan," it reads, "Homeland of Teme-Augama Anishnabai" (see the photo on p. 2). The sign has stood on this spot since 2007, but the Teme-Augama Anishnabai – People of the Deep Water – have called n'Daki Menan home for thousands of years.[1] Nonetheless, many non-Aboriginal people know this same place as Temagami, Ontario, and consider it not the Teme-Augama Anishnabai's homeland, but an iconic site of wild Canadian nature (see the map on p. 3). Temagami is forested with pine and other tree species, including maple and birch, and contains many lakes as well as the rocky shores and thin soils considered typical of the Canadian Shield. It has served as a popular destination for campers and canoe trippers since the turn of the twentieth century. This book examines how n'Daki Menan became a famous Canadian wilderness, even as the Teme-Augama Anishnabai continuously asserted their rights and responsibilities toward a very differently understood territory.

The main argument of the book is that Temagami has been *made* – imaginatively and materially – as a site of wild Canadian nature. Its appearance as naturally wild and Canadian is the result of historical processes and relationships of power that disguised themselves as natural and worked to dispossess the Teme-Augama Anishnabai of their territory. For many generations, the First Nation governed the use of n'Daki Menan according to a system of family hunting territories, where each family had a responsibility to steward its two- to three-hundred-square-mile area in a way that

Welcome to N'Daki Menan –
a road sign on Highway 11 at the entrance to n'Daki Menan. *Author photo*

ensured the continuity of the species upon which the nation depended for survival.[2] As non-Aboriginal people began to encroach in growing numbers upon n'Daki Menan in the late nineteenth and early twentieth centuries, the Teme-Augama Anishnabai found their ways of life and relationships with n'Daki Menan disrupted. Over the ensuing years, they became increasingly excluded from their lands until, with the creation of a reserve in 1971, the federal and provincial governments officially recognized them as having claim to only one square mile of the four thousand comprising n'Daki Menan. Since then, the Teme-Augama Anishnabai have taken legal and direct action to assert control over n'Daki Menan, but according to Canadian law and popular imagination, the region exists, with the exception of the one-square-mile reserve, as part of Ontario.[3]

Temagami's reputation as wilderness has travelled far beyond the boundaries of the region itself. Tourist operators certainly try to tempt visitors

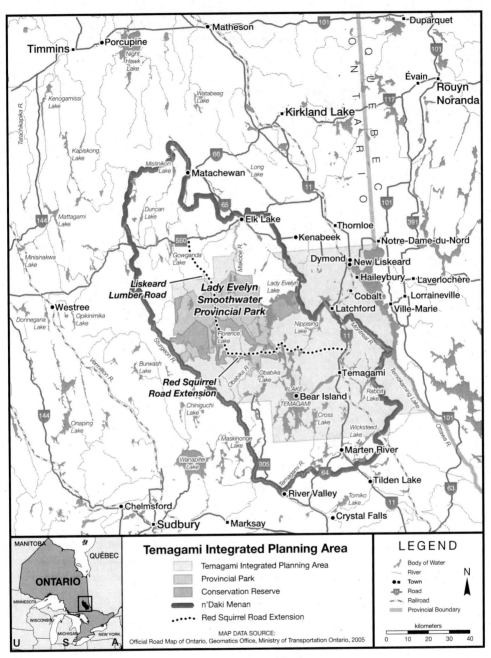

Temagami Integrated Planning Area

LEGEND

Temagami Integrated Planning Area
Provincial Park
Conservation Reserve
n'Daki Menan
Red Squirrel Road Extension

Body of Water
River
Town
Road
Railroad
Provincial Boundary

N

kilometers
0   10   20   30   40

MAP DATA SOURCE:
Official Road Map of Ontario, Geomatics Office, Ministry of Transportation Ontario, 2005

The Temagami Integrated Planning Area.

with the promise of "pristine lakes," "magnificent old pine," and "miles upon miles of unspoiled wilderness to explore," but many people who have never set foot (or dipped paddle) there also know of it.[4] Its fame stems in part from a 1980s conflict that is widely remembered as a fight between environmentalists and the provincial government regarding the construction of a logging road.[5] In 1985, the Ontario Ministry of Natural Resources announced its plan to extend the Red Squirrel Road, which would connect two logging roads and open up new stands of timber south of Lady Evelyn Smoothwater Provincial Park for extraction by local forest companies (see the map on p. 3). Environmentalist critics of the government's plan soon formed the Temagami Wilderness Society and managed to attract national and international media attention as well as a great deal of public support for their attempt to block the logging of what they began to call the "last great pine wilderness." They gained support from prominent Canadians such as Margaret Atwood, David Suzuki, and Bob Rae, which helped to raise the profile of the Temagami issue, as did the arrest of more than ninety environmental protesters who blockaded the logging road in the fall of 1989. (Bob Rae was arrested with other protesters.)[6] The road extension was eventually completed, but it never opened. In response to environmentalist pressure, the province decided to prohibit logging in this "particularly sensitive area" of the Temagami forest.[7] Since then, the issue has faded from mainstream attention. What remains, however, is the idea of Temagami as a wilderness, a wilderness worth fighting for.

My argument – that the Temagami wilderness is a product of history and relationships of power rather than simply of nature – hinges upon the understanding, elaborated in Chapter 1, that wilderness is a social category that works alongside other social categories such as race and gender, gaining legitimacy through its appearance as self-evident, or natural. The naturalizing force of wilderness, race, and gender disguises the exclusionary practices through which places and subjects are created. As I explain in the following chapters, the existence of Temagami as a Canadian wilderness space depended variously upon the Teme-Augama Anishnabai's eviction from n'Daki Menan, their confinement onto a tiny fraction of their traditional territory, their collapse into the category of wilderness, and the denial of their presence in and claim to the region. The creation of Temagami as a Canadian space was also part of a larger nation-building project that attempted, in part through the exclusion, or limited conditional inclusion, of immigrants of colour, to make Canada into a white settler society. To unravel the Temagami wilderness, as I aim to do by revealing the cultural threads holding it together as a site of wild Canadian nature and making it seem self-evidently so, is to remove the naturalizing power of this social construct.

Such an unravelling is a necessary part of moving toward more just futures for those of us living in what has become the Canadian nation. As most non-Aboriginal Canadians now acknowledge, the first explorers in what eventually became Canada did not discover an empty wilderness. Instead, they happened upon territory new to them but familiar to the many First Nations whom they met along the way and who led them to the lakes, rivers, and landscapes that they later named and claimed. The diverse First Nations who encountered European explorers spoke approximately fifty languages, divided lands according to their own systems, and depending on their geographical and cultural circumstances, lived by fishing, trading, trapping, hunting, gathering, and farming.[8] When French, then British, then Canadian governments divided First Nations lands into colonies, a nation, provinces, and territories, they imposed new orders onto pre-existing systems, thus disrupting those systems. And yet, like the Temagami wilderness, colonial and national territorial divisions have come to assume a certain naturalness, at least to the extent that non-Aboriginal Canadians rarely consider, as we drive north on Highway 11 or walk in downtown Toronto, Montreal, or Vancouver, the contested character of these "Canadian" places. The Teme-Augama Anishnabai's sign challenges the *Canadianness* as well as the *wildness* of Temagami, demanding that we examine again the ground we thought we knew.

This book provides such an examination with the hope that readers will understand and take seriously the embeddedness of colonial relations in the present, even in terms as seemingly innocuous as "Canadian" and "wilderness." Colonial relations include a Canadian nation built upon the dispossession of First Nations peoples, the preferential treatment of certain settler groups, and the exploitation of the non-human world. We are shaped by and left with these legacies, albeit in differing ways depending upon where we fit within the nation, but we do not need to pass them along unquestioned to future generations. Indeed, the persistence with which First Nations have demanded lands, rights, and recognition, as well as the efforts by marginalized groups within the nation to have their concerns addressed, has made this virtually impossible. The non-human world has also grabbed our attention recently, forcing us to recognize what some have been saying for generations – that our actions affect the world around us and that if we hope to live in a world with clean air and water, with healthy soil and good food, a world that will sustain the lives of humans and others, we need to live with rather than against the non-human life that comprises and shares our world. Movement toward justice requires not only the recognition that non-Aboriginal people and governments live on Aboriginal lands, but also the establishment of more equitable relations among First Nations, the diverse population of non-Natives who live here as well, and the (again diverse) animal and plant worlds upon which we depend for survival and with whom we inhabit this earth.[9]

This book maps stories. It shows how the making of Temagami as Canadian wilderness had and has everything to do with the (incomplete and always contested) dispossession of the Teme-Augama Anishnabai and therefore with the non-Native Canadians who have benefited from this process. I recognize that non-Aboriginal people living in Canada are a diverse group (as are Aboriginal peoples). Some, many with white skin, have been encouraged to make Canada their home, whereas others have had to fight systemic discrimination to carve out a place in the nation. But in spite of our significant differences, the fact that we all live in Canada, that we all arrived later to this Native land, makes Aboriginal issues our issues as well. The story that I tell is very specific. It transpired as it did because of the particular interactions that occurred over the years among the Teme-Augama Anishnabai, n'Daki Menan, and people from other places. Yet I hope that this specific story also resonates more broadly. The processes through which the lands of particular First Nations became part of the Canadian nation are inextricably linked to a larger story of colonialism and nation building, and this larger story becomes visible through the place-based account I tell.

Learning about the history of n'Daki Menan/Temagami has made it impossible for me to think of the region (or any other) as a Canadian wilderness, but it will always be one of my favourite places on earth. I first visited Temagami as a teenager in 1992, when my fellow campers and I embarked on a two-week canoe trip organized by the summer camp I attended for many years. The purpose of the trip was to develop our leadership skills in a wilderness setting, and we took turns leading the group as we paddled past tree-covered shorelines, portaged along trails carved out of the forest, and camped in small clearings beside big trees.[10] Temagami's wilderness character appeared so self-evident that it never occurred to me to ask questions of wilderness. Instead, I embraced it wholeheartedly and paddled hard, stopping only when we approached a stark treeless slope to wonder what had happened there. Clear-cutting had happened. The experience of seeing this clearcut, devastating and frightening as it appeared, affected me profoundly and helped to shape an environmental conscious-ness that remains with me today. In part because Temagami appeared so wild, the destruction of even a small part of it seemed a crime. For this reason, I find myself sympathetic to the environmentalist efforts of the 1980s: I do not want Temagami destroyed by unsustainable forestry prac-tices either.

And yet my attachment to this place is also connected to the history that first brought me there, a history that I now argue needs to be re-examined in the context of colonialism. We campers travelled through the wilderness region of Temagami, Canada, rather than through the Teme-Augama Anishnabai's n'Daki Menan. Indeed, our canoe trip fol-lowed hard on the heels of a 1991 Supreme Court of Canada ruling that the Teme-Augama Anishnabai had lost any Aboriginal rights they once enjoyed in n'Daki Menan. We paddled through Temagami, then, coming to know and care about it as part of the Canadian wilderness, whereas the Teme-Augama Anishnabai found themselves excluded from the territory that they knew differently, and intimately. I now believe that we campers, and our Temagami wilderness experiences, contributed to the Teme-Augama Anishnabai's difficulties in having their territory recognized by non-Aboriginal governments – and so it is my own implication in the dispossession of Aboriginal peoples that leads me to question and to study this place.

We were not the only campers/environmentalists, however, to participate in the creation of the Temagami wilderness and thus to perpetuate the erasure of the Teme-Augama Anishnabai and n'Daki Menan. In the 1980s, while environmentalists struggled to save it, the Teme-Augama Anishnabai battled in court to have the same land recognized in Canadian law not as wilderness, but as n'Daki Menan.[11] In 1988, the year before the environ-mental blockades, the First Nation set up its own roadblocks to prevent the extension of the logging road. Chief Gary Potts spoke out not only against the industrial logging of the region, stating that it would create "a desert," but also against the environmentalist vision, which would make the region into "a zoo."[12] More fundamentally, the Teme-Augama Anishnabai challenged the assumption that either the provincial govern-ment or environmentalists had the right to determine the future of their territory. They camped in the bush for more than six months to stake their claim, removing themselves only when the province agreed not to begin building the road until after the Ontario Court of Appeal had heard their case.[13] Within environmentalist representation of the conflict, however, the Teme-Augama Anishnabai struggle became invisible. Even after, separately

from environmentalists, they again blockaded the logging road in 1989 to
stake a claim to their homeland – this time over two hundred Teme-
Augama Anishnabai protesters and their supporters were arrested – the
issue was represented, and continues to be remembered, as a contest over
wilderness.[14] Even as I sympathize with environmentalists and share many
of their concerns, I am disappointed by their persistent reliance on the
concept of empty wilderness, particularly given that criticisms of the idea
are no longer new.[15] I write this piece in the hope that those who, like me,
care deeply about the more-than-human world will see in this book solid
reasons to let go of the wilderness concept while continuing to struggle,
in perhaps quite different ways, toward a world in which all of us might
live well.

CHAPTERS

Each chapter of this book focuses on a specific period in the production,
contestation, and transformation of n'Daki Menan/Temagami. The chapters cover differing time frames and differing discourses, following chrono-
logically from scientific forestry in the late nineteenth century to Canadian
law in the 1980s. The chapters reveal multiple constructions of the region
– empty Canadian wilderness, tourist mecca, wasteful old trees, n'Daki
Menan – and make it clear that it has long been a contested space. But it
also becomes apparent that some versions of the region (Temagami as part
of the Canadian wilderness) have come to dominate the imaginative and
physical landscape at the expense of others (n'Daki Menan). By showing
the contestations and fissures in the social construction of national nature,
as well as by demonstrating how particular understandings of the region
have come to exist as the common-sense truth, this work enters into the
struggle for the constitution of the region, aiming in part to help put n'Daki
Menan back on the map.

    Chapter 1 outlines the theoretical and methodological underpinnings
of the book and explains what it contributes to writing on race, gender,
and nationalisms, as well as to writing on Temagami. Chapter 2 traces how
the Temagami forest became a timber commodity in the early twentieth
century and how this process placed the region within the context of resource conservation, the Canadian nation and British Empire, and displaced the Teme-Augama Anishnabai from n'Daki Menan. Chapter 3
investigates tourism at the turn of the twentieth century, showing how
travel writing constructed Temagami as a part of the pristine Canadian

wilderness for white men (and, to a small extent, white women) to explore. Within this narrative, the Teme-Augama Anishnabai, who were vital to the success of tourism, appeared as part of a disappearing wilderness rather than as cultural beings with their own systems and connections to n'Daki Menan. Neither forest conservation nor tourism was an innocent enterprise, and both were implicated in gendered, classed, and racialized relationships of power and inequality through their fashioning of a wilderness. Chapter 4 examines a conflict between the Teme-Augama Anishnabai and the Ontario government that started, in 1929, when the province demanded that Teme-Augama Anishnabai members pay rent for the privilege of living on Bear Island. In the ensuing controversy, the racial and spatial order that had been (imperfectly) imposed through earlier tourist and forestry discourses and practices was uprooted and reconfigured, and the Teme-Augama Anishnabai found themselves spatially confined and temporally displaced in a process that also revealed the instability of categories such as race and wilderness. Chapter 5 focuses on another struggle between the First Nation and Ontario, a legal battle over title to n'Daki Menan/Temagami that took place between 1973 and 1991. More than a contest over a given territory, the court case served as an avenue for the construction and contestation of land and the categories of race and gender. This chapter shows how historical discourses and practices, often colonial in character, emerge in the present to deny subjectivity and land to Aboriginal peoples. The Conclusion revisits the main points of the book, discusses present-day implications of the creation of the Temagami wilderness, and considers how the arguments advanced here might provide an opening for considering alternative futures in n'Daki Menan.

I

Tangled Wild

My argument that, in and through relationships of power, Temagami has been created historically as a site of Canadian wilderness relies on the understanding that race, gender, and nature are social categories that work together and are powerful precisely because of their ability to appear natural. I draw this understanding from two bodies of scholarship that, until relatively recently, have remained distinct from one another: post-colonial theory and social nature scholarship.

Scholars of colonialism have shown that race is an invented thing, tied up inextricably with the history of European imperialism and changing over time and across space.[1] The insight that race *functions* rather than *exists* is central to my study, allowing me to comprehend the often contradictory ways that the Teme-Augama Anishnabai were racialized as "savage" or "civilized," "authentic" or "inauthentic," and part of a "vanishing race" or not really "Indian" at all. In each case, such race-based representations worked to deny them access to n'Daki Menan and to open the region up to non-Aboriginal interests.[2] Race functioned in the service of colonialism. A consideration of the workings of race in Temagami also allows me to connect the region's history to the larger context of European colonialism in which it took place. As scholars have demonstrated, race played a powerful albeit flexible role as a marker of difference central to the operation of European colonial rule. In his classic *Orientalism,* for instance, Edward Said shows that the multifaceted European discourse of Orientalism did not merely present far-off lands to a European public, but rather invented the Orient as an object of Western knowledge, thus both justifying European rule over the so-called Orient and creating a racial other against whom the European self could be constructed.[3] The racializing dualism between self and other was central to imperialism, for the appearance in Orientalist discourse of colonized peoples as lazy, irrational, and barbaric allowed Europeans to seem hard working, rational, and civilized by contrast, and therefore perfectly suited to rule over colonized others.[4]

Under colonialism, race exerted its power by seeming to be a product of timeless nature rather than European culture. Mary Louise Pratt describes one important method through which racial categories were simultaneously fabricated and made to appear natural.[5] In 1735, Swedish naturalist Carl Linné first introduced his influential plant classification system, and by 1758, it had encompassed humans, which were divided into distinct types, including the Wild Man, American, European, Asiatic, and African. Linné's Eurocentric system, which positioned the European as inventive and governed by laws, and the African as indolent and governed by caprice, created racial "types." Yet these types appeared to exist within the realm of science and nature, and thus worked to naturalize the myth of European superiority as well as that of race and racial types. Metaphors that emerged within the context of colonialism also worked to make racial hierarchies seem natural. As Anne McClintock points out, for example, the "Tree of Man" provided racial scientists with a visual representation of the world's peoples that confirmed the European narrative of progress and civilization.[6] "Aryans" were situated at the top branch of the tree, and racially "inferior" groups occupied its lower branches. This power-laden classification system depended upon the symbol of the tree to naturalize the racial hierarchies embedded within it.

The metaphor of the family, McClintock further demonstrates, also helped to maintain and naturalize the racial divisions upon which colonial rule depended. The Tree of Man image appeared alongside that of the "Family of Man," which depicted human progress in familial terms, with the "lower" races, like European women and children, situated below the European male head of household and pinnacle of civilization.[7] The racial hierarchy reproduced in the Family of Man depended not on the naturalness of a tree, but on the assumed naturalness of the patriarchal family and thus on the subordination of women and children. In the family metaphor, then, both gendered and racialized hierarchies appeared natural, and imperial rule seemed inevitable and even benevolent, a kindly father helping his children progress to higher degrees of civilization.[8]

The family metaphor offers an example of how the categories of race and gender functioned together to naturalize colonial power relations. It also hints at the importance of gender to the workings of empire. Indeed, many scholars have explored gendered dimensions of imperialism, taking as a starting point that sex/gender, like race, does not exist outside of history and relationships of power.[9] One important aspect of this scholarship examines the persistent feminization of colonized lands. The feminine form representing the land was not the same in all places and times. For instance, in the late nineteenth and early twentieth centuries, the Canadian West appeared as a young, virginal white woman, whereas in the 1570s, America began to be personified as a naked indigenous woman wearing a feathered headdress.[10] But in each instance, the feminization of colonized lands, and the linked representation of colonial conquest as sexual mastery, served to underwrite the colonial project, to present imperial acquisition and violence as the natural order of gender relations.

Understanding that the feminization of colonized lands played a role in imperial processes is important to my study for two reasons. First, the consistent female gendering of Temagami nature was part of the larger colonial process of Aboriginal dispossession and European territorial appropriation. Second, the social construction of nature – in this case, the European representation of colonized lands as female – is implicated in colonialism.

This brings me to the second body of work upon which the arguments of this book rely: social nature scholarship. Although it seems counterintuitive – what is nature if not natural? – the concept of social nature has in recent decades gained popularity among scholars interested in examining what Donna Haraway calls the "traffic between what we have come to know historically as nature and culture."[11] These scholars contend that the cordoning off of nature from society does not make analytical or practical sense, since, as Bruce Braun states, "Far from two separate domains, there is but one, a hybrid realm crisscrossed by flows of energy and matter and the movements of animals, plants, people, machines, and ideas."[12] Indeed, nature and society are everywhere implicated in one another, from the lake water piped into city-dwellers' homes and the trees-turned-newspapers on their doorsteps, to gorillas who know American Sign Language, to polar bears who walk the streets of Churchill, Manitoba. The appearance of two separate realms is not pre-given, but rather culturally created. Some Western environmentalists fear that understanding nature as socially constructed undermines efforts to save it, thus giving humans licence to transform their environments in ecologically destructive ways.[13] Social nature scholars, on the other hand, consider that positing nature as an external entity that must be protected by (and from) humans does more harm than good.[14] When nature and humanity seem mutually exclusive categories, we are left in a difficult position. To use nature is to destroy it, to save it is to be apart from it, and we find ourselves with no room to negotiate how to live respectfully and responsibly in the "middle ground," the messy mix of nature and culture that humans and non-humans actually inhabit.[15]

Further, and as this book will make evident, the fiction of a culture-free nature hides the decidedly cultural practices – power-infused and historical – through which nature has come to appear separate from culture. In the case of Temagami, this fiction also disguises the cultural practices in which the region has never existed solely as a natural space. In both cases, what is missing is the culture of nature.[16] Part of the motivation for tracking nature's production lies in making apparent the power relations operating to separate out what counts as nature from what counts as culture, and in showing how the division between nature and culture has benefited some groups, human and non-human both, at the expense of others. In revealing the operation of power within discourses of nature, it becomes possible to redefine nature and culture, "to envision," in Haraway's words, "a different and less hostile order of relationships among people, animals, technologies, and land."[17] William Cronon's "The Trouble with Wilderness" does an excellent job of countering the escape from history that lies hidden in the concept of wilderness. He traces Western environmentalism's concern with wilderness to a specifically masculine bourgeois form of nineteenth-century anti-modernism and demonstrates how elite Euro-American subjects constructed wilderness to reflect their own cultural values. Cronon makes it clear that wilderness was not already *there* by pointing out that it depended on the prior removal of First Nations peoples from their territories. He shows not only *that* wilderness was invented, but also *for whom* it was invented and, importantly, whose histories, bodies, and claims needed to disappear before it could become properly wild.[18]

I do not mean to suggest that there exists no external world beyond human imaginings. (Nor do I mean to suggest that humans are the only creatures to construct nature.) We humans, however, can access the world only through the lens of our own cultures, histories, and contemporary realities. Trouble begins when we mistake our lens for the world itself. The insight that humans fabricate nature is central because it brings nature into the analytical frame and shows the non-human world to be central to the story instead of merely the passive backdrop against which the plot unfolds. Certainly, European imperialism involved the transformation of non-European natures on a massive scale.[19] Yet the lack of attention to nature within most post-colonial scholarship makes the non-human world seem peripheral to the story. By showing how the making of race and gender in colonialism went hand in hand with the creation of nature, my analysis is able to comprehend more thoroughly the gendered and racial- ized dynamics of empire and nation building, and also to make clear the fact that territorial appropriation and environmental change were and remain central to colonial relations.

Kay Anderson and others have examined race and nature together as social categories.[20] In *Race and the Crisis of Humanism*, Anderson demon- strates that a consideration of nature as social can lead to a deeper under- standing of the history of race and racism. She traces the long-standing European concern with what distinguished humans from the rest of nature, showing how Western humanism held the ability to transcend bodily and external nature as key to human distinctiveness, and contends that British encounters with Australian landscapes and Aboriginal peoples challenged this view. In spite of British interventions beginning in the late seventeen hundreds, the indigenous inhabitants of Australia showed no signs, ac- cording to colonial officials, of developing from a "savage" to a "civilized" state. Similarly, Australian plants, animals, and lands remained a mystery to European scientists and agriculturalists, who consistently failed in their attempts to classify and cultivate them. Anderson argues that what officials understood as a lack of progress on the part of indigenous peoples and lands caused a crisis in existing European ideas about what it meant to be human. This crisis led not, as it might have, to a fundamental questioning of the shaky foundations of the belief in human distinctiveness, but pre- cipitated instead the oft-discussed but ill-explained nineteenth-century shift from environmental to racial determinism in colonial racism. Anderson's account shows that race worked not only to justify imperialism, but also to maintain in a time of crisis the European belief in the distinc- tion between nature and culture, which was possible only with a change in European thinking about the nature of race. With the shift to racial determinism, or "scientific" racism, colonized peoples came to be viewed within European frameworks as innately rather than culturally inferior to Europeans, and their capacity to become "civilized" was put into question.

In the Canadian context, works by Bruce Braun and Cole Harris consider the politics of race and nature. In *The Intemperate Rainforest: Nature, Culture, and Power on Canada's West Coast,* Braun details historical and contemporary processes through which the British Columbia forest has come to exist as a site of nature. He argues that the making of the forest as a natural space has had the effect of displacing First Nations' cultural understandings of and claims to the same land, thus authorizing non-Native people – the government, the forest industry, and environmentalists – to regulate, harvest, and speak on behalf of the BC forest. His book demonstrates that contemporary ways of thinking about BC's temperate rainforest are products of history and politics rather than simply self-evident truths.

Braun's study and my own rely on similar methodologies and contain interesting parallels; particularly striking are the similarities between the Temagami environmental protests and the Clayoquot Sound protests that Braun interrogates in his book. In the 1980s, environmentalists in British Columbia, as in Temagami, fought to save what they called the "ancient wilderness" of Clayoquot Sound from exploitation by forestry companies. They concentrated their energies on BC's last "intact" forests, an approach borrowed by the Temagami Wilderness Society in its emphasis on the old-growth character of the Temagami forest and its status as the last of its kind in Ontario.[21] Before 1988, when the Temagami Wilderness Society commissioned ecologist Peter Quinby to study the forest that was slated for logging, concern focused on the potential loss of recreational values rather than on the specific character of the forest.[22] Yet by 1989, with the release of Quinby's research results indicating that Temagami contained the "world's largest known stand of old-growth white and red pine," environmentalists, concerned citizens, and even the provincial government seemed to agree that the old-growth status of the forest was what made it worth saving.[23]

Other parallels exist between Temagami and Clayoquot Sound in the 1980s and 1990s. In both places, the blockading of logging roads led to the arrest of hundreds of protesters (in roadblocks Temagami was first, although more than double the number of people were arrested in Clayoquot Sound in 1993 than in Temagami in the late 1980s), and the blockades and arrests attracted an enormous amount of media and public attention. In addition, as Braun's book and this one make clear, environmentalist efforts in both places not only sounded the alarm bell about unsustainable logging practices, but also helped to mask contemporary

Aboriginal claims to land, thus making the forest appear unproblematically a part of the Canadian wilderness. Braun and I challenge the naturalness of the BC and Temagami forest, revealing the colonial processes that made these entities possible and logical. But my study differs from Braun's in important ways as well. In part, the roots of these differences lie in the distinctive histories of the regions we investigate and in part in our different analytical lenses. I focus more on the national character of the forest and thus on the racialized and gendered nation-building project in which Temagami became implicated.

In *Making Native Space: Colonialism, Resistance, and Reserves in British Columbia*, Cole Harris aims to do almost the opposite of what Braun and I set out to accomplish. He traces the creation of Native reserves in British Columbia, detailing the often violent ways that British and Canadian authorities confined Aboriginal peoples onto smaller and smaller reserves, thereby making the majority of the land available for non-Aboriginal British Columbians (to enjoy, for example, as wilderness). Harris employs Edward Said's idea of a "culture of imperialism" to explore how European ideas about race shaped colonial, provincial, and federal government land policies in ways that dramatically affected Aboriginal individuals, communities, and territories.[24] His study demonstrates that the "Indian reserve" is no more natural a place than the "Canadian wilderness." Rather, both are the result of colonial and nation-building projects that made race as well as space and through which, in Harris' words, one human geography was "superseded by another, both on the ground and in the imagination."[25] *Making Native Space* also shows that differing administrations – first, colonial and later provincial and federal – had very different impacts on Aboriginal peoples living in what became British Columbia and thus demonstrates the importance of paying specific attention to the forms, including the nation form, that colonial rule takes.

The understandings from post-colonial and social nature scholarship that race, gender, and nature appear natural and work together in powerful ways lead to a discussion of how these social categories also help to naturalize the nation form, which, as Benedict Anderson has observed, is full of contradictions. The nation is a relatively new historical entity, yet it appears ancient (or natural) to nationalists. Although it has little philosophical coherence, it has great political power: people are willing to cheer for it at sporting events, fight for it at a bar, and die for it at war.[26] Also, in spite of inequalities that exist within the nation and the fact that most members of a nation will never meet the majority of their fellow members, the nation is always conceived of as a community of people who share a "deep, horizontal comradeship."[27] Considering how such a paradoxical phenomenon has come to appear commonsensical is necessary to denaturalize Temagami's status as a national space. And yet the nation must also be understood as connected in significant ways to European imperialism, not only because both depend for coherence upon gender, race, and nature. Nations such as Canada exist due to border-drawing exercises by imperial powers in their fight over land and resources. And imperialism has played an important role in Canadian nationalism, with early nationalists attempting to strengthen rather than sever imperial ties to Britain.[28] But even within Europe, the nation form as it emerged was connected to empire, with national greatness measured according to imperial might.[29]

Critical race sociologists Robert Miles and Malcolm Brown contend that race makes the nation form seem natural: the collective self of the nation is defined against an external other according to race, resulting in the appearance that "the world's population is 'naturally' divided into distinct nations."[30] They trace the connection between race and nation to the nineteenth century, when nationalists in Europe relied on scientific racism to confer the supposed naturalness of national boundaries, since scientific racism allowed for the explanation that differences between nations were attributable to biology. Scientific racism's biological determinism also gave weight to the idea that the nation form was ancient, or at least historically inevitable.[31] Philosopher Etienne Balibar further argues that both race and language play important roles in the naturalization of the nation form. Together, they produce an identity that he calls "fictive ethnicity," which allows individuals within a nation to understand their differences as smaller than their similarities and thus to imagine themselves as belonging to the nation. Although language is important to the nation because it enables members to communicate with one another and therefore to imagine themselves as connected, Balibar argues that the language community is not enough to produce ethnicity, because it is inherently open, which means that "new acquisitions" can easily become incorporated into the nation, thus disrupting the imagined cohesiveness of a naturally exclusive nation.[32] Race offers "an extra degree of particularity, or a principle of closure, of exclusion," which makes it seem, in spite of the fact that "no modern nation possesses a given 'ethnic' basis," that racial unity is the origin of the nation.[33] The link between race and the nation, Balibar continues, allows for injustices within the nation to seem natural and inevitable, as racialized others can appear "falsely" national and racially degenerate. Their exploitation can then be viewed as unrelated to the privileges of the "genuinely" national and as separate from the equality that makes up the national community.[34]

Like race, gender also plays a role in naturalizing the nation form. As comparative literature professor Mary Layoun points out, an understanding of the nation requires attention not only to who is included and who is excluded, but also an examination of how its members are positioned within nationalist discourse.[35] Layoun suggests that the "very basic rhetorical and organizational principles of the nation are tropes for and expressions of gendered power," where heterosexual men are imagined to protect *their* women, children, and land from danger through public participation in defending the private sphere.[36] Men's mobility is contrasted with women's fixedness. Anne McClintock concurs, arguing that whereas men are represented within nationalist discourse as the "progressive agent of national modernity," women are constructed as the "authentic body of national tradition," a practice that naturalizes a gendered status quo even as it makes the nation appear simultaneously ancient and modern.[37] Historian Anna Davin shows how gender also linked empire and nation in turn-of-the-twentieth-century Britain, when British women were made responsible for producing healthy (male) children who would defend Britain and the empire in the face of competition from other nations.[38]

In the Canadian context, race and gender have helped to naturalize the nation in troubling ways. Canada's existence as French and British colonies, then as a settler society, and later an imperial dominion before adopting official multiculturalism was and is neither a phenomenon of ancient origin nor a historical inevitability. Instead, Canada is largely the result, to borrow Teme-Augama Anishnabai chief Gary Potts' words, of a "squabble between white men over land that doesn't belong to them."[39] Yet as critical theorists of the nation have shown, Canada has come to make common sense as a white, predominantly English-speaking country through interacting webs of law, policy, discourse, and practice that are gendered as well as racialized.[40] Enakshi Dua shows, for example, that the early-twentieth-century debate over the emigration of Asian women from India to Canada centred on whether these women posed a threat to a white nation. Those who favoured excluding Indian women asserted that their entry would encourage Indian men to remain in Canada and produce "ethnic communities" rather than returning to India once they were no longer needed as labourers. On the other hand, their opponents suggested that if Indian women were not allowed into Canada, Indian men would become involved with white women, thus threatening the white nation with miscegenation.[41] The argument not only racialized and gendered Indian women as the creators of ethnic communities, but also made a white settler Canada appear natural.

Until well after the Second World War, Canadian nationalist mythology was based on British cultural hegemony and the exclusion of racial and cultural difference.[42] Members of Canada First, an influential nationalist movement that began shortly after Confederation and advocated that Canada should hold a central place within the British Empire, advanced the view that Canada "must ever be ... a Northern country inhabited by the descendants of Northern races."[43] They promoted the immigration of northern Europeans to the newly annexed Canadian west, convinced that only rapid settlement would ensure that it became "British in racial character and institutions."[44] As Eva Mackey observes, the nationalism of Canada First was gendered as well as racialized. Whereas the North and northern races were associated with the masculine virtues of virility, strength, self-reliance, and health, the South and southern races were made inferior and "other" through their feminization.[45] Canada First member William Foster expressed it this way in a celebrated address, published in 1871: "We are a Northern people – as the true out-crop of human nature, more manly, more real, than the weak marrow-bones superstition of an effeminate South."[46]

But, as Homi Bhabha reminds us, far from being a coherent and stable form, the nation is full of ambivalence, ambivalence that stems from the contradictory ways that national unity is constructed within nationalist discourse. The *pedagogical* discourse of nationalism claims the origin of the nation to be fixed in antiquity or nature, and it situates the people as the object of the discourse. But the nation must also exert its authority and unity in the present through the *performative* discourse of the nation. This discourse relies on the people not as objects, but as subjects whose daily activities must be performed as the activities of the nation, thus demonstrating the "living principle of the people as that continual process by which the national life is redeemed and signified as a repeating and reproductive process."[47] The reliance of the nation on the performativity of the people makes it vulnerable to interventions and challenges by those placed on its margins.

Although the Canadian nation was built upon the marginalization of First Nations peoples from their lands and their confinement onto tiny reserves, as well as upon the attempt to attract British settlers and to restrict the entry of black and Asian people, this project has not been entirely successful.[48] The Canadian nation is and has always been an ambivalent (and now officially multicultural) entity, contested by those at the fringes. For one thing, Aboriginal peoples have not gone away and have instead fought for their lands, struggled for legal recognition under Canadian law, maintained their identities, worked for wages, and employed a number of other strategies for survival within a nation formed on their dispossession.[49] Also, as Frances Abele and Daiva Stasiulis have pointed out, from the early days of nation building, the desire of officials to create Canada as a British settler nation conflicted with their need for labourers who would do the work of building it.[50] Since British immigrants failed to arrive in great numbers, Canada permitted the entry of people from throughout Europe and, in limited numbers, from China, Japan, and India.[51] In spite of barriers in the form of head taxes, immigration restrictions, and white settler racism, members of "non-preferred races" persisted in their efforts to enter Canada and to attain citizenship rights.[52] Women have also contested their various places in the nation and thus altered its shape.[53] It is largely because of the struggles of these groups that Canada did not become a white settler society. They performed a different kind of nation.

Particularly important for my study is attention to how nature works alongside race and gender in the naturalization of the Canadian nation. Eric Kaufmann has noted that all nationalisms depend upon the existence of a special relationship between the nation and its geography.[54] But in places such as Canada, the United States, and Switzerland, where large areas of land appear to be wilderness, that special relationship is based on the "naturalization of the nation" rather than on the "nationalization of nature."[55] The nationalization of nature occurs when a community emphasizes the imprint of the nation's culture upon a specific territory. The naturalization of the nation occurs, on the other hand, when a community celebrates wild nature as that which regenerates the nation.[56] In the former, the nation imposes itself onto nature, whereas in the latter, nature is seen as determining national culture. Kaufmann argues that with the rising influence of romanticism over the course of the nineteenth century, Canadian and American nationalists came to understand the wilderness (of the north and the west, respectively) as generative of national character.

Certainly, the type of nationalism articulated by Canada First relied on the idea that the landscape shaped the nation. In an attempt to kindle nationalist feeling, its adherents celebrated Canada's northern location and challenging climate as necessary elements for the building of a powerful country.[57] Yet this environmental determinism went hand in hand with racial determinism, as Canada Firsters asserted that, by nature and by virtue of living in northern climates, people of northern European ancestry were a "healthy, hardy, virtuous, dominant race."[58] Members of the "northern races" were deemed the only ones capable of surviving the harsh Canadian winters, and the climate itself was considered instrumental in the maintenance of racial character.[59] Race and nature thus worked together (in highly gendered ways) to make the idea of a white settler Canada appear natural, and a variety of explicitly racist immigration policies reinforced the northern race idea. The notion of "climatic unsuitability," for instance, was used until 1953 as a reason to exclude immigrants of colour from Canada.[60]

Notably, and as Eva Mackey observes, though Canadian nationalist mythology has changed over time in response to shifting economic, political, and social circumstances, one feature that has remained consistent is the idea of Canada as a northern wilderness.[61] The iconic Canadian wilderness is most famously depicted in the paintings of the Group of Seven. Comprising seven artists based in Toronto who first exhibited as the Group of Seven in 1920, it is often credited with developing a uniquely Canadian form of landscape painting inspired by the rugged character of the land itself and also with stimulating a sense of national identity based on a wilderness aesthetic.[62] Links between Canada and the northern wilderness do not begin and end with the Group of Seven, however. As discussed above, Canada First nationalism of the late nineteenth century also depended on ideas about the relationship between the nation and its northern landscape. And in the late 1920s, Emily Carr began to be considered the Western Canadian complement to the Group of Seven. Carr's works, many of them depicting dense forests, were understood to reflect the landscape and to capture the quintessential character of the Canadian west coast.[63] Today, Carr and the Group of Seven are among Canada's most famous artists, and although they painted very different "wildernesses" – Carr remained focused mainly on the west coast, whereas the Group painted landscapes as diverse as the Rocky Mountains, the Arctic, and Algonquin Park – these and other "wild" places in Canada have collectively come to represent the essence of the nation.[64]

The idea that such varying sites could come together to epitomize the Canadian wilderness, and thus the nation more generally, speaks to one of the tensions of nationalism. As anthropologist Ghassan Hage shows in the Australian context, when people describe their experiences of particular locales, whether they talk about walking down a city street or taking a canoe trip in the wilderness, they often articulate their experiences at the national rather than only the local level.[65] Cultural theorist Lauren Berlant explores the inverse of this phenomenon in the United States, examining how "national culture becomes local" through the "images, narratives, monuments, and sites that circulate through personal/collective consciousness."[66] If people indeed experience very specific localities as national spaces, then it becomes possible for quite diverse places to be characterized as national. A trip to Banff National Park might feel unlike a trip to Niagara Falls, but both can be and are considered quintessentially Canadian experiences. Catriona Sandilands argues that national parks are shaped by this local/national tension. On the one hand, parks are very much local places, both because they are "a fairly haphazard collection of sites that perform a variety of local roles" and because they must market themselves as unlike anywhere else in order to attract visitors. On the other hand, part of what makes parks distinct from their local surroundings and thus important areas for tourists to visit is the fact that they have been designated as sites of national significance. Therefore, parks must, in all their local specificity, do the work of representing the nation.[67] Although Sandilands concentrates specifically on national parks, her insights are relevant for thinking about places not *officially* selected as sites of national nature but which are nevertheless considered to be part of the Canadian wilderness. Temagami is one example. Like national parks, it is a locality, and promotional efforts attempt to attract visitors by focusing on its special character, particularly its distinctive old-growth forest. At the same time, however, like those diverse places painted by the Group of Seven and Emily Carr, Temagami has taken on a broader national significance as representative of the Canadian wilderness.

Though it may be more appropriate to speak of national wilderness in the plural rather than in the singular, one thing that iconic images of Canadian wilderness share is their appearance as empty of human activity. Given that First Nations have lived on these homelands for millennia and have not considered them wilderness, it is fair to say that all Canadian wilderness is invented.[68] Certainly, scholars have criticized the works of both the Group of Seven and Emily Carr for erasing Aboriginal peoples from the picture, thus making possible the idea of a vacant Canadian wilderness and providing a representational justification for the colonization of Aboriginal peoples and lands.[69] The trouble with Temagami as a wild *Canadian* space, then, is that it works to naturalize the nation as well as the wilderness, and in so doing, it makes racialized and gendered dynamics of nationalism appear as products of nature rather than culture.

Like the figuring of Temagami as wild, the representation of the region
as Canadian leaves little room for the Teme-Augama Anishnabai to articulate their alternative perspective on n'Daki Menan. The potent combination
of *Canadian* and *wilderness* doubly denies the Teme-Augama Anishnabai's
claim to land, for whereas the concept of wilderness erases their presence
in the region, the claiming implicit in the term "national" marks the area
as belonging to Canada, not to them. Naturalizing the nation form also
risks making nationalist exclusions, particularly those drawn upon racial
lines, appear equally natural.

   Helpful though they are for exploring connections between imperialism
and nation building, and the processes through which the nation form
and nationalist exclusions are naturalized (and contested), critical studies
of the nation rarely attend to how the land is produced in nationalist
discourse.[70] Bonita Lawrence and Enakshi Dua have recently argued that
anti-racist scholarship on the Canadian nation does not always take seriously the colonization of Aboriginal peoples upon which the nation was
and continues to be premised. In part, they contend, this is the result of
scholars' failure to take up the contested character of "Canadian" land and
to recognize that the reclamation of lands is central to First Nations'
struggles for self-determination.[71] Analyzing how the presence and claims
of Aboriginal peoples are erased to make the land appear "naturally" wild
and Canadian allows us to see anew the processes of colonization upon
which a racialized and gendered Canadian nation rests.

METHODOLOGICAL CONSIDERATIONS

To historicize the Temagami wilderness, I use a genealogical approach, a
form of historical analysis developed by Michel Foucault that describes
the history of the present and concentrates on how power operates in the
production of subjects and truths.[72] Such an approach calls into question
contemporary truths and encourages researchers to examine the conditions
of possibility through which particular truths emerged and came to seem
obvious. By making evident the histories of taken-for-granted truths,
genealogical analyses show that truths are the effects of contingencies rather
than inevitabilities of the past. Such studies also reveal the operation of
power in the creation of apparently timeless truths, and it is this attention
to the intricate workings of power that attracts me to a genealogical approach. According to Foucault, power operates through discourse, and

discourse is defined not simply as language but as "practices that systematically form the objects of which they speak."[73] Discourse is comprised of those utterances, or texts, not always verbal or written, that make some form of claim to truth and are sanctioned as knowledge.[74] The analysis of discourse is central to a genealogical approach, and the purpose of studying it is to understand its effects, to comprehend, for example, how certain discourses come to function as truth in specific places and times while others are cast aside. Discourse is thus connected to power through the mechanisms that allow some to serve as true and constrain others from emerging. Yet these mechanisms of power often remain hidden, and discourses seem to reflect an objective world rather than constituting that world.[75] An analysis of the discourses and therefore relationships of power through which Temagami became a famous site of Canadian wilderness is part of the contest over the meaning of this region, and thus over the region itself. If this story is part of a struggle, other stories necessarily exist as well, which can be recognized only when we understand that this story is not the truth in any straightforward sense. The account of the Teme-Augama Anishnabai's long-standing claim to land cannot be heard when Temagami is only wild and Canadian. By revealing how one story came to have the effect of truth, I aim to make room for alternatives to be heard and for different futures – which include Teme-Augama Anishnabai self-determination in n'Daki Menan – to be imagined.

The discourse analysis that I employ relies on primary materials obtained from a number of archival locations in Ontario. The timeline of this book spans the hundred or so years from the late nineteenth century to the late twentieth century. Although I do not write in depth about this entire period, I did search for and access materials covering it and beyond. From Library and Archives Canada in Ottawa, the Ontario Native Affairs Secretariat in Toronto, and the Temagami First Nation Band Office on Bear Island in Lake Temagami, I accessed Department of Indian Affairs correspondence and reports for the Temagami region dating from 1848 to 2005. The Archives of Ontario in Toronto provided reports, memoranda, and correspondence about forestry, land surveys, cottage leases, and the damming of lakes in the Temagami region. Much of this material dates between the late 1890s and 1934. At the Archives of Ontario and at the Ontario Court of Appeal in Toronto, I was able to access court documents. I was also given permission by the Joint Council of the Teme-Augama Anishnabai and Temagami First Nation to study court documents at the band office, including sixty-eight volumes of trial transcript that I could not locate elsewhere. At the band office, I was also allowed to access reports, speech transcripts, and correspondence about the land claim. Most of this material was produced in the 1970s and 1980s. Finally, at the Toronto Reference Library, the Archives of Ontario, and the University of Toronto and York University libraries, I retrieved newspaper and magazine articles and advertisements dating from the late 1890s to the late 1990s. In conducting my analysis, I looked for common themes in the texts, as well as interruptions of those themes; linguistic choices; links between texts and images; language structure and style; connections between the texts and the documents or conversations to which they referred; and relationships between the texts and the larger political, historical, and discursive conditions from which they sprang.

Though my source materials were quite diverse, most were written rather than oral.[76] One major drawback of this is that relatively few voices are incorporated into my analysis. The views of government officials about early-twentieth-century forest policy, for example, exist in the written record in a way that the perspectives of farmers living near the region at the time do not. Similarly, the opinions of Department of Indian Affairs officials about concerns expressed by the Teme-Augama Anishnabai are recorded, whereas the thoughts of non-Native people living among or in close proximity to the band are generally not written down. The Teme-Augama Anishnabai's perspectives before the 1970s usually appear only when band members petitioned for a reserve in n'Daki Menan or when they had specific complaints related to the policing of their activities by government representatives. Such petitions and complaints were commonly written by chiefs and were sometimes translated and/or recorded by local magistrates or church officials. During and after the 1970s, Teme-Augama Anishnabai perspectives are more diverse, but the voices of chiefs still tend to dominate the record as speeches and in newspaper reports. Court documents are filled primarily with lawyers' arguments and with testimony by non-Native "expert" witnesses, though Teme-Augama Anishnabai testimonies are also recorded. With the exceptions of Madeline Theriault and Mary Laronde, who are discussed below, Teme-Augama Anishnabai women's voices are notably absent from the documents. Non-Native women's perspectives are also uncommon, although in Chapter 3 I examine some travel accounts written by women.

The story I tell in the following chapters is a partial one, then, and not only because of my particular viewpoint on the events and discourses that I explore. It is also partial because of the stories that comprise the written record, stories that are shaped by race, class, and gender. Much of the record upon which I draw has been composed by white men who enjoyed the class privilege of working in government offices rather than turning soil, felling trees, or guiding tourists for a living. Certainly, not everyone shared their views. Indeed, they themselves held a variety of opinions and perspectives. Real life as it unfolded in Temagami was much more complicated than the archival material suggests. Yet the archives remain a source of rich and important information, offering insight into the minds of men who had the power to shape laws and decisions that had and continue to have consequences in the world. Thus, the opinions of these men matter not only for the (partial) perspectives that they offer about (class-privileged white male) views, but also because, more than those of other people, their ideas often had quite wide-ranging effects. In addition, though archives do not offer a complete picture of history, neither do they present a simplistic or coherent account of the colonial and national expansion into and takeover of Teme-Augama Anishnabai territory. It is abundantly clear from the archival record that the creation of Temagami as a site of wild Canadian nature was never a straightforward matter. The Teme-Augama Anishnabai and their supporters *do* write back, and it is evident in many places that they not only respond to colonial processes but actively engage on their own terms with the Indian agents, tourists, fire rangers, and others whom they encounter in n'Daki Menan.

One danger of relying on these written accounts is that I risk centring encounters between the Teme-Augama Anishnabai and non-Native interlopers as the key events determining the lives of both parties – of seeing the power relations of colonialism as the only dynamics shaping the region.[77] This is not my intention, even though encounters resulting from colonialism are significant to the story that I tell. The Teme-Augama Anishnabai had and continue to have multiple relationships with one another, with non-Native people who visit or live in n'Daki Menan, and with the animals, plants, rocks, and waters that comprise it. These significant connections extend far beyond the story that I tell, and I acknowledge them only partly in referring, at appropriate moments, to accounts written by Teme-Augama Anishnabai individuals about their relationships with their territory. My narrative is only one among several, albeit one that is necessary given the still common association between Temagami and Canadian wilderness, and I discuss its links with stories that the Teme-Augama Anishnabai tell and have told about their own and their ancestors' relationships with n'Daki Menan.

I focus my study on a number of key moments in the history of the region, which I selected in two ways. First, I chose periods highlighted on historical timelines created by the Teme-Augama Anishnabai themselves. These are recorded in books and as photocopies in the band office and are repeated when Teme-Augama Anishnabai members give information sessions about the history of their land claim.[78] I chose such instances because they had a considerable impact on the First Nation's experience of the region. Often that impact was negative: the Teme-Augama Anishnabai were made not at home in their own homeland. Since the construction of the region as a national wilderness space depended on their displacement, it makes sense to pay attention to times when they experienced the loss of their lands particularly acutely. Second, I selected moments to study by looking to the historical record for times when the popular press, supporters of forest conservation, the provincial government, or the Department of Indian Affairs paid a great deal of attention to Temagami. These instances often corresponded with events listed on Teme-Augama Anishnabai timelines, which is not surprising, given that non-Native attention to the region often resulted in the regulation of and encroachments onto n'Daki Menan. None of the primary sources upon which I rely was previously untapped – the Teme-Augama Anishnabai spent more than ten years researching their court case alone, and they uncovered thousands of sources from the sixteen hundreds to the 1970s – but my reading of this material provides a fresh perspective on the making of Temagami.

WRITING ABOUT TEMAGAMI

Temagami is not a new site for historical study, although no one has examined the region through my particular analytical lens. *The Temagami Experience: Recreation, Resources, and Aboriginal Rights in the Northern Ontario Wilderness,* by Bruce W. Hodgins and Jamie Benidickson, describes the development of the district and the efforts to implement management plans and policies to regulate forestry, mining, Aboriginal activities, settlement, and tourism.[79] Hodgins and Benidickson argue that from the mid-nineteenth century, recreational users, resource interests, provincial officials, and the Teme-Augama Anishnabai have all contributed to the development of Temagami. They further contend that due to the "relative isolation and ruggedness" of Temagami nature, "those interested in the landscape and resources of the district have preserved or been forced to preserve a balance, at least until recent times [the 1970s]."[80] Hodgins and Benidickson's account is one of competing interests, where various groups have met and clashed over their opposing ideas of what should happen in Temagami nature.[81]

Although *The Temagami Experience* is thoroughly researched and comprehensive, its central claims warrant re-examination in light of the insights of post-colonial and social nature literature. By assuming nature to exist as a stable (isolated, rugged) object over which a human struggle is waged, the authors forego an examination of how Temagami *came into existence* as a site of Canadian nature and do not fully account for the complex power relations that served to make the region available for some people while denying the claims of others. Unlike Hodgins and Benidickson's account, my analysis forefronts the colonial and nationalist relationships of power and inequality that created the Temagami wilderness and dispossessed the Teme-Augama Anishnabai, and it thus adds a new layer of understanding to the historical and contemporary conflicts in the area. This book also makes it clear that some of what Hodgins and Benidickson view as conflicting interest groups actually have more in common than it seems at first glance. As will be discussed in Chapters 2 and 3, though present-day canoeists may oppose logging in Temagami, wilderness tourism and industrial forestry both have their roots in European colonialism and white settler nationalism, and both worked in opposition to the Teme-Augama Anishnabai's, but not to one another's, interests. A solution to contemporary conflicts in Temagami that merely suggests a balancing of diverse interests risks reproducing colonial and nationalist relationships of power and inequality.

Members of the Teme-Augama Anishnabai, past and present, have also written about the history of the region, sometimes in books and other times on the landscape itself in the form of place names and evidence of land use. This writing is important for a number of reasons. First, it clearly reveals that the region is, and has always been, a homeland, n'Daki Menan. The writing therefore offers a rich variety of detailed evidence for the invented character of Canadian wilderness. In her autobiography, *Moose to Moccasins: The Story of Ka Kita Wa Pa No Kwe,* for instance, Madeline Theriault shares vivid memories of her childhood and young adulthood in n'Daki Menan during the early twentieth century, describing how she and members of her community prepared food and made clothing from the resources of their territory, as well as how they travelled through it by canoe and snowshoe.[82] Like Theriault's account, a fairly recent Teme-Augama Anishnabai report about traditional land-use philosophies and practices indicates the enormous extent to which the Teme-Augama Anishnabai used the hundreds of species of n'Daki Menan and how they governed the use of their territory by a complex belief system. The species they relied on included but were not limited to moose, bear, beaver, and rabbit for food, clothing, trade, and medicine; fish and birds for food; red and white pine, cedar, birch, poplar, and maple trees for constructing homes, barns, utensils, baby boards, tables, chairs, toboggans and snowshoes; birchbark for canoes, containers, and cutting boards; pine pitch as an adhesive; maple trees for paddles and for syrup; spruce tree roots for thread and fish nets; and berries and other plants for food and medicine.[83]

Not only did everything in n'Daki Menan have a place within Teme-Augama Anishnabai life, but everything also had a name. The extensive knowledge of n'Daki Menan revealed in place names has been recorded by Craig Macdonald in his historical map of the area.[84] This map, which Macdonald created with the help of Teme-Augama Anishnabai elders and others over a period of twenty-six years beginning in the 1970s, includes the Anishnabai names for over six hundred waterways and landforms, and also identifies hundreds of traditional travel routes.[85] It is testimony to Macdonald's enormous abilities and persistence as a researcher – he consulted old maps, survey reports, and fur trade journals in addition to conducting approximately five hundred interviews with Teme-Augama Anishnabai elders, elders from nearby First Nations, and non-Aboriginal trappers, guides, loggers, and others who knew something about the Aboriginal geography of the region. Further, the map's place names and pathways demonstrate the existence of n'Daki Menan as homeland rather than wilderness. For instance, an outlet at an arm of Lake Temagami (the lake is shaped rather like an octopus with many arms) is called "Ma-kwaw na-gwaw-awk-shing Saw-gi-hay-gun-ning" or "bear-snaring place," highlighting both the familiarity of the Teme-Augama Anishnabai with their territory and the value of this particular spot for capturing bears.[86]

Teme-Augama Anishnabai historical writing also shows that the First Nation's identity, and aboriginality more generally, is a negotiated, contested, and changing thing. Theriault's *Moose to Moccasins* shows that although outside forces attempted to construct an "authentic" Aboriginal identity for her and others, she made her own identity as a daughter, granddaughter, mother, wife, craftsperson, worker, and community member who negotiated the changes in her life with dignity, grace, and humour. In a passage that reveals much about non-Aboriginal expectations of aboriginality, Theriault describes how she and other members of her community participated in the making of *The Silent Enemy*, a 1930 movie that was filmed in n'Daki Menan.[87] Community members appeared onscreen, built the set, and prepared the food for the actors, and Theriault and three other women made "one hundred complete Indian outfits in one month for use in the picture."[88] The film depicts pre-contact Ojibwa life in which a Native tribe struggles against the "silent enemy" of starvation. On its initial run, it sold itself as an authentic depiction of Native life, but Theriault wryly observes that though the "picture was really a lot of fun to do," it was "not very authentic. When I think of some of the things they had us do, from dancing barefoot in the snow to carrying a bear cub in a canoe while shooting rapids, I really wonder. It's too bad they didn't pay more attention to us who knew better."[89] *The Silent Enemy* certainly participated in the creation of an imaginary Indian to be consumed by a non-Native audience, and the irony of Aboriginal people producing sets and outfits for a film written and directed by non-Natives for non-Native viewers about "authentic" Aboriginal life (in which Aboriginal people are represented as nearly starving to death) is rather striking.[90] But Theriault's account reveals that she had no trouble defining Aboriginal identity on her own terms or reflecting with humour on the ridiculousness of Hollywood portrayals.

Finally, writing by band members makes clear the central connections between Teme-Augama Anishnabai identity and n'Daki Menan (although both these links and the use to which members of the First Nation put n'Daki Menan were changing rather than static), and thus demonstrates why an essential component of decolonization must be the transfer of lands from Canada to Aboriginal peoples. In an article about the co-management of n'Daki Menan by the First Nation and non-Native residents, Mary Laronde discusses the special relationships developed over time between the former and its territory. She is hesitantly optimistic about joint stewardship, but she also insists that an essential part of it involves the Teme-Augama Anishnabai as sole stewards of a significant portion of n'Daki Menan.[91] In his history of the Temagami land claim, Gary Potts also centres relationships between the Teme-Augama Anishnabai and n'Daki Menan by explaining land stewardship. According to Potts, stewardship entails using the land in such a way that future generations may also rely on it.[92] In his story, non-Native infringements on Teme-Augama Anishnabai territory and ways of life began not in the 1970s, but in the 1870s, when Chief Tonene first brought the band's claim before the Canadian government.

2

Timber Nature

In 1901, the Ontario government created the Temagami Forest Reserve (TFR) to secure future timber supplies. Centred geographically on Lake Temagami, most of the two-thousand-plus square miles of reserve lay within n'Daki Menan. In 1903, the province expanded the reserve to almost six thousand square miles, and virtually all of n'Daki Menan fell within its boundaries (see the map on p. 34). Resource conservation is widely regarded as an inherently beneficial thing, but this chapter shows that the creation of the TFR, and the forest conservation movement that spawned it, helped to transform n'Daki Menan into a natural and national space, and to dispossess the Teme-Augama Anishnabai of their traditional territory. In making this argument, I join scholars who in recent years have shown that conservationist discourses, policies, and practices must become objects of analysis. Far from regulating or even saving a pre-existing nature, they have shaped social constructions of nature and determined access to land and resources.[1] Particularly remarkable in the Temagami case is the short time it took for the forest reserve to become naturalized on the landscape and for its existence to become a justifiable reason (according to provincial and federal governments at least) for denying the Teme-Augama Anishnabai access to n'Daki Menan, even as non-Aboriginal individuals and companies were enabled to take advantage of its timber, mineral, hydroelectric, and tourism potential. The process of naturalizing and nationalizing the landscape occurred in two main ways – via law and forest conservation discourse – which also worked to naturalize ideas about race and gender.

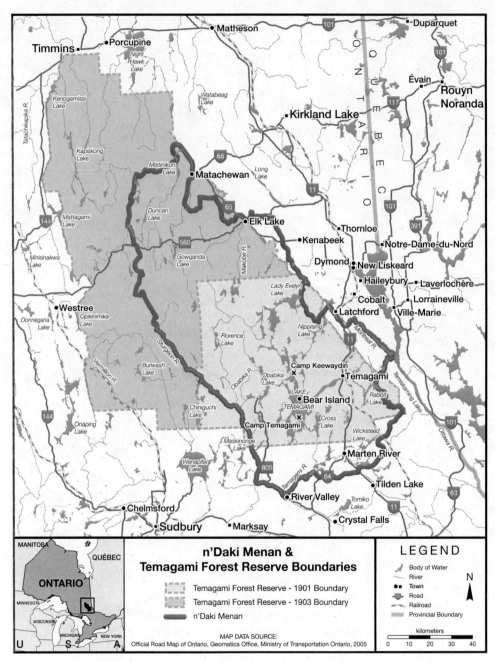

N'Daki Menan and Temagami Forest Reserve boundaries.

N'Daki Menan before 1901

Although increasing numbers of non-Native people encroached upon n'Daki Menan in the second half of the nineteenth century, it remained Teme-Augama Anishnabai territory. Indeed, Bruce Hodgins and Jamie Benidickson contend that in the nineteenth century, it was slowly "brought closer to the orbit of Canadian influences" but remained "just beyond the Canadian periphery."[2]

The Teme-Augama Anishnabai lived upon and regulated their use of n'Daki Menan for thousands of years before non-Native people arrived. They used it extensively and intensively, and also traded with the Wendat (Huron) to the south, often relying on Nipissing intermediaries to transport meat and skins south and to return north with corn, cornmeal, and pottery.[3] Although relationships between the Teme-Augama Anishnabai and n'Daki Menan changed over time and from season to season, and indeed, band membership also varied with intermarriage and adoption, for many generations the region provided the First Nation with the essentials for survival and served as the central site for the construction of individual and collective identity.[4] Since this book is about the processes through which Temagami became a natural and Canadian space, I will not dwell on the pre-contact period. I do not mean to suggest, however, that pre-contact stories are somehow insignificant. Important in and of themselves for describing the rich and varied lives of individuals and First Nations, they are also often vital for First Nations negotiating or litigating their land claims with Canadian governments and courts, and trying to reclaim their histories and identities within the context of hundreds of years of colonial domination.[5] Stories about pre-contact life can also be dangerous, particularly when they are used by non-Native governments, courts, and people to position Aboriginal existence as unchanging and outside of the present moment.[6] The contested character of stories about pre-contact relationships between the Teme-Augama Anishnabai and n'Daki Menan will become clear in Chapter 5. In the court case discussed in that chapter, the First Nation and Ontario mobilized very different accounts of the distant past in order to fight for very different visions of the future.

When Europeans entered n'Daki Menan, it became a "contact zone" in Mary Louise Pratt's sense of the term, a space where mutually constitutive relationships between European colonizers and Teme-Augama Anishnabai began to take place within "radically asymmetrical relations of power."[7] By at least the mid-seventeenth century, the Teme-Augama

Anishnabai began to expand their trading network to participate with Europeans in the fur trade, and they sometimes travelled long distances to reach both French and English traders.[8] In 1834, the Hudson's Bay Company (HBC) established an outpost on Temagami Island in Lake Temagami, which was open intermittently from fall to spring until 1857 when it began to operate more regularly. Certainly, the fur trade affected the band. By 1876, for example, Chief Cana Chintz was forced to ask for government assistance, indicating that beaver and deer once plentiful in the area had been killed by "the white man."[9] Nevertheless, the Teme-Augama Anishnabai retained a good deal of control over the fur trade, since the HBC depended heavily upon them to trade furs with it instead of with the competition and to honour their debts from previous years. They also got good returns for their furs by taking advantage of rivalries between the HBC and independent traders, including Alexis (or Alex) Dokis, who will be discussed below.[10]

As well as largely dictating their own engagement with the fur trade, the Teme-Augama Anishnabai comprised the majority of the population of n'Daki Menan before 1901. Occasional survey parties entered the area, but, like most fur traders, they did not stay permanently, and like HBC representatives, they depended on Teme-Augama Anishnabai to guide them.[11] In the 1870s, representatives of the Geological Survey of Canada explored the Temagami area, and surveyors working for the Canadian Pacific Railway examined possible routes fairly close to Lake Temagami. During the next thirty years, Robert Bell and A.E. Barlow of the Geological Survey travelled to Temagami a number of times in search of minerals and other exploitable resources, but this enterprise was not considered as important as their work in the Sudbury mining area.[12] Although n'Daki Menan officially became part of the province of Ontario with Confederation in 1867, the provincial government considered it, like much of northern Ontario, "practically a *terra incognita*" before a 1900 survey was commissioned to take stock of its exploitable resources.[13] Practically speaking, then, even as government-appointed surveyors assessed Temagami's resource potential, including that for timber and mineral development, the region remained Teme-Augama Anishnabai territory.

In the late 1870s, however, Chief Tonene, who replaced Chief Cana Chintz in 1878, began to express his band's concern about increased lumbering activity close to its territory. He told Indian agent Charles Skene that the Teme-Augama Anishnabai desired to have some land set aside for them before their territory was actually intruded upon by white lumbermen. Skene, who had never heard of the Teme-Augama Anishnabai, feared that unless the Indian Department acted in a timely fashion, the band's land would be taken away and its members would be left with nothing, and so he suggested creating a reserve for them under the Robinson-Huron Treaty.[14] Under the provisions of the Robinson-Huron Treaty, originally signed in 1850, chiefs were to cede their bands' territories, with the exception of reserves to reside upon and cultivate. In exchange for this, bands received yearly treaty payments, or annuities, and were allowed to hunt and fish within ceded territory as long as the Crown rather than private companies or individuals held title to it.[15] In the 1850s, the British government was interested primarily in controlling the mining areas along the shores of Lakes Superior and Huron rather than lands in the interior that few non-Native people had reached, and so it is not surprising that the Teme-Augama Anishnabai and other First Nations living a fair distance from Lake Huron had not participated in the treaty.[16]

Chief Tonene and other members of the Teme-Augama Anishnabai repeatedly asked Skene whether and when a reserve would be set aside for them, and Skene in turn regularly urged his superiors in the Department of Indian Affairs (DIA) to do something about the situation.[17] Underlining the urgency of the matter, Skene forwarded to Lawrence Vankoughnet, the deputy superintendent general of Indian affairs, a letter from an HBC officer that indicated that band lands were "being ruined by whites and others disposed to hunt on them"; later, he reported that Chief Tonene had told him that trees had already been taken from n'Daki Menan.[18] As a result of this pressure, Vankoughnet sent Skene to ascertain from Tonene the extent of country claimed by the band as its hunting grounds.[19] When asked to detail the conditions under which his band would be willing to surrender its lands, Tonene told Skene that the band would like to receive money every year for as long as "you dispose of our Hunting Grounds," as well as a permanent reserve so that it could establish a farm to provide for the children.[20] The reserve desired by the First Nation was a hundred-square-mile area around Austin Bay at the south end of Lake Temagami.[21]

Although the matter of a reserve had apparently been engaging Superintendent General of Indian Affairs (and Prime Minister) John A. Macdonald in 1881 before his departure to Europe, the band had heard nothing definitive about it by 1882, at which time it applied to be placed on the list of annuitants under the Robinson-Huron Treaty. In 1883, it began to receive regular treaty payments.[22]

The reserve itself, however, proved more difficult for the Teme-Augama Anishnabai to obtain.[23] This was related to the jurisdictional division enshrined within the Constitution Act, 1867, under which Indians and lands reserved for them became a responsibility of the federal government, whereas most lands and resources came under provincial authority. Since the territory controlled by the Teme-Augama Anishnabai had passed into provincial hands with Confederation (according to Canadian governments), the DIA believed it needed Ontario's permission to create a reserve for the band.[24] The quarrel that arose between the DIA and Ontario over the reserve was quite typical of disputes between the two levels of government regarding Aboriginal lands. In spite of frequent queries by the First Nation, passed diligently along by the local Indian agent, the DIA seemed in no particular hurry to accommodate the request for a reserve. For instance, DIA surveyor G.B. Abrey was asked by his superiors in the spring of 1883 to survey a potential reserve, but he did not do so until a year and a half later, and did not file a report for another six months.[25] But, though slow to act, the DIA did eventually (in 1885) ask the Ontario government to consider creating a reserve, and over the next decade, it continued to request a response from the province about the matter.[26] Ontario occasionally acknowledged receipt of the letters but otherwise made no attempt to reply.[27] Even when the federal government twice tried to take up the issue with the province through a tribunal or arbitration board, provincial representatives managed to avoid responding to requests to meet and settle the matter.[28]

It was not that Ontario did not receive the letters. In fact, in 1894, Ontario's assistant commissioner of Crown lands, Aubrey White, sent District Forester D.F. MacDonald on a secret mission south of Temagami to Lake Nipissing in order to gather information from local chiefs about the Teme-Augama Anishnabai. White wanted to know whether they had resided at Lake Temagami before the signing of the Robinson-Huron Treaty or whether they were actually part of another band for which a reserve had already been set aside.[29] He reasoned that if the province could show that the Teme-Augama Anishnabai were merely members of another band, separated from it in order to gain access to better hunting grounds, they had no claim to a reserve. MacDonald went to Lake Nipissing and spoke with Chief Dokis and his son Alexis. Dokis was much more interested in discussing how the local Indian agent, Thomas Walton (Skene's replacement), had been attempting to force his band to sell the timber on its reserve than in talking about who lived at Lake Temagami.[30] He did mention, though, that former Temagami headman Peter Nebenegwune had not known about the Robinson-Huron Treaty. Alexis Dokis provided MacDonald with further details about the Lake Temagami people, though he did not offer the information hoped for by White. Instead, he listed a number of families that, in his words, "belonged to Lake Temagami proper," with no indication that they had come from elsewhere. He also mentioned that the Temagami families had started gardens in the locality chosen as their reserve, which he described as "well timbered with hardwood and pine" and containing "very good" soil.[31] After receiving MacDonald's report, White kept quiet about both the secret mission and the province's perspective on the Teme-Augama Anishnabai claim.

The inability or unwillingness of Canadian governments to create a reserve certainly had negative consequences for the Teme-Augama Anishnabai, who nevertheless did their best to ensure that the issue remained a live one. In 1884, for example, when Indian agent Walton pressed upon them "the subject of education," they promised to build a schoolhouse and devote some of their annuity money toward paying for a teacher as soon as they had a reserve.[32] They also expressed an interest in taking up farming, but not before they had a reserve, since, they said, working hard to clear land that might not become part of it made little sense.[33] Given that education and the cultivation of land were central to the "civilizing mission" of British imperialism from which the DIA stemmed, the Teme-Augama Anishnabai's stated willingness to send their children to school and plant potatoes can be seen as a way of appeasing the Indian agent and negotiating a paternalistic system in order to have their needs met.[34] But given that the animals upon which they depended for subsistence had become scarce, their desire to grow crops probably had as much to do with survival as it did with anything else. By 1890, having given up waiting for a reserve, members of the band had cleared over eighteen acres of land, some of which were within the boundaries of the proposed reserve. As Chief Tonene stated, "members of the Band felt so uncertain on the subject of a Reserve that they would wait no longer and commenced during the last 2 years to make clearances wherever suitable."[35] In spite of their creativity in dealing with their situation, not having a reserve was a frequent source of frustration. In 1894, Indian agent Walton reported that members of the First Nation "despairingly deplore[d]" the DIA's failure to obtain a reserve for them.[36]

Clearly, contact with Europeans affected the Teme-Augama Anishnabai before the creation of the TFR. N'Daki Menan was increasingly encroached upon by outsiders during the late nineteenth century, and the provincial government ignored Teme-Augama Anishnabai requests for a reserve. Still, n'Daki Menan remained their territory. By 1904, tourists would be flocking to the area by the thousands, but few reached Lake Temagami in the 1890s. Further, though survey reports indicated mineral and timber potential in the region, very little resource development had taken place, and no outside law enforcement regulated Teme-Augama Anishnabai activities in n'Daki Menan. Although the Ontario government remained silent about its position on a reserve, the logic of forest conservation had not yet become predominant, and members of the band remained cautiously hopeful that they would soon receive a reserve at Austin Bay.

TEMAGAMI TIMBER NATURE

Before the creation of the TFR, any number of options for the region remained possible. One was for the Teme-Augama Anishnabai to continue their existence as a self-governing people in n'Daki Menan. Agricultural settlement represented another possible future, though surveyors who explored the area in the nineteenth century thought that it offered little potential for agriculture due to its rocky soils. Although members of the Teme-Augama Anishnabai and the HBC had reasonable success at growing potatoes on patches of good soil, by 1900 only two other individuals had attempted agriculture in the area. A retired HBC employee grew oats and potatoes next to the Montreal River, and Catholic missionary Charles Paradis grew potatoes and a few other vegetables at the north end of Lake Temagami.[37] Surveyors seemed much more optimistic about the region's timber and mineral supply than they did about its agricultural potential.[38] Department of Crown Lands representatives who toured the area by canoe in 1899 similarly commented on the "surprising quantity of white pine" and "received assurances that the quantity of standing timber exceeded that sold since Confederation."[39]

But it was not until January of 1901 that provincial officials charted the boundaries of the TFR and approved its creation by an order-in-council.[40] The act of legislating the TFR into existence was what made the region, legally speaking, into a natural, national space: a timber commodity under the jurisdiction of Ontario, Canada. The 1898 Forest Reserves Act empowered the province to set aside portions of Crown land for the purpose of securing future timber supplies, and under the act forest reserves were defined as areas whose sole purpose was to produce timber. The following clause excluded virtually every other possibility: "No lands within the boundaries of such reserves shall be sold, leased or otherwise disposed of, and no person shall locate, settle upon, use or occupy any such land, or hunt, fish, shoot, trap or spear or carry or use fire arms or explosives within or upon such reserves."[41] The Teme-Augama Anishnabai had long resided in what had suddenly became the TFR, and their multifaceted knowledge of it involved much more than recognizing its timber value. But Ontario's view of the region differed from theirs. It saw a "virgin territory well timbered with Pine" that had the potential to become a lucrative part of the province and nation, and in creating the forest reserve, it turned its vision into law.[42] The Teme-Augama Anishnabai, on the other hand, found themselves to be outlaws in lands they knew as n'Daki Menan but that now appeared on maps as the Temagami Forest Reserve.

Although the Forest Reserves Act clearly defined forest reserves as areas whose only function was timber production, things were much more ambiguous in practice. This ambiguity was related to conservationist beliefs that some land uses, including mineral prospecting, mining, hydroelectric development, tourism, the protection of the water supply, and the conservation of game animals, were compatible with forest conservation and therefore could be permitted inside forest reserves. Ontario's clerk of forestry, Thomas Southworth, for instance, wrote that the Forest Reserves Act had the dual purpose of securing future timber supplies and protecting the sources of some of Ontario's principal streams, observing that "the areas best suited for one purpose are equally adapted for the other."[43] Aubrey White added that the region's lakes were full of fish and its forests full of birds, game, and fur-bearing animals, and implied that the reserve would protect all these features.[44] Some thought that the Ontario government also intended the TFR to become "a beautiful and healthful resort for our people for all time."[45] Southworth commented that though it was perhaps "inadvisable to exclude tourists or even summer residents from the district," the provisions of the Forest Reserves Act would permit the government "more perfect control ... of the tourist travel as well as the exploitation of the immense timber wealth in the district" and added that mining might also take place in the TFR under the regulations of the act.[46]

The Forest Reserves Act was not the first legislation in Ontario to bring together the seemingly diverse objectives of forest conservation, mineral development, game and wildlife protection, maintenance of the water supply, and recreational use. Similar priorities informed the creation of Algonquin Park in 1893.[47] But under the Forest Reserves Act, at least in principle if not in practice, timber conservation was the primary objective, whereas Algonquin Park was established as "a public park and forest reservation, fish and game preserve, health resort and pleasure ground for the benefit, advantage and enjoyment of the people of the Province."[48]

Not surprisingly, given the multiple purposes the TFR was expected to serve (and as Hodgins and Benidickson argue), it did not become solely a timber preserve.[49] Yet the *idea* of the region as a forest reserve succeeded in gaining the status of truth, with the TFR coming to appear as a product of nature rather than culture, and the Teme-Augama Anishnabai's very different understandings of and relationships with it becoming displaced and erased.

The imposition of one culture of nature onto another occurred not only through law, but also through forest conservation discourse, in which the timber of the Temagami region became naturalized as a commodity of national significance. Forest conservationist ideas grew increasingly popular during the ten years following the 1900 creation of the Canadian Forestry Association, a non-governmental organization dedicated to promoting scientific forestry, and the conservationist discourse I examine comes from the speeches, articles, public education materials, and meeting reports produced by the relatively small group of elite white men – politicians, civil servants, forest industry leaders, intellectuals, bankers, and professional foresters – who spearheaded and popularized the conservation movement.[50] Until late in the nineteenth century, settlers and colonial administrators saw the future of Canada in agriculture. The task before settlers was to carve a space for themselves in the new Dominion by converting forest into farmland.[51] The forest seemed eternal, and though forests were thought of as non-renewable since, once "mined," previously forested land usually became farmland, the general understanding was that the vastness of Canada's forest meant that the timber supply could never be exhausted.[52] This perspective, however, became not only untenable as wood supplies, particularly in eastern Canada, began to dwindle, but also unfashionable as the conservationist perspective began to take hold.[53] Emerging conservationist wisdom held that the forest, properly managed, could become a permanent *renewable* resource.[54]

This change did not occur overnight. Conservation ideas travelled from Europe to North America with people such as Bernhard Fernow, the vocal Prussian-born conservation advocate who became the first professional forester in the United States, and who, in 1907, founded the first forestry school in Canada at the University of Toronto.[55] The goal of forest conservation, according to Fernow, was to ensure the maximum supply of wood in perpetuity through the management of permanent forests by scientifically trained professionals. This idea gained popularity in both the United States and Canada after the American Forestry Congress met for the first time in 1882 (Fernow was in attendance), with a second meeting taking place in Montreal in the same year. At these meetings – the one in Montreal is often cited as marking the beginning of the forest conservation movement in Canada – delegates determined that wasteful cutting practices, forest fires, the clearing of land unfit for agriculture, and poor wood utilization were resulting in the depletion of North American forests. Steps should be taken to ensure the maintenance of the timber supply and therefore the continued existence of the forest industry.[56]

The ideas of the conservation movement found their way into legislation, though not to the extent that conservationists believed they should.[57] In Ontario, the passage of the Forest Reserves Act indicated the province's commitment to implementing conservationist principles.[58] Indeed, Thomas Southworth praised the 1898 act as "the inauguration of a scientific forestry system in Ontario."[59] Since his appointment as clerk of forestry in 1895, Southworth had advocated for Ontario to begin a system of scientific forestry and pushed especially for the government to prevent settlement in portions of the province "that are found to be not well adapted for agricultural purposes."[60]

The Forest Reserves Act was consistent with conservationist goals as established at the 1882 American Forestry Congress meetings, where delegates addressed themselves to two interrelated tasks: to preserve existing forests and to restore forests on lands whose timber had been cut or burned down.[61] Both these goals required that sites thought better adapted to timber growth than to agriculture be maintained as perpetual forest land under public ownership. The act fit these objectives well, since its primary aim was the protection of timber through the exclusion of settlement from land deemed better suited to tree growth than to farming. Also consistent with the objectives of the congress were regulations under the Forest Reserves Act providing for the protection of forest reserves from fire. Ontario's forest fire protection system, developed in 1885 by Aubrey White as a direct result of the "great forestry convention" in Montreal, involved stationing a number of hired fire rangers at places considered to be sources of fire danger and charging them with educating the public about the perils of forest fires, enforcing provisions under the 1878 Fire Act, and extinguishing forest fires that they encountered during their travels.[62]

Although the TFR was not the first reserve created under the Forest Reserves Act, it was by far the largest, as well as the only one that featured considerable quantities of valuable timber. The other two reserves, the Eastern and the Sibley, contained 125,000 lumbered-over and fire-swept

acres between them, whereas the Temagami reserve alone included well
over 1 million acres, many of which were forested. The province created
the first two reserves in hopes that one day, given time and adequate protection from fire, they would become valuable timber resources.[63] The TFR
was another story. Hodgins and Benidickson state that it was the "centre-
piece" of Ontario's new forestry system and its creation a "crucial event
in the history of the North American conservation movement."[64] Indeed,
in a memorandum written to the commissioner of Crown lands in support of the creation of the TFR, Aubrey White observed that it probably
contained the largest body of pine timber left in Ontario's Crown hands
and optimistically stated that, with proper government management, it
could be the most valuable asset in the province and a permanent source
of revenue.[65]

   It is difficult to overstate the significance placed on the TFR within the
Canadian forest conservation movement. In 1901, the Canadian Forestry
Association (CFA) announced that the setting aside of the TFR was one
of the most significant events in Canadian forestry that year and noted
that it "illustrates well the progressive spirit which animates the Government
of the Province of Ontario."[66] According to the CFA, the initiative was
especially remarkable because the province had the opportunity to make
a large revenue by putting the area under licence in the usual way but
chose instead to manage it wisely, without having to concede to other
interests.[67] The CFA went further to say that those interested in Canadian
forestry should watch the development of the Temagami reserve and take
every opportunity to foster public support for its creation, because its
success would have a significant impact on the future of forest administration in the entire nation. An increase in public support for the TFR, according to the CFA, would prompt the government to take further
progressive steps toward a rational system of forestry and would also justify
public spending on fire suppression and the development of a management
system necessary to ensure the regular reproduction of timber.[68]

   The goals of forest conservation did not appeal to everyone equally.
Overwhelmingly, members of the CFA came from cities and lumbering
towns, and the farming classes that made up more than half the Canadian
population were almost completely absent from its membership.[69] Urban-
based men of the upper classes as well as lumbermen joined the movement,
whereas farmers, women, and Aboriginal people did not. Conservationist
perspectives on the forest, then, were certainly partial but nevertheless
need to be examined, for they shaped not only popular thinking, but also

policy, and therefore the land itself and the various relationships that people could have with land. N'Daki Menan was entirely absent from conservationist discourse, which consistently portrayed the Temagami region as a nationally significant timber resource.

Within conservationist discourse, Temagami and Canadian forests more generally became naturalized as sites of valuable lumber in part through their feminization and representation as "virgin." Conservationists stated that "our virgin forests," including Temagami's "territory of virgin timber," were wasteful, decaying, ripe, overmature, excessively lavish, and decadent (certainly all feminized terms, though not all connoting virginal qualities).[70] According to Bernhard Fernow, the "natural forest resource as we find it" was "lying idle and awaiting the hand of a rational manager."[71] The representation of a feminized forest waiting for (rational, masculine) management served to naturalize the goals of forest conservation by making conservationists' concerns appear to stem from nature. The appearance of a virgin forest in conservationist discourse also erased Aboriginal territorialities.[72] The reclassification of peopled lands as virgin negated Aboriginal peoples' presence on and claim to forested land, thus making "Canadian" forests available to be managed according to the principles of scientific forestry.

Forest conservation discourse worked not only to make Canadian forests and forest conservation appear natural, but also to naturalize the Canadian nation and its place within the British Empire. Conservationists called the woodland wealth of Canada "our greatest heritage," arguing that since Canada had been "blessed by Providence with a wealth of forest," it must adopt a rational forestry system.[73] The nation, it appeared, was always in existence, bestowed upon Canadians by chance, nature, or divine intervention, its resources available for citizens to use. But conservationists also argued that Canadian forests, with proper management, could meet Great Britain's needs for lumber as well and thus fulfill Canada's duty to its mother country.[74] The British Empire and Canada's place as a colony within it thus appeared only natural.

INDIANS RESIDENT IN THE FOREST RESERVE

The Teme-Augama Anishnabai still lived in what had become the TFR, but they and n'Daki Menan had been discursively displaced by the construction of the area as natural and national space. The region came to be thought of as a timber reserve, and the Teme-Augama Anishnabai were unable to persuade Canadian governments to recognize even a small part of it as their territory.

When provincial authorities created the TFR, they knew that "a small band of Indians" lived there but did not consider band members to have "actual ownership" of the area or "proprietary rights over any particular territory."[75] This view, consistent with the British imperialist perspective that shaped Canadian Indian policy more generally, held that "uncivilized" peoples, particularly those who did not cultivate their lands according to European standards, were not landowners or settlers, but were mere occupants of the areas they inhabited.[76] This understanding of landownership meant that government officials saw no contradiction in outlawing the settlement of lands they knew the band had resided on for many generations. Yet the Teme-Augama Anishnabai could not easily be ignored by provincial authorities, who responded for the most part by constructing them in relation to the forest reserve. Southworth, for instance, thought that their presence would benefit both them and the government, since "the work of caring for and operating the territory will be profitable for them."[77] Further, he believed that they would be "put at no disadvantage from the creation of the Forest Reserve," since some of them already worked as guides for tourists, and the creation of the TFR would allow more of them to be so employed.[78] White seemed less sure. He feared that the Indians might become enemies of the forest, ready to set fire to do harm (he did not consider that they had their own reasons for setting fires, one of which was to encourage the growth of berries). He agreed with Southworth that they should be hired as tourist guides, but his reasoning had more to do with trying to dissuade them from burning down the forest than anything else.[79]

Regardless of whether the Teme-Augama Anishnabai were positioned as potential helpers or hinderers of the forest reserve, their relationship to the land was defined by conservationist ideals for the forest. N'Daki Menan was a source of timber, not the homeland of the Teme-Augama Anishnabai. Although they remained in place after the creation of the TFR, the previously indissoluble link between them and the land was torn apart and the parts placed (separately) into the context of conservation. Thus, the Teme-Augama Anishnabai and n'Daki Menan could be considered without reference to one another, and the band's long-standing claim to and relationships with the area could be rendered invisible. N'Daki Menan became part of the Ontario and Canadian forest, and the Teme-Augama Anishnabai became the "Indians who are resident in the Forest Reserve."[80]

As a result, Aubrey White was able to say in 1911 that the Department of Crown Lands had "treated the Indians there [in the TFR] in a very generous way."[81] He assured the DIA that his department had not disturbed the Indians, who "are permitted to roam about there over a much larger area than they could expect to get in an Indian Reserve, and they are employed as fire rangers and guides and our information is that they are quite contented to be left as they are."[82] The Teme-Augama Anishnabai, who did not see themselves or their claim to n'Daki Menan as existing in relation to the TFR, did not perceive their treatment by the Ontario government as generous in the least. Band members expressed their frustration at being asked to vacate their houses, at being forced to get permission from the chief fire ranger even to cut firewood, and at being forbidden to fell trees and build houses.[83] They continually pressed their claim for a reserve, and by the time White made the above statements, they had sent delegations, petitions, and a number of letters to the DIA, all in an attempt to urge a decision from the department about the reserve.[84] One fairly typical petition, written in 1907, read, "We have been asking for a reserve on Lake Temagami for [illegible number] years. We were offered a reserve a few years ago, but did not get it. We see that the Government gave reserves to all the Indians north of us last summer, and we do not know of any Band but ourselves who have not their own reserves. We have no land that we can settle on. We wish you would help us to get a reserve."[85] The petition was signed by fifty-one Teme-Augama Anishnabai women and men.

Whereas the Teme-Augama Anishnabai found their activities in n'Daki Menan to be severely restricted, non-Aboriginal people were able to access the area with ease. Sturgeon Falls Pulp and Paper Company was permitted to cut enough pulpwood to supply its mills for twenty-one years.[86] Smaller-scale logging took place within the TFR as well. In 1901, Temagami fire rangers built a headquarters on Bear Island, using lumber and shingles "manufactured on the spot."[87] They also cleared portages of trees.[88] In December of 1902, the Department of Crown Lands made new regulations under the Forest Reserves Act designed not to advance scientific forestry, but to control other activities in reserves. The regulations permitted mineral prospecting and mining in the reserves, as well as cutting timber to facilitate mining activities. Other regulations were meant to prevent fires in reserves and to prohibit people from felling trees without government authorization. The new regulations also provided for the licensing of guides, making it illegal for anyone to guide tourists through forest reserves without a licence, and mandated that visitors to reserves must give rangers personal information and details about their travel plans.[89]

These regulations were spurred because the TFR was about to be opened up by the Temiskaming and Northern Ontario Railway (TNOR), a government line that would extend from North Bay through the TFR and pass by the end of Lake Temagami's northeast arm.[90] The Department of Crown Lands (correctly) expected that the construction of the railway would bring large numbers of tourists and prospectors to the TFR, and it therefore wanted to ensure that rules were in place to control their behaviour. Tourists and prospectors were not discouraged from entering the TFR. Indeed, the TNOR was partially intended to encourage mineral development and tourism.[91] In 1903, railway construction workers came upon veins of cobalt-silver ore quite a distance north of Lake Temagami and outside the TFR. This discovery led to the founding of a mineral camp appropriately called Cobalt; by 1905, prospecting was taking place on a large scale in and around it.[92] The government opened the TFR for prospecting in 1906, and soon many prospectors began to explore it. By 1909, they had staked thousands of claims and begun substantial mining work.[93]

In 1903, the Department of Crown Lands decided to license felling timber (as distinct from pulpwood) in the TFR for the first time, explaining that "a reserve from which no lumber is taken would not be serving its full purpose."[94] The department also gave permission and money for trees to be cleared along the railway line where it passed through the TFR.[95] When Southworth successfully petitioned to have the TFR expanded, the department had already given out several pulpwood licences for lands within the new boundary. Of the 3,700 square miles to be added to the reserve, 1,850 of them were covered by pulp concessions.[96] Over the decade, Ontario granted several timber and pulp licences in addition to those that already existed within the TFR. Parties were permitted to cut wood for railway ties, mature pine or pine damaged by fire or wind, and timber for mining and power-generating purposes.[97] In addition, portions of the TFR were withdrawn from the reserve to facilitate mineral development, and companies were allowed to dam lakes, provided that they cleared the shorelines of trees killed by raised water levels.[98] The Department of Crown Lands also permitted summer residence in the TFR and began leasing out islands in Lake Temagami to people interested in building summer homes and camps there.[99]

The fact that so many non-timber-related activities took place within the TFR was not a sign that forest conservation had failed. Settlers had been excluded, fires kept under control, and activities understood as compatible with forest conservation regulated, although, as government officials recognized, many activities permitted in the TFR threatened to destroy the timber that the reserve was designed to protect. In 1910, for example, White noted that the TFR was in great danger of fires due especially to prospecting, silver mining, and tourism, and suggested that the numbers of rangers be increased to protect the forest from fire.[100] That a variety of activities were occurring within the TFR, all authorized by the provincial government, does indicate, however, that the region had become part of the province of Ontario and the Canadian nation. It had been marked for resource development and tourism rather than settlement. Because only two non-Native agricultural settlers lived in the area prior to the creation of the TFR, its establishment as a forest reserve did not greatly affect the non-Native farming class (the two settlers were allowed to remain). Teme-Augama Anishnabai lives, on the other hand, were drastically changed. Although non-Native forestry interests, mineral developers, hydro companies, and tourists were authorized by Ontario to reap the benefits of the region's resources, the Teme-Augama Anishnabai were prevented from cutting down even a few trees to build houses for themselves.

There was still the matter of a reserve for the band, which it would not let the government forget, a matter that challenged both Ontario's assertion of control over the region and the region's existence as a natural space of timber (and other resources). Yet by 1910, Ontario was able to cite the TFR as the *reason* for refusing to create an Indian reserve. By 1897, White had received at least three letters from the DIA outlining the Teme-Augama Anishnabai claim and requesting that representatives from the two governments meet to discuss the matter of an Indian reserve.[101] Although White ignored or responded only cursorily to those letters, in his memorandum recommending the creation of the TFR, he stated that Ontario had refused to cooperate with the DIA in creating the Indian reserve in part because it was aware of the "great quantities of Pine" in the area.[102] It was not until 1906, when the DIA, pressured by Teme-Augama Anishnabai who had taken the train to Ottawa to further their claim, again petitioned Ontario about creating a reserve, that White finally responded for Ontario by stating that the province could not "see its way" to granting the DIA request.[103] White offered no explanation for this decision, even when asked by the deputy superintendent general of Indian affairs.[104] When, in 1910, the Teme-Augama Anishnabai again reminded the DIA of their claim, and the DIA again wrote to the province, White responded with a tentative answer explaining that since the Robinson-Huron Treaty did not provide for a reserve, and since preserving the area's timber was important, he could not promise a favourable reply to the department's request.[105] The DIA wrote back, saying that although the Teme-Augama

Anishnabai were not represented at the signing of the treaty, this should not "prejudice their right to the benefits arising from that treaty."[106] Nevertheless, Ontario's response was that the minister was "unable to recommend the setting apart of an Indian Reserve in the Temagami Forest Reserve" for the reasons given in White's previous letter.[107]

Not surprisingly, the reasons White offered to the DIA were the same as those in his internal memorandum recommending the setting aside of the TFR: that Ontario had no legal obligation to create an Indian reserve, and that great quantities of timber existed in the area, which needed to be protected. What is interesting is *when* the Ontario government chose to explain its refusal to create the reserve. The DIA first requested that Ontario consider establishing a reserve for the band in 1885, and, at least by the time White wrote his 1901 forest reserve memorandum, the provincial government had arrived at a firm answer. Yet for the next nine years, it refused to answer federal requests about its position on the matter. This time lapse was significant, because by 1910, enough time had passed to enable Ontario to cite the existence of the forest reserve and the need to protect it as central reasons for denying a reserve to the Teme-Augama Anishnabai. White's 1910 declaration could not have been made in 1901, because the forest reserve was then too new to make sense as a reason to deny a reserve to an Indian band that everyone recognized as having resided in the area long before the creation of the TFR. Yet in 1910, despite the continued protests of the Teme-Augama Anishnabai, Ontario's reasoning made enough sense to the DIA that instead of pursuing the Teme-Augama Anishnabai's claims, the department informed them that Ontario "positively refused to set apart an Indian reserve in the Temagami Forest Reserve."[108] The fact that the Teme-Augama Anishnabai had continuously pressed their claim since at least 1877, twenty-four years before the TFR was created, was forgotten in this historically reversed logic. This reasoning became possible not simply with the passage of time, but through the active steps taken by Ontario within this period to legislate and regulate non-Native people into, and the Teme-Augama Anishnabai out of, the TFR.

Before Any Government Was Born in Canada

The TFR continued to affect Teme-Augama Anishnabai life profoundly after 1910. In 1911, Ontario banned shooting and fishing there. When the DIA followed up on a request by the band to find out what provisions would be made for it regarding hunting and fishing in the TFR now that those activities were banned, White wanted to know "under what authority they [the Indians] claim the right to fish and shoot there, and what their expectations are."[109] In response, the band again requested a reserve at the south end of Lake Temagami as well as fishing and hunting rights as outlined in the Robinson-Huron Treaty. Though DIA secretary J.D. McLean conveyed this message to White, he did not respond.[110] Ontario remained intransigent, and the DIA did not put a great deal of pressure on the province to create a reserve for the Teme-Augama Anishnabai, in spite of their frequent letters, petitions, and delegations to the department. In 1912, Chief Alexander (Aleck) Paul complained to the DIA that the chief forest ranger in Temagami would not permit the Teme-Augama Anishnabai to erect dwellings on Bear Island, even though they had to send their children to school there. Paul insisted that it was "our right to live as people and surely it is only fair that we should be allowed to build for our own use on Bear Island."[111] In response to this, the DIA merely asked Ontario to "indicate some suitable spot to which it may be possible to induce these Indians to remove and to build homes for themselves."[112]

Left with no reserve and only precarious fishing and hunting rights, the Teme-Augama Anishnabai became increasingly dependent for their livelihoods on working as guides for the tourists, prospectors, and surveyors who travelled to n'Daki Menan in increasing numbers during the first decade of the twentieth century. But, as they repeatedly insisted, they wanted more than to work for wages: they wanted a reserve and hunting and fishing rights as outlined in the Robinson-Huron Treaty.

In part because the Teme-Augama Anishnabai worked as guides in the TFR, the Ontario government did not feel obligated to facilitate the creation of a reserve. Southworth, for example, felt assured that the creation of the TFR would put the band at no disadvantage.[113] Yet the band clearly was disadvantaged once the TFR became the reason for denying it a reserve. Still, White confidently suggested that the Teme-Augama Anishnabai were better off without a reserve, since this permitted them to roam about and work as fire rangers and guides.[114] Thus, guiding, which the Teme-Augama Anishnabai did at least in part *because* they no longer had land in their own territory, and because their subsistence activities were policed and regarded as criminal by officials now patrolling n'Daki Menan, became a reason that they did not need their own territory. But guiding benefited Ontario more than it did the band, since guides worked in the service of forest conservation by safeguarding the area from fires set by tourists and prospectors. This arrangement served Ontario well, for guides provided the government with free fire protection services, and the province did not surrender any valuable pine timber by creating an Indian reserve. Under the Forest Reserves Act, the government required that people working as guides in the TFR must carry a licence, which could be revoked if they disobeyed the Fire Act and the Forest Reserves Act.[115] Thus, by functioning as guides, the Teme-Augama Anishnabai found themselves in the awkward position of playing a role in a forest conservation scheme that depended on the erasure of their claim to n'Daki Menan.

Unlike the government, the Teme-Augama Anishnabai did not suffer from historical amnesia. As Chief Aleck Paul stated in a 1913 speech, part of which appeared in a Philadelphia newspaper, "If an Indian went to the old country and sold hunting licences to the old country people for them to hunt on their own land, the white people would not stand for that."[116] Similarly, in 1917, Paul directly challenged the province's reasoning for not allowing the band a reserve. Upon learning that Ontario refused to grant the reserve because of the value of the timber in the region, he stated that "We think that we deserve to have something on our reserve. We have been here before any government was born in Canada."[117] The Teme-Augama Anishnabai not only saw through Ontario's logic, but consistently insisted upon their own claim to n'Daki Menan. In spite of their efforts, however, they remained unheard. The establishment of the TFR was not only a matter of introducing rational management – however poorly it was achieved – into an empty forest, but was part of a larger process through which Aboriginal title to the land began to be forgotten and legislatively removed. Indeed, the introduction of the forest reserve not only limited Teme-Augama Anishnabai access to and control over their lands, but it also helped to place them in a service role with respect to white tourists who were attracted to Temagami because of its supposedly pristine wilderness.

3

Virgin Territory for the Sportsman

During the first decade of the twentieth century, the tourism industry blossomed in Temagami. As late as 1899, the region still seemed to many outsiders a "little known district amid the wilds of Canada," but perhaps as early as 1905, when the railway first stretched north to Temagami, and certainly by 1910, it had become a "far famed sportsman's paradise of the north," with thousands of tourists visiting each summer.[1] Travel writing played a central role in this transformation and in the creation of the region as a natural and national space. At the same time, it hastened the erasure of n'Daki Menan as Teme-Augama Anishnabai territory and fostered non-Aboriginal territorial appropriation. In travel writing, Temagami was typically presented as a wilderness space to be consumed by tourists, especially by white male tourists, suggesting the *multiple* ways in which nature is constructed in the service of colonialism and demonstrating that race and gender operate flexibly in the making of national natures.

Travel writing produced between 1894 and 1915 reveals how Temagami came into existence as a natural and national wilderness space, a construction that has proven remarkably durable. This literature offers the perspectives of those who visited the area and wrote about their experiences. It provides neither an objective depiction nor a clear window into the actual experiences of the writers. Like all narratives, travel accounts are products of their time and of authorial choice (often constrained by editorial demands and the expectations of the genre).[2] As Patricia Jasen has demonstrated, pre–First World War tourism in Ontario was dominated by a romantic sensibility, including a fascination among upper- and middle-class white tourists with people and places they considered wild or primitive.[3] Visiting such places gave them an opportunity to reflect on the nature of civilization and usually to find their own culture superior to the "wild" peoples and places they encountered.[4] Turn-of-the-century travel writing both reflected and reinforced the culture of imperialism in which it was situated. Indeed, European travel writing is now acknowledged to have played an important part in the colonization of non-European peoples and lands.[5] Still, travel accounts do give an indication of how tourists experienced Temagami, and they show how writers chose to describe their experiences. These descriptions matter because they shaped the ways that readers, many of whom never ventured into Temagami, comprehended it. As Mary Louise Pratt shows, and as will become clear below, European travel writing was a product of "transculturation" rather than of one-way (Europe-to-colony) knowledge production, but the "imperial eyes" of travel writing were no less implicated than other techniques of imperialism in shaping economic and political realities.[6]

CLASS, GENDER, AND RACE IN TEMAGAMI TOURISM; OR, WHO WENT, WHO WROTE, AND WHO WORKED

Tourism in Temagami, as in the rest of Ontario before the First World War, was largely an activity of middle- and upper-class women and men.[7] Upper-class boys also spent their summers in Temagami beginning in the opening years of the twentieth century, when two private boys' camps, the American Camp Keewaydin and the Canadian Camp Temagami, opened on Lake Temagami (see the map on p. 34).[8] The directors of these camps, A.S. Clarke and A.L. Cochrane respectively, held positions at prestigious private schools from which they recruited their campers.[9] Before the railway reached Temagami, getting to the area via train, steamer, and portage before even putting a canoe in the water was something only those with leisure time and spare money could afford. Even after railway service began, the more than day-long train ride from Toronto or Buffalo made Temagami largely inaccessible to urban working-class people, who usually did not have paid holidays and typically worked six days a week until well into the First World War.[10] Some rural people who lived close to Temagami visited it for day trips, as, for example, with the annual excursion organized from nearby New Liskeard by the Independent Order of Odd Fellows.[11] They did not, however, tend to write about their experiences, and members of the more privileged classes were both the writers of, and the target audience for, Temagami travel writing.

Although white women and boys went on wilderness vacations in Temagami, all but a few of the several dozen travel narratives written about the area between 1894 and 1915 were penned by white men. Jasen suggests that this was not because women did not go on such vacations, but because the wilderness travel narrative was typically gendered male, and women were at least sometimes actively discouraged from writing in this form.[12] Boys probably wrote of their Temagami camping adventures and canoe trips in letters home, but such accounts did not find their way into the pages of popular camping, hunting, and fishing magazines such as *Rod and Gun*.[13] In both Canada and the United States, camps were thoroughly implicated in the sorts of imperialist and nationalist processes described in this chapter, including the linked ideas that Aboriginal peoples and cultures were dying, and that white men were the natural leaders of the nation. At private boys' camps such as Keewaydin and Temagami, "Indian programming" encouraged campers to appropriate (often invented) aspects of Aboriginal cultures and to perform them in a manner that indicated that authentic Native people lived only in the distant past. "Playing Indian" at camp provided boys with an antidote to the "overcivilizing" and "emasculating" effects of modernity that so concerned social observers, but it also assisted in the naturalization of colonialism by making campers appear as the descendants of the Indians and therefore as the natural and Native inheritors of the nation.[14]

In part because women wrote so few of the published travel narratives about Temagami, it is difficult to assess how many women and girls travelled to the region. This difficulty is compounded by the fact that, as both Pratt and Jasen point out, men's narratives are not always reliable sources of information about women's and girls' participation in travel.[15] As a woman writer recalled about her hunting trip in Temagami, "I went out to call my husband to breakfast, when one of them [a party of hunters from Toronto] exclaimed, 'Is that a woman's voice? Why, we're not out of civilization yet!'"[16] When a white woman was acknowledged as entering wilderness space, the space ceased to be wild. Here, the woman stood as a "boundary marker" in Anne McClintock's sense of the term, a threshold figure through which "men oriented themselves in space, as agents of power and agents of knowledge."[17] If white women marked the boundary between civilization and wilderness – where they were, wilderness was not – it makes sense that white men writing about their wilderness experiences and the masculinity required to survive them would avoid mentioning the presence of white women. Acknowledging white women in Temagami, especially far from "sign[s] of civilization" such as the railway, meant challenging the notion that only men had the ability to enter into nature's wildest places.[18] Few writers seemed interested in making such a challenge, and sometimes even when male authors did reveal the presence of white women on their camping trips, the women remained peripheral to the story. One man opened his article by stating that "the fit of restlessness ... came over me and, abandoning my duties, the daily worries for the daily bread, I set forth to hold communion with nature, and, as a fitting setting for such a quest, I chose as my companions nature's own children."[19] Yet his wife accompanied him on this trip. The absence of women in men's travel narratives had the effect of making wilderness appear not only wild, but also a domain for white men, even though white women also visited Temagami.

The few travel accounts written by women offer insight into their experiences of Temagami, although these must be read, as must men's (in different ways), with the understanding that gendered expectations played a role in what they considered appropriate to write (usually with the help of editors).[20] Perhaps some women were inspired to camp in Temagami by claims such as Ella Walton's (in an 1899 essay called "A Woman's Views on Camping Out") that "primitive instincts are the same in a woman as in a man" and that camping was "a perfect rest for weary mothers, energetic housekeepers, brain-workers, and fagged-out society women."[21] As Jasen observes, white women's participation in wilderness holidays was connected to feminist concerns of the day.[22] Women who went camping challenged the prevalent view that girls and women had neither the capacity nor the enthusiasm for the pastime that boys and men did, a view that rendered it "quite natural" that boys' camps far outnumbered girls' camps in Canada and the United States.[23] One young woman on a Temagami canoe trip recounted with relish the "wild exhilaration singing at your heart and thrilling through your blood at every lunge and rise of the bow" as she paddled in swift wind across a lake.[24] Wilderness tourism gave some girls and women room, at least temporarily, to challenge or take a break from the gender roles they were expected to fulfill at home. On such trips, Aboriginal guides often performed the cooking and cleaning generally done by women, which freed the latter to hunt, fish, and participate in other activities in the male realm.[25] The idea that women could find emancipation through travelling to wilderness spaces, a privilege very few could afford, reveals the class bias of this particular version of feminism. It also gives some indication of the race politics at work in Temagami, where some white women could access greater freedom by hiring Aboriginal guides to cook and clean for them, and to help them travel through Teme-Augama Anishnabai territory.

When Teme-Augama Anishnabai participated in tourism, it was work. Indeed, they did much of the labour that made the leisure of white tourists possible and enjoyable (see the following page). As they became increasingly marginalized from n'Daki Menan, tourism became an important means of economic survival. There are indications, however, that some would have preferred to get by in other ways. They petitioned for a reserve in part because band members were being "annoyed by people," and an elder recalled in a 1973 interview that before the introduction of the railway, "I had a nice life. I'd like to see that again, no game warden, no white people, only two white people at the Hudson's Bay, only two white people."[26] Others, though, looked forward in the winter months to seeing "their tourists" again the following summer and viewed the days of working for tourists as good times.[27]

Whether they despised, enjoyed, or felt ambivalent about outsiders entering n'Daki Menan, the Teme-Augama Anishnabai did not choose to have tourists invade their territory in the summer months. By participating in tourism, they were making the best of a situation largely not of their own creation. But the introduction of tourism in Temagami did not mean that the band gave up its other activities. If most band members worked in tourism during the summer and sometimes fall months, they spent their winters hunting and trapping on their family territories.[28]

Encounters between tourists and Teme-Augama Anishnabai individuals in the contact zone of n'Daki Menan/Temagami were highly ambivalent affairs. Although band members did not publish their accounts of tourism, they influenced what tourists could write, as well as where they could travel in n'Daki Menan. They also had and continue to have their own stories about their territory, stories into which vacationers sometimes fit. Tourists' experiences of the region were definitely shaped by the formidable amount of "cultural baggage" they brought with them (which, as we shall see, they expected their guides to carry along with the rest of the luggage) but also by their encounters with real places and with real people who were active participants in tourism and who variously assisted, resisted, and ignored tourists' imaginations of themselves and their lands.[29] Because of the multiple roles played by the Teme-Augama Anishnabai, tourists did not always get the vacation they had in mind. Travel writers had much more

VOL. LXXX., No. 8   FEBRUARY 22, 1913   Price 10 Cents

FOREST AND STREAM

PORTAGE NO. 7, BETWEEN TEMAGAMI AND STURGEON RIVER
Photograph by S. S. Sangster.

This 1913 cover of *Forest and Stream* shows some of the work that Teme-Augama Anishnabai members did to assist tourists' vacations. On portages, guides usually carried the canoes, tents, food, and equipment, leaving tourists with only cameras, guns, and fishing rods to carry. *Courtesy of Toronto Reference Library* control over their writing than they did over their trips per se, and it was the writing more than encounters between Natives and tourists that produced the region as a wild national space.

Teme-Augama Anishnabai men and boys worked as guides (women did not, probably in large part because of tourist expectations about "proper" gender roles), securing decent wages because the demand for guides far outmatched the supply. In fact, some visitors complained that the guides were paid too much and felt that wealthy American tourists were "spoiling the guide market for the tourist of moderate means" by outbidding one another and paying guides as much as $3.50 per day.[30] In spite of the Ontario government's (seemingly failed) 1906 attempt to fix guides' wages in the TFR at $2.50 per day and to ban guides from abandoning one party to join another that offered better pay, guiding tourists remained an important and well-paying occupation for Teme-Augama Anishnabai men well beyond 1915.[31] Teme-Augama Anishnabai women also found employment in the tourism industry, working as cooks at camps such as Keewaydin and Temagami, and as helpers and waitresses at hotels on Lake Temagami. They also did laundry and staged plays for tourists, cleaned cottages at private camps, and sold butter, homemade bread, and handicrafts to tourists. The men also ferried vacationers from Temagami Station to Bear Island and cut ice and wood in the winter months for camp owners to use during the summer.[32] Men and women participated in dances that frequently took place on Bear Island at least in part for the entertainment of tourists. These dances were well attended by Native and non-Native people alike.[33]

Aboriginal people played large parts in many white men's travel narratives and also in those few accounts written by white women. Native guides figured particularly prominently in accounts of Temagami wilderness holidays, but writers often commented as well on the Native people they met during their journeys or saw from a distance. Authors seemed to take every possible opportunity to philosophize about the character and habits of Aboriginal men, women, and children. Less evident in this literature are the work-leisure relationships between Teme-Augama Anishnabai women and tourists. This comparative invisibility of women speaks both to the common erasure of work done by women and to the particular fascination of white male writers with their male guides. This preoccupation cannot be separated from the culture of imperialism in which tourists travelled. Raised on fiction and other media that featured the imaginary Indian (noble, solitary, male, dying), most writers focused on *this* figure rather than on trying to explode the very notion that it existed

Cover of a Grand Trunk Railway advertisement booklet from 1908.
Like travel writing, promotional material attempted to attract tourists to Temagami
by drawing from and reinforcing stereotypes about Aboriginal people and Aboriginal
guides in particular. *York University Libraries, Clara Thomas Archives and
Special Collections, Toronto, CPC 1908 0139, image number ASC 02012*

(see above). Teme-Augama Anishnabai who worked as guides fulfilled the
role for writers, at least in published narratives, of the Indian that tourists
had in mind.[34]

Guides served many other roles in Temagami tourism as well, particularly
that of servant. They did so because vacationers left their own servants at
home.[35] As one contented tourist commented, "the trip was the best I have
ever taken, the guides could not be beaten. They were gentlemanly, intelligent, excellent hunters and at the same time good servants."[36] Many
writers considered guides absolutely necessary for journeys through what
one author called "Temagami's Tangled Wild."[37] Another recommended
that a "canoe and guide should be provided for each of the party, and an
extra guide with canoe to carry supplies, cook and attend to camp." This
would leave "the 'sports' ... and their personal guides, free to get away from
camp in the morning or come in late at night, without the domestic

economies being upset thereby."[38] Many, though not all, visitors heeded this kind of advice and hired at least one guide per person. In 1905, the regional Indian agent reported that guides were so highly sought-after that the Teme-Augama Anishnabai could not supply more than half the demand, and Aboriginal people came from elsewhere to fill the gap.[39]

Not all writers thought it necessary to travel with guides. One suggested that the adequate maps of the area made them superfluous, and another asserted that the "highest degree in the order of campers" was achieved when (male) campers were unaccompanied by guides.[40] Nor did the writers agree that the best guides were Aboriginal. Most preferred them – one author bragged that his hunting party, which was led by Aboriginal guides, succeeded in seeing and shooting many moose, whereas a party led by white guides came back empty-handed – but a few writers thought that white guides were superior. One extolled the virtues of his white guide by saying, "As for Hec, he was an ideal guide; not a full blood, nor even a half breed Indian to loll around and grunt out guttural and monosyllabic answers to your questions. He was a Scotchman: bright, intelligent, truthful, honest almost to a fault, and very energetic."[41] Tourists' opinions, both positive and negative, about Aboriginal guides were shaped by and productive of contemporary racial thinking, which included particular ideas about progress, civilization, and nationhood. A few discovered that, as a writer remarked, "one of our Indians turned out after being washed to have been born in Bond Street, London." Grey Owl, who became Canada's favourite British-born imaginary Indian, also guided tourists in Temagami during the early 1900s.[42]

WILD TEMAGAMI

Temagami consistently featured in travel literature as a feminized wild place. Authors called it "utterly wild," an "as yet wholly unsurveyed" region where nature "is to be found in practically her virgin state." Even after it had become a well-known tourist destination, writers continued to represent it as "thousands of square miles of primitive forest intersected by innumerable lakes and rivers, many of them practically unexplored."[43] Temagami figured not only as virgin, but also as part of the past. One author described a voyage down the Temagami River as a tour through "regions of grand antiquity," where it became possible to "lose yourself among the shades of former ages when the forest patriarchs and the red-man dwelt in unmolested security."[44]

Somewhat ironically, given the representation in forest conservationist discourse of virgin forests as wasteful and degenerate, the construction in tourist writing of virgin Temagami nature as glorious and unspoiled became possible in part because of the creation of the TFR. Although the Ontario government set aside the reserve primarily for the purpose of ensuring future timber supplies, it allowed a wide variety of resource-extractive projects to take place within it, including mining and logging. These enterprises, along with the activities and presence of the Teme-Augama Anishnabai, made Temagami far from unspoiled and uninhabited. But as wooded areas in much of southern Ontario and the eastern United States were rapidly being converted into agricultural lands (much to the dismay of forest conservationists), Temagami remained relatively well treed, and so tourists were easily able to describe it as "covered with virgin forest." Thanks to its "untouched and unscarred" forests standing in "all their primeval glory" (or at least their appearance as such), visitors could feel that they were deep within the wilderness and "far from the haunts of human beings."[45] The Ontario government took steps to maintain the image of Temagami as a wild place. Although it permitted power companies to dam lakes and cut timber in the TFR, it imposed restrictions to ensure that tourists encountered the wild Temagami of their imaginations rather than a landscape altered by industry. Companies were required to remove trees that had been drowned by raised lake levels and to log in areas sufficiently distant from the shoreline that vacationers could not see the deforested sites from their canoes.[46] Thus, the physical space of Temagami was shaped by tourist expectations, which became reality through the regulations designed in response to them.

Temagami tourism did not occur in a vacuum, and the romantic sensibility that Jasen reveals as fundamental to tourism in Ontario from the 1790s very much determined how travel writers represented Temagami.[47] Jasen describes romanticism as the tendency, prevalent among upper- and middle-class Europeans by the late eighteenth century, to value what they considered wild nature, to hold a new respect for imagination and feeling, and to associate with the secular realm feelings formerly understood as religious. She discusses various elements central to romanticism, such as the appearance of the sublime and the picturesque as important aesthetic categories, a growing interest in Aboriginal peoples, and linkages among ideas of history, landscape, and nationalism.[48] Places that fit into romantic ideals – for example, those that contained sublime elements such as waterfalls and dark forests or picturesque features such as roughness and variety in the natural landscape – became imbued with meaning, and tourists travelled to them to experience the sights and sensations associated with romanticism. Promoters of tourism in turn packaged and sold romantic images in an attempt to so stimulate tourists' imaginations that they would travel via train and boat to distant places to spend their money on experiencing the wild in nature.[49]

It is no coincidence, then, that the commodification of Temagami occurred through the selling of the romantic. Those with vested interests in tourism relied on romanticism to promote the region because promoters in other parts of Ontario had already successfully commodified the romantic. When it came to railway advertising, the same companies sold different places at the same time (often in a single advertisement) by using the language and images of romanticism. The Canadian Pacific and Grand Trunk Railways advertised Temagami alongside other well-known "wild" places such as the Kawartha Lakes, Muskoka, the French River, and Georgian Bay. Independent promoters of tourism also represented Temagami in accordance with the romantic sensibility.

Travel writers relied on romantic tropes to describe Temagami. Even though they had no financial stake in representing the region in romantic terms, they conformed to the norms of the genre and the expectations of their readers. Most often, they invoked romantic notions of the picturesque, characterizing Temagami as a "bit of nature in her wildest, most picturesque dress" and as a "wondrous nature picture" produced by "the mighty World-Maker."[50] Authors also portrayed it in sublime terms but did so less often, as the popularity of the sublime declined in the latter half of the nineteenth century.[51] Typical was a description of "the awful stillness of the recesses of the dark interior of the forest" that "was all so thrilling and gently exhilarating." Similarly, an encounter with the Temagami wilderness was averred to bring "the spirit face to face with the primeval and eternal."[52]

The idea that wild places were transitory or doomed increased their attraction as destinations.[53] Banking on the idea that these "silent places" were disappearing with the "march of Empire" and the "white man['s] ceaseless search for the earth's endowments," promoters advertised Temagami as a place where tourists could escape the forward movement of time and access both traces of a past era and the nostalgia associated with its erasure. Embedded in such understanding is a narrative of progress, in which the destruction of the forest appears as the necessary result of European history's inevitable unfolding. Both conservationists and travel writers took it for granted and thus made it seem natural that the emergence of "civilized conditions" in Canada mandated the disappearance of the wild forest. But whereas conservationists called for the replacement of the virgin forest with an ordered timber commodity, travel literature merely encouraged tourists to visit before it was too late. As a Grand Trunk Railway ad put it, "A little while and the 'forest primeval' shall be no more. In all probability we of this generation will be the last to relate to our grandchildren the stirring stories of the hunt in the wild forests of Canada. Therefore, it behooves you, O mighty hunter, to go forth and capture your caribou or moose while you may."[54]

However inflected, representations of a virgin forest in travel narratives emptied Temagami of agency. As the moose, waterfalls, and old trees became incorporated into a tourist gaze that valued them according to their ability to conform aesthetically and imaginatively to romantic ideals, they could no longer have their own reasons for being or uses for one another.[55] The virgin forest also had no room for the territorial claims of the Teme-Augama Anishnabai. With no other reasons for its existence and no prior claims impinging upon it, n'Daki Menan could be reinvented within travel literature as a tourist destination. Forest conservation and tourism discourses both depicted the land as virgin, naturalizing their (differing) visions of it, and both worked to erase n'Daki Menan and to open up the area to Euro-Canadian male authority and control.

Forest conservation discourse allowed the government and conservationists to ignore the territoriality of the Teme-Augama Anishnabai and to construct them in relation to the TFR. Tourism discourse, by contrast, acknowledged an indigenous presence in Temagami but failed to recognize its *present*. Here the diversity of contemporary Teme-Augama Anishnabai circumstances disappeared, and local indigenous people were rendered as generic "Indians" who existed as part of the wilderness, and as part of the past. Whereas the idea of a virgin forest enacted a *spatial* displacement, that of the forest as part of the past and "the Indian" as part of the forest displaced the Teme-Augama Anishnabai *in time*. This process allowed writers to accept, and indeed celebrate, the presence of Indians (especially guides) in Temagami, even as they denied an Aboriginal presence in the contemporary moment.

Writers reinforced this banishment by assuming the inevitable disappearance of Aboriginal people and ways of life. To illustrate: an article reflecting on the considerable assistance that the "woods Indian" had given white people in the north concluded by regretting that Aboriginal people "led the way and did the work for the civilization which eventually will swallow them up." Other writers regretted that the "race [was] dying out" and some effected the disappearance of Aboriginal people, stating that "here it was that the Ojibways had their home ... The wigwams, with the circling smoke, have disappeared, and in their place are the tents of holidaymakers or prospectors."[56] A particularly telling advertisement encouraged tourists to hire Aboriginal guides in Temagami, stating that "they will be the best guides you ever had, and they will take you through the rivers, lakes, forests and hunting grounds their forefathers once called home." This ad, in which Aboriginal people exist in the past and yet are required in the present to "paddle your canoe in their own superb way," nicely reveals the work that went into imaginatively emptying peopled lands of people in making room for white tourists.[57]

Writers also constructed Aboriginal people as uncivilized by depicting them as both part of the wilderness and as fixed at an early stage of development. As Louis Armstrong stated in 1900, "Many will sympathize with us in the delight we experienced in being in an uninhabited country; uninhabited, that is except by those oldest families of the north." Another writer echoed Armstrong's sentiments, stating that his party craved land "untrammeled by the foot of man, unsullied by his hand," and was fortunate enough to find Temagami, which was inhabited by "the bears, the moose and even Indians."[58] Aboriginal people consistently appeared in travel writing as "children of the wild" and as "children of nature, ... notwithstanding that some of them are grey."[59] As one writer stated bluntly, "the average Indian differs from the average white in character as the child differs from the man – he is less developed." Others offered more nuanced analyses. Among them, C.C. Farr believed that context was everything. When he travelled in the bush with his guides, he was impressed by how "spontaneously and unconsciously [their] knowledge would peep out ... without effort, instinctively." In their "natural habitat," Farr let them handle everything, as a matter of course. In town, on the other hand, he thought they "appeared somewhat ungainly, and incongruous," and he felt "obliged to extend a kind of protectional aegis over their ignorance of surrounding conditions." Another writer saw the "wild and unspoiled Indian ... [as] a mass of contradictions." "Capture one of these wild men of the woods," he said, "bring him to our civilization, and his intelligence seems far below that of a child; but in his own wilderness he is a different creature, and, pitted against him, we are forced to acknowledge his infinite superiority."[60]

The message that Aboriginal people were a part of and belonged in the wilderness but could not survive in civilization worked to contain them in the past, and in the Temagami wilderness. (Interestingly, this was the same place from which government officials attempted to evict them, or at least to severely restrict activities unrelated to the forest reserve.) This discounted the possibility that Aboriginal people had the potential to become "civilized" and thus to survive the modern era. In fact, when tourists found evidence that Teme-Augama Anishnabai negotiated modernity quite well – one writer commented, for example, that many spoke fluent English and French – they seemed unsure of how to respond, and generally tossed it off as out of keeping with true Aboriginal character.[61] Conversely, writers savoured moments when Aboriginal people appeared "properly" Aboriginal. Upon dropping his camera into the lake, one remarked disappointedly that he would not be able to photograph "a few favorite poses of my guide David, which I knew would interest my friends."[62] By insisting that Native people belonged in the wilderness, travel writers attempted to keep them in wilderness time (the past), a period, as they presented it, that was nearing its end.

Even when the writers extolled the virtues and bush skills of Aboriginal people, and particularly of Native men, they simultaneously asserted their own cultural superiority. One admired the "wonderful power the adult Indian possesses" but contended that the "Anglo-Saxon spirit of adventure ... more than any other force under Providence, has been the civilizing factor in the world's progress."[63] He was willing to grant brute strength to Aboriginal people but restricted the ability to move forward to British colonizers. Thus, European culture was made to appear civilized and progressive through the construction of Aboriginal people as savage and fixed in time and space.

Generally, writers discounted Aboriginal peoples' capacities to develop or learn skills and characterized their guides' abilities in the bush as innate instincts. Thus, journeys through the forest and across lakes offered many opportunities for "our Indians to display their ability of keen scent" and their "instinctive sureness."[64] In this way, travel narratives depicted Aboriginal people as having more in common with wild animals than with white tourists. The representation of Temagami as *wild with* Aboriginal people made it easy to imagine it as *wild for* white tourists. It also allowed vacationers to forget that guides participated in tourism for work rather than pleasure – one writer commented that the "Indians each carried a canoe over those six miles with apparently as much ease as we did our rifles and fishing-rods" – a lapse that enabled tourists to ignore the fact that guides were people trying to make a living on their land in the present.[65]

Yet writers also valued the savagery and wildness that they believed they found in Temagami and its Aboriginal inhabitants. Many tourists visited Temagami for such encounters. Their appreciation of savagery and the wild must be understood against contemporary fears that modern life was artificial and meaningless, and that it threatened the racial health of the nation. Such anti-modernist concerns permeated middle- and upper-class culture in North America and beyond, and have been examined by many scholars.[66] Louis Armstrong voiced them when he asked, "Are we Anglo-Saxons degenerating? Is the Englishman, the American and the Canadian less hardy than his forefathers?" His answer was a clear yes. North American men were "becoming effeminate, as [had] done so many of the advanced civilizations of the past." The cure, many thought, for the "over-civilization" of modern urban life lay in "the outdoor life," where camping, canoeing, and portaging allowed men to become physically and mentally fit like their forefathers, who had been "hewers of wood and drawers of water" instead of office workers. Armstrong called for outdoor activities to become "national pastimes."[67] Contact with wild nature thus became increasingly associated with a healthy, white, male-led nation. The author of an article entitled "Why We Take to the Woods" predicted that it would be "a shame and a blow to the health of the nation when hunting is a thing of the past." After all, he continued, no other activity removed men from civilization entirely. Travel writers insisted that it was imperative, particularly for men, to take regular breaks from civilization in order to recuperate from the pressures of modern urban life and to become "energized and built up, stronger in body and mind."[68]

Given the perceived effects of modern life and the promise that a wilderness vacation could prevent degeneracy, tourists and travel writers came to appreciate what they saw as the savage in nature. Particularly attractive was the idea that a wilderness encounter could bring out the savage assumed to be embedded in every civilized man. As two contented tourists said of their Temagami vacation, "With each mile breath came freer; with each hour we grew delightfully more savage."[69] Tourists appreciated wild Temagami nature for what they perceived it did to them: made them (temporarily) uncivilized. This positive evaluation of wilderness was also connected to their appreciation of supposedly savage Aboriginal people. They not only enjoyed regarding Native people's abilities in the bush, but also valued the extent to which wilderness trips allowed them to approximate their own ideas of Aboriginal people. One young canoe tripper found himself "as free as the wind to act like the original red-man himself."[70]

For all that they valued wilderness, however, travel writers simultaneously drew a sharp boundary between civilization and savagery, placing themselves on the side of the former and Aboriginal people on the side of the latter. They did this primarily by asserting that encounters with wilderness helped enable the success of their own civilization. White men, unlike Aboriginal people, became savage for a reason: to become more effective contributors to civilization. As one writer put it, a wilderness vacation allowed "the brain-fagged, nerve-racked, denizens of our great cities" to recover from "the hurry and the worry of the ten months' grind in the treadmill of business life" so that they might return to work with "added zest and vim."[71] Tourists also remained separate from the area's Aboriginal inhabitants through their status as visitors to rather than residents of the Temagami wild. They encountered nature, became temporarily savage, and emerged from their experience better fit for the challenges of civilization. Aboriginal people, on the other hand, were at home only in the wilderness and unfit for the civilization that vacationers assumed would eventually overcome both the Temagami forest and its indigenous inhabitants.

No matter how writers characterized Aboriginal people, the very act of defining them and their cultures in the context of European colonial expansion was an assertion of control.[72] But the specific ways that travel writers depicted Aboriginal people and Temagami mattered too, since these representations influenced how readers understood the region and its inhabitants. For many, reading travel literature was as close as they came to Temagami, and such writing made it easy for tourists to imagine the area as a wild space existing only for them to discover. Although some representations challenged the idea that Aboriginal people were anachronistic or savage – for example, the Teme-Augama Anishnabai's self-representation in letters to the DIA, in which they articulated themselves as a creative and intelligent group coping in the present and planning for the future – these did not circulate widely, freeing outsiders from confronting the possibility that other people might have a prior claim to Temagami, or that it might not be a wilderness at all.

Tourists' sense of entitlement to Temagami also rested on the larger project of imperial expansion and white settler nationalism in which tourism was situated. Elite white subjects visited it in droves, believing that they had the right to do so. For them, the trip posed a logistical rather than an ethical question: how to get there, not whether they should go. This question was answered as soon as the railway reached the area. According to a 1905 *Toronto Daily Star* article, now that "the pathfinder has passed that way, has opened a steel trail," it only made sense that "you, who are tired of the old, worn trails, may have your first peep into this new sportsman's Paradise."[73]

Travel literature encouraged this kind of thinking, placing Temagami tourism within the context of the Canadian nation and naturalizing the national as well as the wilderness character of the region. A Temagami canoe trip was a "typically Canadian" form of vacation, for no "other civilized country has a great north woods, combined with lakes and rivers, where the lover of nature can study her unadorned loveliness in all its grandeur." One writer contended that, due to the Ontario government's decision to lease islands in Lake Temagami, the area would become "an ever increasing[ly] valuable national asset," the success of which would have an effect upon the whole nation. Another hypothesized in 1900 that Canadians had begun to travel in increased numbers to other parts of the country for a variety of reasons, primary among them being that patriotism had broadened from provincial to national boundaries. Thus, vacationing in Temagami and other parts of Canada became a nationalist activity, and Canadians who spent their holidays in other countries were disparaged as "not made of the stuff which counts for so much in the upbuilding of the nation." Canadians, it was said, owed it to their country to become "a strong and vigorous race, men and women whose minds shall only be equalled by the power and development of their bodies."[74]

Temagami tourism naturalized the white settler nation in other ways as well. There was no question within travel writing but that the Temagami wilderness belonged to Canadians – was in fact their "natural birthright," according to one author – and it and other wild places were often promoted as gifts that the nation had to offer the rest of the world, something that Canadians should be proud to have and to share.[75] Whether they journeyed to remote places or merely encouraged others to do so, tourists and travel writers assumed that the land was theirs to consume as they pleased in the cause of national expansion. This was most obviously evidenced in the relationship between tourism and resource extraction. The best way to publicize Canada's "immense resources, our unrivaled scenery, and our delightful summer climate," suggested one author, was through "the tourist sportsman," a man of means whose endorsement of a particular area inevitably led to its development through investments in extractive industries such as forestry and mining. National development was understood as a force for good, and in this context, it was imperative to ensure that the tourist sportsman was satisfied with his Canadian wilderness vacation, so that he would return on business to invest his capital in Canada.[76]

As though following this script, Dan O'Connor, a prominent Temagami business owner, became interested in mining in the area through his involvement in the tourist industry. Eventually, he gave up the direct running of his hotel and steamboat company, though he remained a shareholder, in order to pursue his mining interests.[77] Similarly, C.C. Farr,

who enthusiastically endorsed tourism in Temagami and authored many
Rod and Gun articles containing advice for tourists, simultaneously promoted white settlement and railway development in the area. He founded
the village of Haileybury in the late nineteenth century, naming it after
the school he attended in England, and set about attracting British settlers
by giving lectures in England and producing pamphlets directed at those
who were considering leaving England for one of its "numerous colonies."
One advantage of Canada, Farr stated, was that, unlike the United States,
it was "essentially loyal to the mother country." Even though Haileybury,
which was situated on the western shore of Lake Temiskaming and sometimes served as a jumping-off place for Temagami tourists, did not become
the thriving metropolis that Farr envisioned, his various roles as wilderness
tourist and promoter of tourism and settlement reveal not only his entre-
preneurial spirit, but also links between tourism and a white settler Canada.
Jasen contends that the many roles played by Farr also captured the "dynamics of wilderness tourism on the larger colonial stage"; though Farr
expressed a (paternalistic) fondness for local Aboriginal people, his determination to open up the region for white industry and settlement was
part of the process through which Aboriginal people became marginalized
from their lands.[78]

THE ANTI-CONQUEST OF TEMAGAMI TOURISM

Travel literature presents Temagami wilderness vacationing as an innocent
activity and confers the region unproblematically upon the Canadian nation and its white citizens, but tourism was a power-laden venture directly
connected to the expansionist cause. It seems similarly innocent, however,
in Bruce Hodgins and Jamie Benidickson's *The Temagami Experience*. The
authors celebrate the development of wilderness camping and tourism,
even as they argue that the Teme-Augama Anishnabai have a just claim to
land in Temagami. Their narrative makes it difficult to assess the impact
of non-Native activities on the band.[79] They treat tourism at the turn of
the twentieth century separately from Teme-Augama Anishnabai pursuits,
and they fail to consider the common role that resource and tourist industries played in the marginalization of the band in n'Daki Menan.
Instead, they state that the first signs of conflict between resource industries
and those who had an "environmental concern" about the region emerged
during the early twentieth century.[80] Here they trace an argument regarding
the damming of Temagami lakes that began around the turn of the century

and continued for more than two decades, asserting that while industrial users north and south of Temagami fought over the water resource, "an unorganized but persistent community of recreational users endeavoured to safeguard the natural environment of the forest from the impact of manufactured fluctuations or alterations in water levels."[81]

My reading of this controversy is quite different. Although tourists did worry about the rising water levels resulting from damming the lakes, their focus was on potential damage to the "*scenic beauties* of the lakes" and the quality of fishing.[82] Their apprehension reflected their own interests in Temagami, and it is a mistake to conflate "aesthetic values, environmental concerns, and the habits of vacationing campers" and to assume that these were necessarily in conflict with "the priorities of the forest industry."[83] Such logic renders tourism innocent, benevolent even, as it presents the interests of tourists as springing from nature.[84]

To argue that tourists' interests were "seldom in harmony with the priorities of the forest industry" or the hydro industry ignores the ways in which resource extraction and tourism worked symbiotically in Temagami. Vacationers' occasional complaints about resource development did not fundamentally challenge industry or its underlying logic of progress. Tourists generally supported (national) development. For one thing, they relied on it (in the form of the railway) to get to Temagami. Rather than challenging industrial development, they generally felt that it should be sufficiently hidden so as not to ruin their wilderness experiences. Both summer visitors and power companies abstracted and extracted n'Daki Menan from the Teme-Augama Anishnabai and placed Temagami into a new set of economic and cultural systems, even as they made it appear that their visions of nature were written into the land.

Late-nineteenth- and early-twentieth-century Temagami tourism was an "anti-conquest"; it simultaneously asserted European hegemony and rendered its own power invisible.[85] It seemed innocent in part by depicting Temagami as wild with Aboriginal people, and thus by implication as wild for tourists. More directly, Temagami appeared to be wild for tourists because God or nature had created it for their pleasure, particularly for men. As one writer asserted, the fact that Temagami lacked cultivatable soil was an indication of God "decreeing and setting apart this whole region of hundreds of miles in every direction as a great game preserve." God had provided its "most beautiful scenery ... for the refreshment of his children." The title of this article, "Timagami, a Region Organized by Nature for Real Sport," clearly revealed its author's perspective. Other writers shared his point of view, characterizing Temagami as "the northern Ontario paradise ... truly a sportsman's Garden of Eden," and as "practically virgin territory for the sportsman."[86] The construction of Temagami as a natural space made for tourists implicitly rendered tourists innocent subjects who merely received this place, and created tourism as an instance of passive consumption rather than of active appropriation. Even as travel writing helped to make Temagami into a natural space that could be consumed by visitors, this process remained invisible, allowing Temagami to appear wild for tourists precisely because travel writers were able to "subsume culture and history into nature."[87]

Such innocence was reinforced by the implication that sportsmen had no choice but to travel: they had to respond to the call of the wild. A member of the canoeing club organized through Camp Keewaydin explained the call of the wild as "a strange feeling of unrest" that came upon men during the spring. Initially unable to understand its meaning, they soon realized that "the wild has begun to call" them "back to the free life of the natural man." Contemplating the call of the wild, another Temagami canoe tripper concluded that, since the current industrial age discouraged individuals from conducting activities that did not produce material wealth, the call must be instinctive in men, touching "the most responsive chords of a man's nature."[88] Even as he ignored the increase of wilderness vacationing in industrial society, he demonstrated both the gendered character of the call of the wild and the way that it reinforced tourists' sense of innocence. Although some women insisted that men and women had the same instincts and that women also required wilderness holidays, travel writers generally constructed Temagami as a region for sports*men*. One went so far as to claim that "*the* story of Temagami" was "a story of men, rods and fish."[89] Whether tourists understood the call of the wild as a primitive instinct insisting that they travel, as Temagami nature calling them to visit, or as a combination of the two, the idea that they did not journey entirely of their own volition worked well for them. To borrow McClintock's phrase, the call of the wild represented "nature's invitation to conquest," and as such, it justified tourist infiltration of Teme-Augama Anishnabai territory, simultaneously obscuring the connections between this onslaught and the larger colonial processes of which it constituted an important part.[90]

When Does Possession Happen?

Years before the first tourists began to trickle into Temagami, colonial and then provincial and national governments had claimed the area as their own, had possessed it in theory. But this claiming had little to do with the reality lived by the Teme-Augama Anishnabai. Not until the late 1870s, when non-Native people began cutting timber on the fringes of n'Daki Menan, did the Teme-Augama Anishnabai begin to feel concerned about the encroachment of others onto their land. Another twenty-five years passed before the railway brought thousands of tourists to Temagami each summer. These incursions certainly affected the band, but its members did not simply step aside and hand their territory to tourists. According to them, n'Daki Menan remained, as always, their own territory. Vacationers, however, had other ideas. They travelled to Temagami to experience the last of the Canadian wilderness before it faded away, along with its Aboriginal inhabitants, in the face of modern civilization.

In creating Temagami and its Aboriginal population as part of the vanishing Canadian wilderness for white men to visit, travel writing simultaneously rendered unintelligible both the contemporary presence of the Teme-Augama Anishnabai and their claim to land. Yet, for all that tourists expected to find a picturesque wilderness on their Temagami vacations (including noble, and dying, Indians), they encountered a confusing new place, full of lakes and rocks and dense forests, one they did not know how to negotiate, but that the Teme-Augama Anishnabai knew well. And, as some writers acknowledged, tourists were "helpless to get about" without the assistance of Aboriginal guides, who occasionally deserted one party for another offering higher pay, but more often carried tourists' luggage, set up their tents, cooked their food, taught them how to fish and hunt, did their laundry, and waited their tables.[91] Travel writers seem to have dealt with this awkward situation by controlling the actions of the Indians on the page, voicing satisfaction when they looked and acted like the Indians they had in mind and expressing anxiety and displeasure when they did not.[92] Frank Carrell, for instance, wanted to photograph favourite poses struck by his guide but was offended when a guide sat with his party on a hotel veranda.[93] The anxiety expressed by some writers in their Temagami travel narratives was caused by going to a place imagined as a Canadian wilderness tourism destination and finding that it was no such thing. Temagami became part of the Canadian wilderness less through tourist encounters with the region – which were full of ambivalences, of un-imaginary Indians, of getting lost in an unfamiliar landscape – than through writing and reading about those encounters. Over time, and by the repetition of stories, Temagami came to be imagined as a site of national nature. But possession and dispossession, like the stories themselves, were never complete. Other stories existed.

4

A Rocky Reserve

In June 1929, the Ontario government charged rent to a number of Teme-Augama Anishnabai who resided on Bear Island in Lake Temagami. According to the province, Pete Misabi, John Katt, William Pishabo, and Alex Mattias had no title to the lands upon which they lived, and their illegal occupation was holding up development on the island. Ontario offered these residents an opportunity to lease and thereby "acquire some title" to the lands they occupied, but they refused to comply.[1] This episode sparked, or more accurately reignited, a struggle between the Teme-Augama Anishnabai and Ontario over Temagami, a struggle that continues to the present.

Between 1929 and 1943, the dispute reconfigured Temagami, as earlier discourses about the region were reconstituted in and through the rent issue. Although the Temagami of 1943 did not differ much from that of 1915, conceived as a site of Canadian nature for tourists to visit and lumber companies to log, by the later date provincial and federal governments had concluded that Bear Island was the only part of it to which the Teme-Augama Anishnabai had any claim, even though the band continued to insist that its territory encompassed all of n'Daki Menan.

THE CANADIAN NATION IN CONTEXT

Following the First World War, a firmer sense of Canadian nationalism emerged alongside a desire to wash away the memories of war. The landscape paintings of the Group of Seven are widely credited with developing a distinct sense of Canadian identity, and increasing numbers of Canadians took vacations in the wilderness landscapes that seemed to epitomize the nation.[2] Post-war prosperity also meant that more people, many of them travelling by automobile on roads built to serve the needs of a growing car culture, could visit previously inaccessible places. With the completion of a gravel highway to Temagami in 1927, tourists could drive up from Toronto within a day, and the number of summer visitors soared until the Depression of the 1930s.[3]

Although Canadian nationalism became more clearly defined after 1914, it was no less racialized. Aboriginal peoples continued to be erased from the landscape of the nation. As well, legislation – such as the 1910 Immigration Act, which allowed the exclusion of immigrants deemed racially undesirable, and the 1923 Chinese Immigration (Exclusion) Act, which prevented almost all immigration from China – attempted to ensure that Canada would remain a white settler nation.[4] Meanwhile, increasing numbers of *white* Canadians were encouraged to travel to wilderness spaces, where they came to know themselves and were defined as Canadian not only by being welcomed into the space of the nation (as Aboriginal people and racialized others were not), but also by experiencing these wild places as their own.

(Re)making Temagami Nature

Although logging took place in the Temagami Forest Reserve early in the twentieth century, exploitation quickened markedly during the late 1920s. Critics of the forest reserve system, including William Milne, whose lumber company had profited since 1905 from the clearing of trees along the railway line in the TFR, charged in the early 1920s that the Forest Reserves Act had not encouraged timber production so much as timber hoarding in Temagami and elsewhere, with the result that "millions of feet of excellent pine [were] going to waste in the northern country."[5] Shortly thereafter, Ontario began to sell timber and pulpwood licences in the TFR at a brisk pace, beginning with a 1927 timber licence that granted the Gillies Brothers Lumber Company permission to cut pine trees from a 115-square-mile area east of Lake Temagami along the railway line.[6] As in the early twentieth century, the provincial government relied on the language of forest con-servation to explain its land-use decisions – Minister of Lands and Forests William Finlayson stated that the timber sale to Gillies was "based upon the principles of rotation of crop and perpetuation of forest wealth" – but later assessments suggest that political and economic reasons were more important than scientific forestry principles in shaping policy.[7] As timber and pulpwood licences covered increasing amounts of the region, Temagami was more deeply inscribed as a site of valuable timber and as part of the province and the nation.

All of this worked to deny the Teme-Augama Anishnabai access to the forest. In the first written correspondence in a decade between the band and the DIA, George Friday requested permission to "cut logs" for building purposes after the chief forest ranger had warned him against doing so. Friday's letter implied that he had a right to cut trees in the region, a right that came, presumably, from his understanding that his band had a claim to n'Daki Menan. In reply, Indian agent G.P. Cockburn convinced him to make a frame rather than a log building, thus seeming to settle the matter.[8]

Tourism also increased dramatically in Temagami. Camps Keewaydin and Temagami continued to run, and two additional boys' camps, Wabun and Wigwasati, opened in the early 1930s.[9] More lodges and resorts also opened, some along the new highway and others on islands in Lake Temagami.[10] After Ontario issued additional leases during the late 1920s, a new group of cottagers arrived to take up islands in the lake. With approximately 60 new leases issued in the six years before 1933, the total reached 223.[11] Promotional materials and articles highlighting the wonders of the region further encouraged tourism, reinforcing the idea of Temagami as an intact wilderness. According to a 1928 *Toronto Globe* article, for instance, it was an "unbroken forest primeval ... untouched by the hand of man." A few weeks in this "Land of Virgin Beauty" would "reconstruct a broken-down physical constitution and give a tired, worn-out man a new lease of life, sending him back to his work with such a store of energy that he finds the following months of toil a thing to be enjoyed rather than feared."[12] As before, and perhaps not surprising given advertisers' interest in the bottom line, Temagami was represented primarily as a site for sports-*men*. It was, according to the government-run railway company, a "veritable paradise for the Tourist, the Fisherman and the Hunter," a place where even the "black bass, lake trout and maskinonge [lay] in wait for the fisherman."[13] And once more the Teme-Augama Anishnabai were either erased from the "virgin" landscape or constructed as part of the national past. Advertisers encouraged tourists to visit the "quaint Indian settlements" as well as the HBC post where "the Indians generations ago brought the fur wealth of the hinterland to barter for blankets and traps." The Teme-Augama

Anishnabai continued to trap on their family hunting territories and to sell the furs at that very HBC post (which had moved from Temagami Island to Bear Island), but it was said that the post "stands ... ready to serve the needs of the modern explorers of the watery trails and green glades."[14] With Indians consigned to the past, visitors could experience Temagami as part of their national wilderness in the present, "under the care," of course, "of an experienced [Native] guide."[15]

With the increased popularity of tourism came the consolidation of Temagami as a (now especially) Canadian destination, with the result that the Teme-Augama Anishnabai and n'Daki Menan existed in even more isolation from one another. In fact, white cottagers began calling themselves "settlers" and "the permanent residents of Lake Temagami and the Temagami Forest Reserve." They referred to the Teme-Augama Anishnabai, by contrast, as "Bear Islanders."[16] Some band members did reside on the island during the summer months, when they were not out on their hunting territories. Bear Island was, after all, the focal point of Temagami tourism, where vacationers often picked up supplies and engaged guides. Since band members continued to guide tourists, it only made sense that they would be on Bear Island some of the time. The cottagers' inscription of the band as Bear Islanders, however, functioned to fix it onto a tiny fraction of n'Daki Menan. With this, the rest of the territory became available to "settlers," who also identified themselves by island. Although tourists in the past had considered Temagami a paradise to visit, the cottagers' claim to it as permanently their own signalled a more definite territorial appropriation, which further undermined the Teme-Augama Anishnabai claim to n'Daki Menan.

Like other tourists before them, the settlers constructed n'Daki Menan and the Teme-Augama Anishnabai in relation to themselves. In 1931, a group of cottagers started the Temagami Association, the primary purpose of which was to ensure the protection of summer residents' increasingly valuable properties. Robert Newcomb, the association's founding president, thought that the cottagers should maintain good relationships with the Teme-Augama Anishnabai.[17] He therefore suggested that cottagers "be interested in [the Teme-Augama Anishnabai's] welfare and help them when the opportunity offers" by giving them work, shoes, and clothing. Cottagers owed them this "help," according to Newcomb, not only because they were "simple, honest, friendly people," but also because they were the "natural guardians" of "*our* [cottagers'] property."[18] Evidently, Temagami Association members saw no relationship between the "want and suffering" of the band and their own encroachment onto its territory.[19] In the logic of the association, the cottages and the land on which they stood appeared to belong "naturally" to cottagers, just as the Teme-Augama Anishnabai appeared as the "natural" guardians of cottagers' property. No further explanation seemed necessary.

A 1940 letter from Teme-Augama Anishnabai member Joe Friday to the DIA tells another story, however. Friday described being approached by two American men at the island where he had lived "since [he] was a kid" and where he had built cabins and was running a lodge. The men told him that the island was up for lease, and that if they decided to lease it, he would have to leave.[20] As the Indian agent explained, when the rental was not paid for islands, those inhabiting them "are considered squatters and can be removed by Provincial authorities."[21] Thus, as Ontario leased more Lake Temagami islands to cottagers, more cottagers became "settlers," whereas the Teme-Augama Anishnabai were considered squatters, or at the very best Bear Islanders, and evicted from (most of) their land. Neither the American men's ability to lease this island and to build a cottage on it, nor Friday's removal from it were natural. Both were the result of the provincial decision to lease islands in Lake Temagami to cottagers.

The Temagami Association was not opposed to logging but did not want its impact to be visible from the shores of Lake Temagami.[22] Fortunately for it, William Finlayson, minister of lands and forests from 1926 to 1934, had a cottage on the lake, and he assured the association that any logging would neither "be noticed from the shore" nor "offend settlers."[23] Thus, the cottagers began to exercise a significant influence over the activities that could take place in Temagami, and logging companies had to abide by the following restrictions: "No lumber camps or buildings of any description to be erected along the shore of Timagami Lake. No land will be cleared for skidways or rollways along the shore of Timagami Lake. Trees within 300 feet of portages and shorelines of inland lakes are reserved, excepting where these are marked to be cut by a representative of the Department. No booming or towing operations will be permitted in Timagami Lake during the months of July and August."[24]

Ontario also created a skyline reserve on Lake Temagami, prohibiting cutting from the shore to the top of the skyline.[25] With such restrictions in place, cottagers and tourists could continue to imagine Temagami as their pristine wilderness, even as timber and pulp companies removed increasing quantities of wood from it. By advertising the government-run railway line as a vehicle for wilderness tourism while granting timber and pulpwood licences, Ontario helped to create the idea of Temagami as both a wilderness for tourists and a site of valuable timber. Similarly, fire rangers hired to protect TFR timber cleared and marked portages for tourists.[26]

In 1929, when Deputy Minister of Lands and Forests Walter Cain informed Misabi, Katt, Pishabo, and Mattias that they would have to pay rent to live on Bear Island, he was seeking to make room for the growing number of cottagers and tourists interested in Temagami. Instead of complying, the four men consulted the local Indian agent and revived the question of their reserve, contending that band members could not be forced to vacate Bear Island when they had nowhere else to go. They also found it unfair to be charged rent for lands they had lived upon for generations.[27] In response, the DIA asked Ontario whether band members could remain on the island without paying rent until a reserve was set aside for them elsewhere. Ontario replied that "these Indians have the same privileges to occupy these lots as do businesses and other people," and should therefore not hold up development by refusing to pay rent. Further, provincial surveyor general L.V. Rorke opined, even if a reserve were created, the band would not vacate Bear Island, since "the Indians on Lake Timagami are more in touch with civilization than any other band" and would therefore not want to leave the centre of the tourist trade. For that reason, Ontario concluded that "as time goes on there seems to be less and less reason why lands should be set apart for the Timagami Indians in Austin Bay, Timagami Forest Reserve." Not only did the Indians "make their livelihood not so much through trapping, as being appointed guides, boat-men and general handymen for the tourists and cottagers who locate in that part of the country throughout the summer season," but also, according to Rorke, they "have been fairly well treated in their occupation of Crown lands on the lake."[28]

Ontario's statement that there seemed no reason to create a reserve depended upon earlier constructions of the region as a provincial forest reserve rather than as the Teme-Augama Anishnabai's n'Daki Menan. Indeed, by taking for granted the existence of the area as a forest reserve, Ontario avoided discussing the historical reasons that the Teme-Augama Anishnabai both demanded and were owed (much more than) a reserve, and instead emphasized its kindness in allowing them such a long free stay on Crown lands. Yet the province also relied on new strategies of racialization to argue that the Teme-Augama Anishnabai did not need a reserve, asserting that since they made "their living by guiding and exploring in the ordinary way of the white man," and had more contact with civilization than did any other band, it was "very doubtful" that they "would be satisfied" with living on a reserve.[29] By stating that the Teme-Augama Anishnabai were too civilized to be contented with life on a reserve, Ontario reversed its prior construction of them as too savage to own land, a representation that enabled the government to ban settlement in a region the band had occupied for thousands of years. Now, by associating reserve life with savagery and the Teme-Augama Anishnabai with civilization, Ontario attempted to make all of Temagami into a space that it regulated and to make this desire for control appear as the Teme-Augama Anishnabai's craving for civilization. The construction of the band as uncivilized in 1901 and as civilized in 1929 shows not only the instability of these racialized categories – although this instability is mitigated somewhat through the assumption that the band had *become* more civilized thanks to its years of contact with white tourists – but also how placement in either category can work to deny Aboriginal claims to land.

Ontario's assertion of government ownership of Temagami through the construction of the Teme-Augama Anishnabai as *like* civilized (white) subjects was not entirely successful, for the Teme-Augama Anishnabai refused both to pay rent and to participate in Ontario's forgetting of history. In 1932, Chief William Pishabo wrote to Indian agent G.P. Cockburn, asking him to forward his letter "to the Indian Department in Ottawa to record [his] protest" against the government's latest imposition on band life. Pishabo reminded Cockburn that the "Government promised to give us a reserve some years ago and we are still hoping that this promise will be fulfilled."[30] Indian inspector Thomas McGookin similarly reported that paying rent was "out of the question," because band members felt it "unfair and unjust that they should be required to pay rent for lands occupied by their forefathers for over a hundred years."[31] In 1935, and again in 1936, the Temagami band sent petitions to the DIA asking for the Austin Bay reserve that had been surveyed for it in 1884.[32]

The DIA acceded to Ontario's request to use "moral persuasion" to urge "these Indians ... to pay their indebtedness to the Crown" and later commented that "Bear Island is the property of the Province and these Indians are of course residing thereon without any right or authority."[33] But the department also concurred with the Teme-Augama Anishnabai, as H.W.

McGill, deputy superintendent general of Indian affairs, wrote to Deputy
Minister Cain that they "consider themselves justly entitled to reserve
lands of their own and this Department is in accord with this opinion."
He added that the DIA "considers that the Province has a moral as well
as a legal obligation to provide these Indians with a reserve." After not
receiving a satisfactory response from Ontario, McGill reiterated in 1938
that "the claim of these Indians to the land within the Robinson-Huron
Treaty, as well as their aboriginal hunting rights, has never been extinguished and it never will be till they subscribe to the Treaty and are allotted
a Reserve on the same conditions as were provided for the original
signatories."[34]

VALUABLE TIMBER VERSUS A ROCKY RESERVE

Although Ontario long refused to give "serious consideration" to the matter
of creating a "special reserve" for the Teme-Augama Anishnabai, it finally
agreed to do so in 1938 when government officials realized that the indigenous residents of Bear Island would not make rental payments. The con-
cession to grant a "small reserve" marked Ontario's significant failure to
consolidate its ownership of all of n'Daki Menan and to reconfigure racial
categories in the service of that project.[35] But it did not mean that the
Teme-Augama Anishnabai had won a major victory.

In 1939, provincial government representatives began to investigate the
suitability of "certain areas on Lake Temagami to be used as a reserve for
the Indians of that region."[36] They stated their particular interest in determining the value of the timber on the potential reserve.[37] Chief Forest
Ranger R.H. Bliss was "without reservation, strictly against" the allocation
of any land at Austin Bay to the Teme-Augama Anishnabai, in large part
because the area was "very valuable ... from the standpoint of pine and we
should not increase the hazard in this area by allowing it to be occupied."
He also stated that the DIA could not possibly ensure that the Indians
remained at Austin Bay, for they would "go back and hang around Bear
Island, where the Hudson Bay store is located and naturally where all their
guiding work comes from." Bliss concluded, therefore, that the Teme-
Augama Anishnabai "should not be moved off Bear Island" and that setting
aside a reserve at the south end of Lake Temagami was "unnecessary."[38]
The report accompanying Bliss' letter noted that, with the exception of
three small clearings, Austin Bay was covered with "virgin bush," including
many pine trees over 150 years old.[39]

Drawing on such reports, Cain informed the DIA that Ontario "cannot consent" to disposing of any land around Austin Bay for a reserve, on the grounds that the area was "altogether too valuable from a timber point of view to even consider the question and for that reason this feature of it must be dismissed from the picture now." Taking the advice of his colleagues, Cain suggested that part of Bear Island be established as a "permanent area for the Indians" because it would remain the "rendezvous of the Indians," who would refuse to "stay put" on any other reserve granted to them.[40]

With the Teme-Augama Anishnabai demanding a reserve, Ontario could no longer pretend that they did not want one. It decided to deal with the "problem" of the Bear Island Indians by confining them there. That way, the band would be kept away from the timber around Austin Bay, and Ontario could profit from leasing that land to forestry companies while giving up only a small area that, as Indian agent J.A. Marleau noted, contained "little timber" and rocky ground.[41]

Unfortunately for the Teme-Augama Anishnabai, and without their prior approval, the DIA immediately agreed to Ontario's Bear Island proposal.[42] Indian agent Marleau told an Ontario government employee that the purpose of securing a reserve for the Teme-Augama Anishnabai was to "group them at one place to endeavour to lower the cost of maintenance."[43] When the Teme-Augama Anishnabai caught wind of the plan to locate their reserve on Bear Island, they objected vehemently: Chief John Twain stated that the "place we wish to have has been picked out by the Temagami Band of Indians long before there was any forest reserve in the Temagami district."[44] Nonetheless, the DIA purchased a portion of Bear Island from the Ontario government in 1943, thus transforming most of the island, in government eyes, from a part of Ontario to land owned by the federal government and reserved for the use of the Teme-Augama Anishnabai.[45] In spite of the land transfer, though, the federal government was unable to convert the area into an official reserve for several years, until Ontario cancelled conditions it placed upon the transfer. The conditions are discussed below. Indigenous resistance to paying rent for traditional lands led Ontario to reassert ownership of the entire Temagami region, except for one square mile of Bear Island. Significantly, however, the government acknowledged that "by the Robinson-Huron Treaty the lands of the Timagami Band of Indians were, through inadvertence and without their consent, improperly removed from their control," and also that Ontario "has benefited by the terms of the said Robinson-Huron Treaty."[46]

A Conditional Transfer

The racial and spatial order of n'Daki Menan/Temagami was transformed in other ways during this period. When Ontario agreed to transfer a mere square mile of land on Bear Island to Ottawa for the use of the Temagami band, it placed a number of conditions on the transfer, including the provision that timber and fuelwood could be cut only under permit and for the personal use of the island residents. Prices for the wood were determined by Ontario. Further, Teme-Augama Anishnabai residents of Bear Island could reside only on the part of the island that had been subdivided by the provincial government prior to the transfer of land.[47] Ontario cited "preservation of beauty of the landscape" as the main reason for the conditions.[48] The lawyer for the Department of Lands and Forests further explained that "the Province does not wish the shoreline of Bear Island to be studded with Indian shacks ... and there should not now or at any other time be any necessity for either isolated buildings or anything in the nature of an Indian village springing up on any part of the Island ... , and particularly on the lake front."[49]

Initially opposed to the timber and fuelwood condition, the DIA suggested that the provincial "Forest Service harvest the present crop of merchantable timber, a lot of which would appear to be mature, within the next five years" and leave the remaining timber to the band. The DIA felt that, unless the band were granted "ownership of the timber, ... [Bear Island] presents a pretty barren reserve."[50] Ontario responded that the "difficulty encountered in this is that the Timagami Tourists' Association [Temagami Association] have in the past and probably would in this case object very strenuously to the removal of what they consider to be a valuable scenic attraction to Lake Timagami." Ontario added that the timber and fuelwood condition was not intended to profit the government from the sale of wood to the Teme-Augama Anishnabai, but was necessary because "it is felt that some control must be exercised as we feel the responsibility to the Tourist Association of Timagami is one to which we must answer."[51] Much as it did in placing conditions on timber licences, Ontario employed these stipulations on the Bear Island transfer to preserve the tourist (and especially "settler") vision of Temagami as an unspoiled wilderness. This vision entailed a shoreline covered with pine trees, not "studded with Indian shacks," and the transfer provisos successfully brought it to fruition. So Temagami nature, and especially its trees, came to exist as a commodity to be visually consumed by tourists. The forest's simultaneous construction as a site of timber to be extracted for profit did not conflict with the tourist image, because of the government specification that "no timber shall be removed from islands nor within 300 ft. of the shoreline of Lake Timagami."[52]

But Bear Island as part of the tourist scenery did not co-exist well with Bear Island as a home and source of livelihood for the Teme-Augama Anishnabai. According to the DIA, they were allowed to live there "without let or hindrance," but Ontario's conditions greatly hindered their activities.[53] Although permitted to live on the island, they could not sell timber or build houses where they pleased, and instead were "limited to the taking of wood for fuel purposes, hunting, travelling over, grazing animals, etc., over the portion of the Island outside the subdivision."[54] If the transfer of the island to the federal government worked to fix the Teme-Augama Anishnabai in space, these conditions not only further contained them, but also restricted them temporally to activities that conformed to tourist expectations of what traditional Aboriginal people did. Visiting the "Indian village" remained a high priority for tourists. As Indian inspector Thomas McGookin stated, "I talked with a number of the businessmen in Timagami and some tourists who were in the hotel and all were definitely of the opinion that the Indians were an added attraction to the tourist business in this community."[55] By preventing the band from living as it chose, the government helped to create it as an attraction for tourist consumption, and vacationers thrilled at the opportunity for contact with Native people such as young Charlie Misabi, who "is very bright and popular with the tourists ... Charlie runs beats for Mr. Stevens, dances and makes himself generally entertaining."[56] Ontario's restrictions did not go so far as to erase the Teme-Augama Anishnabai from the landscape, but they produced aboriginality for the convenience of visitors, insisting that the band had no use for or claim to land outside Ontario's prescription.

RESERVE SPACE

In some ways, little changed in Temagami between 1929 and 1943. In 1929, Ontario understood the region as provincial land. In 1943, it understood the region, with the exception of Bear Island, as provincial land. In 1929, the Teme-Augama Anishnabai wanted a reserve at Austin Bay. In 1943, the Teme-Augama Anishnabai wanted a reserve at Austin Bay. Yet Temagami was significantly reconfigured during this period. The Teme-Augama Anishnabai's refusal to pay rent challenged the notion that n'Daki Menan was a wilderness or timber site belonging to Ontario. In trying to reassert control, Ontario constructed the band both as too civilized to deserve special treatment and too uncivilized to require access to lumber. The marking out of civilization and savagery thus had little to do with the character or behaviour of the Teme-Augama Anishnabai and much to do with Ontario's political and economic interests in land.

When Ontario finally sold Bear Island to the federal government, business owners expressed grave concerns about the possibility that the island would become a reserve. John Turner wrote that "it would be a handicap to continue my business in a reservation, also further should I desire to sell what property we have nobody would want it," and J.P. Lanoie added that "your tourist trade is done for [on] this lake if this Island is made into a reserve."[57] Similarly, the vice-president of the Temagami Association, H.S. Shannon, after having heard that Bear Island had been designated an Indian reserve, wrote to inform the DIA about "certain conditions" that the association considered as requiring the department's immediate attention. The first pressing concern was "the extent to which liquor is available to the Indians on Bear Island." This was a problem because it endangered the lives of summer visitors, who "due to the complicated geographical layout of this district, and also because of numerous submerged rocks which represent hazards to the uninitiated," had to hire Indians "as guides in charge of fishing and camping parties and as drivers for various types of motor-boats." Shannon maintained that "tragedies and near-tragedies have been reported year after year," which had been "traced directly to intoxication on the part of these Indian guides." The second concern was "that of health conditions among the Bear Island Indians." Though members of the Temagami Association did "not want to give the impression that we are definitely aware of any infectious condition," they did feel that since it was "necessary for all summer residents to visit Bear Island periodically for the purchase of supplies at the Hudson Bay Post, it is obvious that general health conditions at that point are a matter of vital importance in this area."[58]

These anxieties certainly seem disproportionate to the transfer of land between governments, especially given that the conditions stipulated by the province worked to ensure that the tourist experience of Temagami would not change. Yet they also hint at a deeper concern about the racialization of Bear Island as an Aboriginal space. When the island belonged to the provincial government, at least according to Ontario, business owners felt pleased about running their companies there. They also found the Teme-Augama Anishnabai an asset and an added attraction to their businesses. Similarly, cottagers hired Aboriginal guides and bought supplies on Bear Island, seemingly without complaint. Suddenly, however, everything changed. With the transfer of land from one level of government to another, the island became imagined as a space no tourist would ever visit, one filled with contagious disease and rampant alcoholism, where no one would consider buying property. The apprehension expressed by the Temagami Association and business owners could not have been about physical changes on the island following the transfer, since the most obvious change was the transfer itself, which occurred on paper. What the transfer represented, however, was a transformation of Bear Island from part of the Temagami wilderness (for tourists to visit) to an Indian space (for Indians). Unlike a quaint Indian village, which could exist for sightseers in the present as part of the past, a reserve carried with it an undeniable Aboriginal presence in the present. The complaints about the transfer must then be seen as part of a contest over the racialization of space. When Bear Island was in the wilderness, cottagers and business owners could imagine that it was for them (or their guests), but when it turned into Indian space, they could no longer imagine it as theirs.[59]

Interestingly, the DIA responded to these complaints by insisting that nothing had changed: business owners still had the same privileges as always, and Indians remained tourist attractions. As a DIA representative wrote to Ontario's Department of Lands and Forests, "May we assure you that the plans of this Department will not in any material way alter conditions on the Island with respect to summer residents from what they have been in the past. It is not our wish to disturb anyone." The department added, "You refer to the fear some summer residents might have that the creation of the Island into an Indian Reserve might make it less desirable as a summer colony. There are instances where the converse has been true. American tourists have often expressed pleasure that their vacations in Canada were spent in close association with the native population."[60] The DIA thus responded to the criticisms on the same level as the criticisms themselves. Instead of challenging the idea of Aboriginal space as degenerate, it insisted that Bear Island was not really an Aboriginal space.[61] It remained a place for vacationers and for business owners who facilitated the tourist trade on Lake Temagami.

WRITING BACK

The remaking of Temagami as a site of nature for the enjoyment of lumber companies and tourists, and the spatial confinement of the Teme-Augama

Anishnabai onto Bear Island, did not go unchallenged. The Teme-Augama Anishnabai articulated their own ideas of the region and the relationships between n'Daki Menan and its inhabitants. In 1942, for example, they sent a proposal to the Department of Lands and Forests outlining a strategy in which they and the provincial government would jointly manage the Temagami Forest Reserve. Because of the significance of the proposal in challenging dominant imaginings of the region, and because relatively few available documents reveal Teme-Augama Anishnabai perspectives, it is important to include the proposal in full. It reads,

> *From:* The Indians of the Timagami Forest Reserve
> *Subject:* A proposal for improved administration of the conservation program.
>
> We, the Indians of the Timagami Forest Reserve, present the following proposal of joint control of forest and game conservation, believing that it will be to the best interests of both the Indians and the Ontario Government. It is the desire of the Indian as well as of the provincial government to preserve the timber and game in the most effective way; however, we are convinced that the present system leads to misunderstanding and lack of good feeling, and that as a result of this, efficient administration is made impossible.
>
> Before presenting our suggestions, we should like to review the conditions which have led to the present situation. In a verbal agreement made by the Ontario Government with the Timagami Indians in about 1902, when the Timagami district was made a forest reserve, the Indians were to be allowed unrestricted settlement, game, and fishing privileges. In the course of the following years, restriction after restriction has been placed on the Indian, until he is now treated more as an alien than as the original owner of the land. Indians are not allowed to establish homes on the mainland under any conditions. They can build on islands only through the purchase of land from the Government. Only on Bear Island, where the terrain is rocky and barren, do the Indians have free settlement rights. In order to build new homes and keep up old ones, timber is necessary. But it can be cut only with the permission of the Government, and must be paid for at a price set by the Government.
>
> The Indian's chief source of meat is deer and beaver, which he is allowed to hunt only during the brief one month season. Although he is supposed to be able to trap without licence, he is unable to sell the furs without them. Hunting and trapping being the Indian's principal means of support, these restrictions are unjustly severe.

Since we Indians feel keenly that the Government has not lived up to its part of the agreements and has in fact denied us a means of support, it becomes increasingly difficult to co-operate fully with the Government's conservation program. We therefore offer the following suggestions in the belief that their adoption would result in increased understanding between the Indians and the Government. Their purpose is to give the Indian a greater share of the responsibility in a program which is as important to him as it is to the Provincial Government.

We Propose:

1. That the Indian Chief of the Timagami Forest Reserve, in co-operation with the Chief Forest Ranger and the Chief Game Warden, determine the conservation measures which the Indians must follow. The Indian Chief will be advised by a council of the Tribe at a meeting held at least twice a year. At these meetings the Chief Forest Ranger and Chief Game Warden are to be present. The necessary measures having been decided upon, the Indian chief, rather than Government officials, shall direct his people to what they may or may not do.

2. That the Indian Chief will keep a record of all timber cut and game taken with his permission, which shall have been granted according to each Indian's individual needs.

3. That, should the Indian Chief prove incapable of his task, a new election of Chief will be held.

4. That the chief shall be paid an adequate salary for his service, so that it will not be necessary for him being away for long periods of time on trapping and guiding trips. Thus he will be free adequately to administer the conservation program.

We present these proposals in the belief that by having a voice in the game and timber regulations, we Indians will be able to achieve full and whole hearted co-operation with the conservation program such as is impossible when our own legitimate needs are not taken into consideration. The conservation program is of as vital concern to us as it is to the Provincial Government, and, since our aims are the same, administration will be both easier and more effective if the Indian and the Government are enabled to work together on it.

Respectfully submitted,
Joe Friday[62]

Friday's proposal shows that the Teme-Augama Anishnabai understanding of the region differed fundamentally from that of Ontario officials.

Although Friday argued that the band and the provincial government had the same interest in forest and game conservation, the rest of his proposal reveals that they did not. Ontario wanted to conserve the forest for lumber extraction and the game for the sport of non-Native tourists. The Teme-Augama Anishnabai presented their "own legitimate needs" as central to any conservation program. Whereas Ontario understood all of the Temagami region except Bear Island as Crown land, the band conceptualized it as shared between Aboriginal and non-Aboriginal people, with the responsibility of governance resting with the chief of the First Nation and the province. As the "original owner of the land," it saw itself as having allowed Ontario to create the TFR on the condition that band members could settle, hunt, and fish where they pleased. Upon being "treated more as an alien than as the original owner of the land," the Teme-Augama Anishnabai found it "increasingly difficult to co-operate fully with the Government's conservation program." Yet their response to what they perceived as "unjustly severe" restrictions was to seek cooperation with Ontario by suggesting a management plan that would meet both their needs and those of the provincial government.

The Teme-Augama Anishnabai, then, saw themselves as having a special relationship with n'Daki Menan based on their unique position as its original owners, yet they accepted the possibility of working respectfully with another government. Nonetheless, Ontario would not be the dominant partner in this arrangement, for, as the proposal insisted, "the Indian chief, rather than Government officials, shall direct his people to what they may or may not do." Whereas Ontario saw the band as a problem that impeded its management of the region, the band saw Ontario's presence merely as a fact. Rather than attempting to remove it, the band tried to work with the province in mutual cooperation and respect. The joint management proposal suggests an alternative way to conceptualize Temagami and the relationships between its differently located inhabitants. But this proposal did not go far. Upon receiving it, the Department of Lands and Forests simply sent a letter to the DIA stating that any application made by Friday should go through Indian Affairs.[63] Although multiple visions of the territory existed at this time, Ontario was more successful than the First Nation at turning its conceptualization into reality. Friday's proposal stands both for the continued effort of the Teme-Augama Anishnabai to articulate their special relationships with and claim to n'Daki Menan, and for the continued attempts by non-Native governments to stake their own claims to land.

Conclusion

After Bear Island was transferred to the federal government, the Teme-Augama Anishnabai continued to petition for a reserve at Austin Bay. Chief John Twain asked how it was possible that Bear Island had been set aside for them when they had not been consulted and added that the "Temagami Band want only one reserve, and that is Austin Bay." They also solicited the advice of a lawyer to help determine which treaty governed them and later approached Ontario premier George Drew to inquire about moving from Bear Island to a more suitable spot on Lake Temagami. In 1946, they instructed the North American Indian Brotherhood (a predecessor to the Assembly of First Nations) to take steps to secure the Austin Bay reserve surveyed for them in 1884. They further resolved that "Austin Bay was never surrendered by the said Band, nor neither was a Party to any Treaty making convention. We also declare that our forefathers were not a Party to the Robinson-Huron Treaty of 1850 and we further state that our Band never gave consent to a surrender or ceded any tract of land or lands of what we occupied from time immemorial."[64]

Although Ontario and Ottawa may have considered the matter resolved with the setting aside of Bear Island for the Teme-Augama Anishnabai, the band did not share this thinking. Finally, in 1960, the DIA agreed that one of its representatives would meet with Chief John Twain to discuss "the band's need for further land." Before this meeting occurred, however, Twain was admitted to hospital and died.[65] Shortly thereafter, and again in 1964, the band council stated that "it is the unanimous wish of the members of the Temagami Band that Bear Island be declared officially an Indian reserve."[66] This statement seems very odd, given the band's long struggle for a reserve *not* on Bear Island, but it was apparently made upon the advice of DIA representatives, who pointed out that administrative programs such as economic development, nursing, and medical transportation were available only to Indians living on official reserves.[67] Bear Island officially became a reserve in 1971 after the Ontario government cancelled the conditions it had placed on the transfer of the island to the federal government.[68] That the Teme-Augama Anishnabai did not intend Bear Island to replace their larger claim became obvious in 1973, when they challenged the provincial government's authority over the territory by filing cautions in the land titles offices for the land titles divisions of Nipissing, Temiskaming, and Sudbury.[69]

5

Legal Landscapes

In 1973, the Teme-Augama Anishnabai filed cautions signalling their objection to Ontario's claimed ownership of Crown lands within n'Daki Menan. The cautions meant that Ontario could not dispose of lands in the region by, for example, selling property to potential cottagers or mining interests. This action was to prevent the province from going forward with a plan, announced during the early 1970s, to build a massive resort complex on Maple Mountain in the middle of n'Daki Menan. The Teme-Augama Anishnabai considered Maple Mountain, or Chee-Baiging, to be sacred, "the place where the spirit goes after the body dies."[1] They wanted to protect this significant place from development and had had enough of Ontario's long-standing disregard for them and for n'Daki Menan.[2]

Before the cautions were resolved, the province began a separate legal action in the Supreme Court of Ontario, seeking, among other things, a declaration that the Teme-Augama Anishnabai had no right, title, or interest in the lands placed under caution. Thus began what is known as the Bear Island case, a lengthy legal battle between the two parties. While it moved through the courts, the cautions remained on the register and prevented Ontario from transferring lands within the cautioned area. The Bear Island trial, heard at intervals from 1982 to 1984 after a number of preliminary hearings, lasted almost 120 days. The decision in favour of Ontario was appealed to the Ontario Court of Appeal and then to the Supreme Court of Canada.

In 1991, the Supreme Court upheld the two lower court judgments in declaring that the Teme-Augama Anishnabai had lost any Aboriginal rights they once had by adhering to the Robinson-Huron Treaty of 1850.[3] The legal battle was not merely a struggle over whether the Teme-Augama Anishnabai or Ontario had a better right to possess a territory. The character of the territory itself, along with racialized and gendered identities, was contested in and through the case, revealing Canadian law as a site where race, gender, and nature are constituted and made to appear natural. The court rulings, though seeming simply to determine who had legal ownership of the region, actually functioned to remake it as a natural part of the Canadian nation and to erase n'Daki Menan from the landscape.

THE CHANGING CANADIAN NATION

Following the Second World War, Canada and many other Western nations began to abandon racially discriminatory policies. Labour shortages in the post-war period of economic growth prompted Canada to look beyond Europe for labour, and immigration from the rest of the world increased substantially.[4] Also, in the post-war era of decolonization and civil rights, publicly defending either racist citizenship and immigration policies or genocidal practices toward Aboriginal peoples was no longer possible.[5] An "international crisis of whiteness" followed the war, as Western nations that had fought against fascism were forced to question the racial thinking embedded in their own national myths and state policies.[6] This questioning, along with pressure by groups marginalized in and by the nation, led to changes in both policy and national imagining. Sunera Thobani makes the important point, however, that although non-European immigrants often experienced European colonialism in their countries of origin, they also contributed to the colonization of Aboriginal peoples as they fought for inclusion in dominant Canadian society.[7] Thus, though Aboriginal peoples and people of colour made a white settler Canada impossible, they did not necessarily share similar goals. Nevertheless, by the 1960s, the efforts of people of colour for citizenship rights and Aboriginal peoples for self-determination coalesced with a number of other forces, including Quebec's sovereignty movement, to cause a "crisis of legitimacy" for Canada.[8]

Changes in immigration and citizenship policies during the 1960s and 1970s, and the constitutional recognition of Aboriginal rights in 1982, can be seen as moves away from a white settler Canada, but scholars have argued that the multiculturalism policy that emerged during the 1970s actually worked both to manage the crisis brought about by the challenges of marginalized groups and to recentre whiteness as the normal mode of being in Canada.[9] Multiculturalism not only allowed Canada to reconstitute itself as a tolerant and generous nation in the face of changing political times, it also made cultural difference the most significant defining characteristic of those considered multicultural. So defined, the political identities of marginalized groups became reduced to cultural identities that could then be managed by the very state responsible for their historical colonization and/or marginalization. Discussions of historical discrimination were elided in favour of celebrations of difference, with the result that white citizens appeared as national subjects who graciously tolerated the difference surrounding them. Within this framework, people of colour and Aboriginal peoples were again positioned as outsiders to the nation, a positioning that continues today: white Canadians are expected to be tolerant, and racialized others are people who must be tolerated.[10] The limits of this tolerance were brought sharply into focus in the treatment of Muslim Canadians by state officials, the popular media, and white Canadians following the 2001 attacks on the World Trade Center.[11]

Yet no matter how powerful its pedagogical discourse, the nation is never a finished project. The Bear Island court case took place within and played a part in the worldwide indigenous struggle for self-determination that gained ground after the Second World War. A Supreme Court of Canada decision on the Nisga'a land claim in 1973 allowed that Aboriginal title had existed prior to the arrival of Europeans, and three judges held the view that this title might still exist.[12] The Nisga'a decision, along with First Nations' vehement rejection of the 1969 White Paper on Indian Policy, which was designed by Ottawa to eliminate the distinct legal status of Aboriginal peoples, prompted an overhaul of Canada's system of negotiating land claims.[13] Claims proliferated, though their resolution has been slow, and recent court decisions in favour of First Nations, however imperfect, are marks of some success in Aboriginal peoples' struggles for land and recognition, and indicate that a multicultural Canada that recentres whiteness is not set in stone.[14]

THE SPACE OF THE LAW

Like other discourses, the law does not exist outside of culture, but is "a part of the cultural processes that actively contribute in the composition of social relations."[15] Yet the truths produced in law, unlike those of other discourses, carry with them the authority of the state. This is not to deny that other discourses have material effects. They do. But it is worth noting the very direct relationship between legal discourse and material reality. As David Delaney puts it, "What the law says is, well, the law."[16] In some cases, of course, legal and non-legal discourses cannot be adequately understood as separate from one another. For example, the early-twentieth-century production of Temagami as an empty wilderness for the enjoyment of tourists depended on its legal construction under the Forest Reserves Act as a site of timber. Because this designation prohibited the clearing of land inside the Temagami Forest Reserve for agricultural settlement, Temagami appeared and could be produced as wilderness. *"Law matters,"* because truth in law becomes truth in the world.[17]

Before taking their claim to a Canadian court, the Teme-Augama Anishnabai spent almost a century attempting various strategies to get non-Native governments to recognize it. The major difference between the filing of the cautions and the many other tactics employed by the band over the years was that the cautions succeeded in stopping the province from doing exactly what it pleased with the lands: leasing, selling, and developing without the permission and against the wishes of the band. For Aboriginal peoples, as for members of other marginalized communities, the Canadian legal system is a complicated place to fight for social change. At the very least, entering into a legal battle means temporarily accepting the language and rules of the court, neither of which were invented by First Nations communities.[18] Some scholars argue that the current court system offers little possibility of furthering the goals of First Nations communities, whereas others note that Aboriginal peoples have very little choice but to engage with the courts, given the limited number of avenues open to them.[19] That the cautions were the *only* strategy employed by the band that succeeded in forcing Ontario to alter substantially its land-use activities – the Maple Mountain resort was not built – reveals that the dominant legal system can be a powerful tool even for marginalized groups.

For the Teme-Augama Anishnabai, mobilizing Canadian law meant entering into a high-stakes game. Legal subjectivity is created through the granting of rights. When the law grants rights, an entity is created as a subject, and when it denies them, an entity is created as an object. Further, the "idea of nature is conventionally used to distinguish objects from subjects ... That which we call nature has no rights."[20] Thus subjects are differentiated not only from objects but also from nature. Or, looked at from another angle, nature *is* an object in law, something to which subjects have rights. Indeed, Adriel Weaver argues that law produces nature as an object of rights and, in so doing, simultaneously constitutes subjectivities

through the recognition or denial of rights to nature.[21] It matters profoundly whether one becomes a subject or an object in law. As Delaney
points out, "The physical realization of the views that nature is an exploitable resource and that animals are appropriate objects of experimentation
is inseparable from the legal conception of property that confers on legal
subjects the right to use and even destroy their property objects."[22] To be
an object of law is to be subjected to the will (and rights) of legal subjects.
To the extent, then, that the Teme-Augama Anishnabai could convince a
judge of their rights to n'Daki Menan, they had the opportunity not only
to become subjects in law, but also to gain the right to act on nature.
Obtaining rights to nature would give authority to make n'Daki Menan
exist on the ground. But their failure to persuade a judge that they had a
legal right to the land would mean both losing n'Daki Menan and existing
as objects under the law, subjected to the will of the provincial government. Of course, they had been subjected to Ontario's will for many years,
and so ostensibly they had little to lose by entering into the legal arena.
In fact, going to court required Ontario to devote time, energy, and money
to prepare an argument and fight for the right to do what it had been
doing for one hundred years.

THE BEAR ISLAND CASE

The arguments in the Bear Island case centred on three main questions.
First, did the Teme-Augama Anishnabai have Aboriginal rights in the lands
in question? Second, if they did have rights, what did the rights entitle
them to do there? And finally, if Aboriginal rights existed, had they been
extinguished? Ontario argued that neither the present-day members of
the band nor their ancestors had ever had any rights to the lands claimed.
In case the judge disagreed, however, Ontario argued in the alternative
that if the Teme-Augama Anishnabai were found to have any right in
n'Daki Menan, that right consisted only of a "bare and revocable licence
to inhabit the lands and to hunt and fish thereon as their predecessors had
done." The province further stated that if the Teme-Augama Anishnabai
had once had hunting and fishing rights within the land claim area, those
rights had been surrendered.[23] For their part, the Teme-Augama Anishnabai
asserted that they were the "descendants of the Indian people who, since
time immemorial, have possessed and occupied as their own, lands known
and identified as 'n'Daki Menan' (our land)." They also argued that n'Daki
Menan was not public land as Ontario contended, but was territory to

which their own rights had never been extinguished and that their rights guaranteed them exclusive possession not restricted to any specific use.[24]

Before we turn to analyze the case, a word about precedent is needed. The Canadian system of common law is based on judicial precedent, meaning that in coming to a decision, a judge applies her interpretation of the findings and reasoning of judges who have dealt with issues similar to those before her.[25] Legal precedent is not, however, a straightforward matter.[26] One complicating factor is the distinction between binding and persuasive authority. Under the doctrine of *stare decisis,* the rule by which courts follow precedents, the decision of a higher court within the same jurisdiction as a lower court acts as a binding authority on the lower court. The decision of a lower court or a court of another jurisdiction, on the other hand, is a persuasive authority, which means that a judge may choose but is not obligated to rely on such a precedent when it is relevant to the case at hand.[27]

In the Bear Island case, the relevant persuasive authority was the Baker Lake case, heard by Justice Patrick Mahoney in 1979. In it, a group of Inuit claimants sought both recognition of their Aboriginal right and title to the Baker Lake area and an order restraining the issue of mining-related permits by the government.[28] Mahoney determined that if the claimants were to establish that they had Aboriginal title to the region recognizable in common law, they must prove the following: that they and their ancestors were members of an organized society; that the organized society occupied the specific territory over which they asserted the Aboriginal title; that the occupation was to the exclusion of other organized societies; and that the occupation was an established fact at the time sovereignty was asserted by England.[29]

Legal tests for Aboriginal title predated the Mahoney decision, but the Baker Lake test added a new level of complexity to Aboriginal rights cases. It was no longer enough for First Nations to show that they had rights stemming from their historical occupation and use of the lands they claimed.[30] Now they also had to give evidence about their social organization and membership, law and governance, spiritual attachment to land, language, and cosmology. The Baker Lake test dramatically influenced how the Teme-Augama Anishnabai and Ontario prepared for and argued their cases, with the former trying both to prove their historical occupation and use of n'Daki Menan, and to show who they were as an Aboriginal people. Ontario, on the other hand, attempted to disprove the Teme-Augama Anishnabai's Aboriginal rights by arguing that the band failed to pass the Baker Lake test of aboriginality.

As a result of the Baker Lake test, the contest over racial categories, and over aboriginality specifically, was not a secondary matter in the Bear Island case, not a by-product of the conflict over land, but one of the primary grounds upon which the court battle was waged. Of course, the struggle over aboriginality cannot be disentangled from the contest over land, since the Baker Lake test dictated that Aboriginal rights to land depended on proof of a particular version of aboriginality. In order to become subjects in law with Aboriginal rights to nature, the Teme-Augama Anishnabai had to pass the legal test for aboriginality. To pass the test, they needed to establish themselves as subjects capable of passing the test (that is, as an organized society of Aboriginal people exclusively inhabiting n'Daki Menan when Britain asserted sovereignty). Thus, in a two-part process, the Teme-Augama Anishnabai had to make themselves as particular subjects according to the law, which necessitated establishing that they had specific relationships with nature, so that they could be granted legal rights as those particular subjects, thereby becoming subjects (and owners) instead of objects in law.

For its part, Ontario tried to ensure that the Teme-Augama Anishnabai failed the Baker Lake test, thus denying them access not only to land but also to subjecthood. Given that the "idea of rights depends conventionally and conceptually on the idea of humanness, which is conceptually dependent in turn on its distinctiveness vis-à-vis nature," it is little wonder that Chief Gary Potts described the Bear Island trial as a "very de-humanizing thing."[31] Ontario's legal strategy was exactly to dehumanize the Teme-Augama Anishnabai, to make them objects rather than subjects in law. The default position created by the Baker Lake test was also striking. Though Ontario's primary claim was that the lands in question were public property, the attorney general did not need to prove this assertion in the positive and argue for the legality of Crown ownership of the territory. Rather, Ontario had only to convince the judge that the Teme-Augama Anishnabai failed the Baker Lake test and that they therefore had no Aboriginal title to the lands. The unspoken but nevertheless obvious assumption was that if the Teme-Augama Anishnabai could not prove that n'Daki Menan belonged to them, it existed, by default, as public land under the authority of Ontario.

Aboriginal Rights

The Teme-Augama Anishnabai argued quite simply that they and their ancestors, as an organized society, had always lived in n'Daki Menan and that they therefore had continuing Aboriginal rights in the land. But though their argument was straightforward enough, it did not merely describe an obvious place and group of people, but rather constituted non-human nature and the racial category of aboriginality for the court. In the statement of defence to Ontario's original claim, the Teme-Augama Anishnabai defined the lands in question as "'n'Daki Menan' (our land)."[32] During his testimony, Gary Potts described in extraordinary detail the geographical boundary of n'Daki Menan as defined by lakes, rivers, and watersheds.[33] He called this a "geo-political boundary" because it was defined by the "natural setting of the land" and by agreement between the Teme-Augama Anishnabai and the "four adjacent tribal Anishnabai nations."[34] In presenting their case, the Teme-Augama Anishnabai thus constituted the non-human nature in question as n'Daki Menan – that is, the land belonging to them. In constructing the region as their land (and, notably, in using their own language to do so), they simultaneously created it as a unified whole that was integrally linked to themselves.

They presented evidence in court to reinforce the inextricable connection between themselves and this specific area, as well as to meet the demands of the Baker Lake test: everything connected to their life occurred in n'Daki Menan, and the land itself bore the marks of their presence. Three elders as well as Chief Potts testified that, according to its oral history, the band had always lived in n'Daki Menan.[35] Scholars from a number of disciplines also supported the band's claim. Historian James Morrison testified that fur trade, marriage, and other records for the Temagami region invariably mentioned ancestors of the Teme-Augama Anishnabai.[36] Craig Macdonald, the n'Daki Menan mapmaker, gave evidence about place names and canoe routes to demonstrate the band's extensive use and knowledge of its territory. The document that he eventually produced literally mapped n'Daki Menan onto the landscape, and his testimony aimed to do the same.[37] The testimonies of linguists John Nichols and John Chambers indicated that the Teme-Augama Anishnabai spoke a unique Ojibwa dialect, which supported the conclusion that they had lived as a distinct society in n'Daki Menan for at least five hundred years.[38] The Teme-Augama Anishnabai also attempted to show that their ancestors comprised a distinct (and ancient) society by giving anthropological and archaeological evidence of myths, rock art, and canoe styles unique to their region.[39]

The Teme-Augama Anishnabai constituted aboriginality by relying on the evidence presented by anthropologist Edward Rogers, who testified in court that "traditional Ojibwa band[s]" in northeastern Ontario tended to remain in the same place over long periods of time, that the Temagami

band demonstrated all signs of being a traditional band, and that therefore it had probably existed as a socially bounded entity in the region
before 1763. Rogers based his conclusions in part on the work of Frank
Speck, an anthropologist who visited the Temagami band in 1911 and recorded information about its social organization, family hunting territories,
customs, myths, and folklore.[40] According to this evidence, a traditional
band was defined by the following: possession of its own geographically
defined territory, which was subdivided into family hunting areas; the
practice of totemism; reliance on the extended family group as the main
social unit; meeting as a band during the summer and splitting into family
hunting groups in the winter; close relationships among the people, often
through blood; the practice of intermarriage and of bringing spouses in
from neighbouring bands; the common practice in which women rather
than men moved to new territories upon marriage; the usual practice of
lands passing from father to son rather than from mother to daughter;
a system of chieftainship; and the possession of a long common history.[41]
The Teme-Augama Anishnabai used this definition to argue that their
ancestors possessed all of the above characteristics of a traditional band.[42]
By defining themselves in this way, they hoped to convince the judge that
they existed as an organized society in n'Daki Menan at the appropriate
historical time and thus deserved rights in the present.

   Yet they did not portray themselves as trapped by the designation of a
traditional band: instead, they constructed aboriginality in a flexible, and
largely Teme-Augama Anishnabai–defined, way. This came across most
strikingly in discussions about the racialized and gendered character of
their identity and control of land. As mentioned above, anthropologists
stated that, in traditional Ojibwa bands, married women typically left the
lands upon which they grew up, and territories were handed down via the
male line. The Teme-Augama Anishnabai did give evidence that, among
their ancestors, lands passed from father to son, stating, for example, that
"Wabimakwa, Cayagwogwsi and Kanecic were brothers who received their
allotments after the death of their father. These contiguous territories
previously formed one."[43] Yet they did not *define themselves* according to
patrilineal descent patterns: instead, they stated that, in "accordance with
the customary law of the Teme-Augama Anishnabai," control of land and
membership rested with the full council of the tribe. The council was made
up of "those Teme-Augama Anishnabai inhabiting and claiming the land."[44]
Gary Potts cited examples in which band law permitted lands to be passed
down through the female line and where non–Teme-Augama Anishnabai
men, including those who married Teme-Augama Anishnabai women,

were accepted as band members.[45] He also discussed the practice of adopting people into the band.[46]

According to Potts' testimony, the Indian Act, not the Teme-Augama Anishnabai, restricted the definition of aboriginality, particularly along the lines of gender, in ways that had negative impacts on the band. To illustrate, he talked about how Madeline Theriault lost her Indian status by marrying a non-Native man. "As far as the government is concerned," he pointed out, "she is a non-Indian," but according to the band, "she is an Indian. She is a Teme-Augama Anishnabai member and there is no purpose to it. She just is."[47] Thus, aboriginality, as constituted by the band, depended first and foremost on the will of the First Nation. Significantly, the Teme-Augama Anishnabai did not characterize aboriginality according to the Indian Act or scholarly definitions except as those suited their courtroom needs and their own understanding of their history. Instead, they perceived aboriginality as flexible and changing, rooted in the notion that they were the people, through blood or adoption, "who grew from the land" and who thus had a special relationship with it.[48]

Against the Teme-Augama Anishnabai's assertion that they had Aboriginal rights to n'Daki Menan based on their historical occupation of it, Ontario contended that the ancestors of the band had never had Aboriginal rights and therefore that their modern descendants had none either. Like the band, Ontario actively constituted definitions of non-human nature and aboriginality in making its arguments, in part through the (re)production of other signs of power such as gender and race. Ontario consistently referred to "the lands in question," not surprisingly avoiding "n'Daki Menan," given the association between that term and the Teme-Augama Anishnabai. Whereas the Teme-Augama Anishnabai defined the region as inherently specific to their nation, Ontario did precisely the opposite by constructing it as part of an undifferentiated provincial space within Canada; government lawyers described the region variously as "within the Province of Ontario," as "public lands," and as "ordinary Crown lands open for settlement, disposition and use."[49] By making the lands ordinary (public) instead of special (reserved for Indians), Ontario could argue that the province, not the Teme-Augama Anishnabai, had the right to control them. Indeed, it counted the Bear Island reserve as special land in which the band had some right, title, or interest but stated that in the rest of the region, only Ontario had the right to "issue letters patent for or grant, sell, lease or otherwise convey or dispose of said lands or any of them."[50]

In support of its claims, the province declared that by the 1763 Treaty of Paris, all right, title, and interest in the lands had passed from the king of France to the king of England and that, subsequently, through the Constitution Act of 1867, the territory came to belong to the Crown in right of Ontario.[51] It bolstered this argument by providing a laundry list of ways that, from the late nineteenth century "to the present, the lands in question have been considered to be, and have been dealt with as, ordinary Crown lands open for settlement, disposition and use pursuant to the *Public Lands Act*, the *Mining Act*, and the *Crown Timber Act* and their predecessors and other statutes."[52] The list included but was not limited to the granting of timber berths to various lumber companies, the employment of fire rangers and the application of scientific forestry concepts, the creation of the Temagami Forest Reserve, the staking of mining claims, the opening of the railway, the introduction, continuation, and regulation of tourism as a major economic factor, the sale of lands for residential, commercial, and recreational purposes, the sale of timber licences, the creation of provincial parks, highways, and dams, and the regulation of hunting and fishing.[53] In this way, Ontario attempted to prove its right to treat Temagami as ordinary Crown land by demonstrating that the province had consistently, and with constitutional authority, exercised that right. In so doing, it produced the region as a multiple-use space of nature, unique perhaps in the kinds of uses made of it, but unexceptional because, as in the rest of the province, Ontario governed those multiple uses. Whereas the Teme-Augama Anishnabai placed a firm boundary around n'Daki Menan, Ontario drew its boundary around the province and the Canadian nation, conceiving of Temagami as merely one small part of a nationally defined and provincially controlled space. Within that space, a number of activities could and did take place, including industrial forestry and tourism. Again, as in previous times, these seemingly opposed activities fit together with no contradiction. What united them was provincial control as authorized by Canadian law.

In the service of its claim to Temagami, Ontario constituted aboriginality as an authentic, untainted essence, fixed in space and in a prior time, and passed along through the male line. Ontario attempted to disprove the aboriginality of the Temagami band by arguing that it had not existed in the proper space at the relevant time. Anthropologist Charles Bishop testified that many Aboriginal groups moved from their "aboriginal territories" shortly after contact with European colonists. Cree peoples living north of Lake Superior, he said, moved west during the eighteenth century and were replaced by Ojibwa peoples.[54] This migration, which postdated contact and continued to the early nineteenth century, occurred "in some areas clearly after 1763." Extrapolating from this information, Ontario argued that although no sources specified a movement of Ojibwa speakers into the Temagami region, "it is more probable than not that the Temagami area would have experienced similar migrations."[55] Thus, if Aboriginal people had lived in Temagami in 1763, they would have been Cree rather than Ojibwa and therefore could not have been the ancestors of the Teme-Augama Anishnabai. Ontario even suggested that the region was completely uninhabited until 1799, presenting as evidence a document from 1790 about a fur trader who travelled through Temagami for a month "without seeing a single Indian."[56] Fixedness in space and time was definitive of aboriginality as established by the Baker Lake test, and by relying on this test, Ontario subscribed to this definition, implicitly constructing the Temagami people as non-native Natives against an imagined group of real Aboriginal people who existed in one place for all of time (or at least since 1763). Whereas early-twentieth-century Temagami tourists never questioned the existence of Aboriginal people in the past, and tourism discourse actually worked to fix the Teme-Augama Anishnabai in a prior time, Ontario's legal argument worked to evict the band from the past, and from the category of "authentic" aboriginality, in order to deny it rights in the present.

Ontario's argument depended in other ways upon the creation of an authentic aboriginality and the exclusion of the Temagami band from that category. Ontario lawyer Blenus Wright asserted that there was a correct way to present an Aboriginal claim: many Aboriginal people testified and the claim was proven through the "concurrence of [their] many voices."[57] Compared to other Aboriginal rights cases, that of the Teme-Augama Anishnabai was all wrong, primarily because the wrong people had supplied its evidence. "Why," Wright asked in his oral argument, "did the evidence of place names and canoe routes et cetera come from [a] non-Indian, Craig Macdonald?"[58] The evidence that was "lacking in this case" should have been given by genuine Aboriginal people.[59] Not enough Indians took the stand, with the result that "your lordship doesn't have in evidence a number of Indian witnesses coming and saying, 'Yes, my father hunted here and my grandfather hunted here and my grandfather told me and this is how we feel about this land, we are aboriginal peoples.'"[60] Also, Chief Potts' evidence appeared suspect because he was of mixed descent, raised by a non-Native mother, did not speak the language of his people at home, and had "no blood relationship to any original Temagami

Indian."[61] By holding Potts up to an imagined real Indian (a pure-blooded Indian whose ancestors had always lived in the same place and who had spent his childhood listening to oral history in his Native language), Ontario both presented aboriginality as a pure essence and excluded Potts from it. To a lesser extent, Ontario did the same thing with the other Teme-Augama Anishnabai witnesses, attempting to show that because they could not name all their ancestors or tell the court exactly where each ancestor had come from, they could not be properly Aboriginal. Ontario was also concerned about the failure of these witnesses to perform aboriginality properly. They came and they testified, but not for long enough and not about the correct things. Instead of describing their band's organization, way of life, hunting grounds, and so on, "all they were basically asked [by the band lawyer], was two questions about treaty money and what they knew about Iroquois war stories."[62]

Gender also played a role in Ontario's exclusion of the Teme-Augama Anishnabai from aboriginality. According to the province, "the usual aboriginal practice of an Algonquin hunting people ... was patrilocal residence (i.e. upon marriage wives moved to the lands of their husbands' families) and patrilineal descent (i.e. descent was determined through the male line)."[63] Though Ontario denied the existence of an eighteenth-century Temagami band, it nevertheless argued that "when the specific aboriginal practice of the Temagami Indians who were present on the lands in the 19th century is examined, it is clear that 'the facts pertinent to' them are [that] the sons remained on the lands of their fathers and descent was determined through the male line." Further, Ontario did not find that there existed "an aboriginal practice whereby men, certainly not substantial numbers of men, come to the lands of the defendants ... and, through some process of osmosis over the years, become considered members of the band."[64] Although it conceded that men had come from elsewhere and became part of the band, Ontario stated that this was "not an aboriginal practice": it resulted from contact with "the Europeans" and with "the broader Canadian society."[65] Against the Teme-Augama Anishnabai's testimony that their customary law dictated that people could become tribal members in a number of ways, including through "adoption, marriage or acceptance" and not only via descent in the male line, Ontario held that patrilineal descent was a "basic feature of the society."[66]

In this line of argument, Ontario not only created aboriginality in highly gendered and racialized ways, but also constructed it as unchanging and fixed in the past.[67] Although, following European contact, Aboriginal people might have traced descent along the female line or adopted men from elsewhere, these "new" practices had "nothing whatever to do with a claim for aboriginal title."[68] Aboriginality thus included only pre-contact practices, since those dating from post-contact times did not count as Aboriginal. Aboriginality was also static, since any changes in Aboriginal practices occurred only through contact, not because of any historical or ongoing adaptability of First Nations peoples.

By defining aboriginality in such circumscribed ways, Ontario put itself in the position to argue that the Temagami band had no claim to aboriginality, because so few of its contemporary members could trace their ancestry along the male line to before 1850. Yet Ontario attributed this racialized and gendered definition of membership to the band itself, in spite of the Teme-Augama Anishnabai's contention that this was not their law. The province argued that under Indian Act legislation, it was "not just a fluke" that Indian status depended on descent through the male line but that this followed "the aboriginal practice."[69] Thus, the well-known sexism and racism of the Indian Act, where women lost their status by marrying non-Native men, and Indian men could become white (or at least no longer legally Indian) by acquiring a university education or entering a profession, but white men could not become Indian, was displaced from Euro-Canadian law onto Aboriginal law.[70] Aboriginality, then, appeared not only as static and fixed in the past, but also as sexist and racist. In the end, though, how the Temagami band did or did not define its identity was largely irrelevant to the province's argument, since only the law of Canada, and particularly the Indian Act, had the power to define Indian status, and it did so according to patrilineal descent.[71] For Ontario, then, aboriginality existed centrally as something that Canadian law, not its Aboriginal counterpart, had the power to determine.

Aboriginal Rights to Do What?

In answer to the second main question of the case – if the Teme-Augama Anishnabai did have Aboriginal rights, what did those rights entitle them to do in the lands? – the Teme-Augama Anishnabai argued that their Aboriginal rights entitled them to use n'Daki Menan exclusively and however they saw fit. According to them, the Royal Proclamation of 1763 constituted "letters patent," thus either recognizing or creating their ownership of n'Daki Menan.[72] The proclamation, issued by King George III shortly after the British conquest of New France, included the provision that "the several Nations or Tribes of Indians" living within the vast region of North America now claimed by Britain should not be disturbed in their possession of territories that had not been ceded to or purchased by the Crown. The proclamation further dictated that the Crown could acquire these lands from the Indians only if and when "the said Indians should be inclined to dispose of the said Lands," at which time they would be purchased by the Crown at a public meeting or assembly.[73] Because they had never sold their lands to the Crown, the Teme-Augama Anishnabai contended that they owned n'Daki Menan and that, as owners, they had the right to do as they pleased on and with their territory.

Having established the non-human nature in question as n'Daki Menan in their argument that they had Aboriginal rights, the Teme-Augama Anishnabai continued through this second argument to constitute nature as integrally related to themselves. As Chief Potts testified, "we own everything on our lands. We own right to the centre of the earth, from the surface, and we own right to the stars above our lands."[74] Here in the legal arena, the Teme-Augama Anishnabai emphasized their rights as owners of n'Daki Menan. Interestingly, though, in other contexts they focused on their responsibilities to their territory and to future generations. For example, in reports to the DIA and band members, Potts observed that development initiatives in n'Daki Menan could "take place only in accordance with enlightened attitudes toward protection of the environment," since "our descendants are entitled to have the land to enjoy a hundred centuries from now as our Native ancestors, one hundred years ago, hoped that we would enjoy the land today and not damage it beyond repair."[75] In the context of the courtroom, where they were attempting to gain the right under Canadian law to enact their vision of n'Daki Menan onto the land, the strongest argument they could put forward was that the rights granted to Indians under the Royal Proclamation were equal to fee simple, which would give them the exclusive power to make decisions about the territory. Thus, demonstrating specific relationships with n'Daki Menan that they envisioned for the future (even as the legitimacy of their claim depended on their intimate knowledge of *past* relations with the territory) was less important than convincing the court that they themselves should decide how to use their lands, at which point they could (re-)establish their own laws without interference from non-Native governments.

In arguing that their rights to n'Daki Menan included the right to do as they pleased on and with it, the Teme-Augama Anishnabai constituted aboriginality as fundamentally human. As their lawyer, Bruce Clark, stated, the "essence of human societies" is their ability to adapt, their aptitude for acting under the assumption that "today we may make that use; tomorrow we may make different uses. Times change."[76] If, he continued, the sulphur from Sudbury's Superstack killed the lakes and all the fish in Temagami, the Teme-Augama Anishnabai "would still continue to survive, they would adapt and maybe the form of adaptation would be to use the sub-surface uses and sell them back to the white man."[77] According to Clark, the human ability to adapt made ridiculous the idea of a cut-off date for Aboriginal rights, which would mean, for example, defining those rights according to how the Teme-Augama Anishnabai used n'Daki Menan at the time of the proclamation. To delineate Aboriginal rights in this way was to deny that Aboriginal people had the capacity to adapt and thus to deny their humanity. Clark hoped that a Canadian court in the 1980s could not accept such a proposition. He further argued that limiting Aboriginal rights to 1763 practices also meant assuming a racial hierarchy of rights, where, for example, non-Native people could receive a grant to start a mine, but Aboriginal people could not, because they were "the wrong colour." Clark asked rhetorically whether the assumption that "Indians had some lesser degree of rights to use and enjoy land than do white people" was a good one.[78] The Teme-Augama Anishnabai's negative answer directly countered colonial constructs, challenging the court to step up to the somewhat new and supposedly not racist idea of the Canadian nation, in which the colonial views (that helped to dispossess the band in the first place) that Aboriginal cultures were unchanging and that Aboriginal people *had* fewer rights to land than did Europeans were no longer acceptable.

By arguing that the "essence of human societies" is their ability to adapt, the Teme-Augama Anishnabai implicitly separated humans from the rest of nature, which then appeared as that which was unable to adapt, or at least as that whose essence was not defined by adaptability. The purpose of constituting aboriginality as humanness was to construct the Teme-Augama Anishnabai as subjects rather than objects in law, so that they could secure the highest possible definition of Aboriginal rights – to objectify nature as they pleased. Thus, though they argued that no racial hierarchy of rights should exist in law, the constraints of a rights-based legal system led them to maintain a hierarchy of rights according to species, working to include themselves in the category of those with rights by constructing themselves, and all Aboriginal people, as human.[79]

Ontario disagreed with this version of what Aboriginal rights included and argued that if the band had Aboriginal title, that title might include the right to compensation for lost use of the land but did not entail any existing right, title, or interest in the land itself. Further, if title existed, it consisted of "a right to occupy the lands and continue to carry out the traditional land uses of their ancestors, i.e. the taking of game and fish for their own use and fur bearing animals for purposes of trade." Ontario asserted that title did not extend over all the territory claimed by the Teme-Augama Anishnabai and that only status Indians who resided on the lands in question could exercise it.[80]

In arguing for a limited definition of the Aboriginal rights of the Temagami band, Ontario reinforced its earlier conception of the lands as belonging to the Crown. Here it used the Royal Proclamation to argue that even if the lands existed as special lands reserved for Indians under the proclamation, they were not all that special. The proclamation stated that it was the king's "Royal Will and Pleasure" that "for the present, and until Our further Pleasure be known," the lands should be reserved for the use of the Indians. Ontario took this to indicate "that it was the very nature of the rights of the Indians under the *Royal Proclamation* that they were subject to change by the Crown at any time."[81] The province also relied on the 1888 St. Catherine's Milling case decision, in which Lord Watson stated that under the terms of the proclamation, "the tenure of the Indians was a personal and usufructuary right, dependent upon the goodwill of the Sovereign."[82] Thus, Indian lands, like all lands in British North America, belonged to the Crown, with Aboriginal title existing as a personal right to hunt and fish until the Crown decided to revoke that right, at which point the territory ceased to be special and became part of undifferentiated Crown lands in right of the province. The term "usufruct," which refers to the legal right to enjoy the profits of something belonging to another, is particularly revealing in this regard: as a right of *temporary* possession, usufruct highlights the transitory character of Aboriginal title; as a right to use *someone else's* property, it emphasizes the dependence of Aboriginal title on underlying Crown ownership. Indian lands, then, were not particularly special, since they existed only to the extent that the Crown permitted them to exist, and they ceased to exist whenever the Crown chose to end them.

That Ontario constructed the lands as belonging to the Crown is also evident in the argument that the proclamation created Aboriginal title. The Teme-Augama Anishnabai understood that, in Canadian law, the proclamation either recognized or created Aboriginal title but did not think that it had anything to do with their own law, in which there was no question but that they owned n'Daki Menan. As Bruce Clark explained, according to "Indian law," Indians on unceded land "feel they are as sovereign as before the white man 'discovered' their continent."[83] Ontario, on the other hand, suggested that the "sole source" of Aboriginal title was the proclamation.[84] The assumption here is that prior to the proclamation, Aboriginal people did not own land (for how could the proclamation have created something that already existed?). Ontario thus presented the lands as belonging to the Crown in part through relying on the understanding that prior to Crown ownership, the lands were completely unowned and thus there for the taking, a construction that not only elided the imperial processes (including legal processes) through which the British acquired North America, but also reinforced the racialization of Aboriginal people as too uncivilized to own land.

Ontario simultaneously created aboriginality in its restricted definition of Aboriginal title. According to the province, if the Teme-Augama Anishnabai had Aboriginal title,in the lands, that title consisted of "the taking of game and fish and other natural products for their own use" but not the commercial use of any products except for furs, the selling of which "undoubtedly is a very longstanding practice of the Algonquian hunting peoples."[85] By labelling Aboriginal title as the right to engage in traditional activities, Ontario presented aboriginality as fixed in the past: Aboriginal people had the right to fish and hunt for their own survival but not to sell the fish, farm the lands, engage in mining, or conduct any other activity not practised by their ancestors. Although Ontario's definition of band membership had limited aboriginality to pre-contact practices, such was not the case where title was concerned, as indicated by its statement that the sale of fur was an Aboriginal right. Indeed, when it came to Aboriginal title, Ontario constituted aboriginality as fixed in 1763.[86] The selection of this date makes sense only under the assumption that the proclamation did in fact create Aboriginal title. The differing dates assigned by Ontario to determine membership and title reveal not only the difficulty the province had in deciding what counted as properly Aboriginal but also the created character of essential racial categories. Yet by denying the aboriginality of any practices not undertaken for centuries by the ancestors of the Temagami band, Ontario maintained that to be Aboriginal was to be in the past (whether that meant 1763 or earlier).

The placement of aboriginality in the past is most evident in Ontario's argument that, in the present, the band had the *same rights* as anyone else to obtain a mining licence but that no Aboriginal right to subsurface minerals existed. Nowadays, the province argued, "the Indians should be able to use these lands as everybody does," and an Indian band has "the same opportunities [to start a mine] as anybody else in Ontario." This opportunity, however, existed under the Mining Act and was unrelated to

Aboriginal rights.[87] Here Aboriginal people could be Aboriginal only in the past. The moment they attempted to access rights in the present, they ceased to be Aboriginal, with their "special" rights disappearing and being replaced by the same rights as those enjoyed by everyone else in the province. In order to argue that the band had no rights as a group in the present, then, Ontario accepted the possibility that individual members of the band could have individual rights – that is, they could become subjects in law, but there could be no modern Aboriginal legal subject.

Whereas Ontario's argument regarding the existence of Aboriginal rights worked to construct the band as ordinary (not quite Native enough to deserve special rights), here the province emphasized the extraordinary character of the band's ancestors by highlighting their past activities as follows: they took game and fish for their families and other products necessary for survival; prior to contact with Europeans, their "way of life had not changed significantly for more than 7,000 years"; they were hunter-gatherers who lived by hunting, fishing, and trapping; and they did not exploit resources commercially until after contact with Europeans.[88] By defining what was special about aboriginality as that which existed in the past, Ontario thus asserted that the preservation of aboriginality meant barring it from the present. What is particularly striking here is the no-win situation created for the Teme-Augama Anishnabai. To prove that they had Aboriginal rights, they needed to supply evidence that they were a traditional band. Yet this allowed Ontario to argue, using the very evidence they had provided, that they existed as Aboriginal people only in the past. Thus, though aboriginality existed solely in the past, the Teme-Augama Anishnabai moved through time in Ontario's argument, existing only in the present when existing in the past meant having rights in the present, and existing only in the past when existing in the present meant having more rights in the present. The province also limited Aboriginal rights by defining them in the gendered and racialized ways discussed above, so that only those descendants in the male line who lived on the lands could access Aboriginal rights.

Extinguished Rights?

The final question addressed by the Teme-Augama Anishnabai and Ontario was whether the Aboriginal rights of the former, provided that they had once existed, had been extinguished. This discussion focused to a large extent on the Robinson-Huron Treaty of 1850 and its effects: Had the

Teme-Augama Anishnabai participated in the treaty, thus surrendering
their lands? And if they had not, had their lands been surrendered anyway?
The Teme-Augama Anishnabai stated that their ancestors had never surrendered any rights in the lands in question by the Robinson-Huron
Treaty.[89] In contrast, Ontario argued that any rights once held by the
predecessors of the band had been surrendered by the treaty.[90]

An analysis of the arguments about the Robinson-Huron Treaty does
not add significant insight into the two parties' representations of nature
and aboriginality. Instead, similar constructions re-emerge. Such an analysis does, however, reveal the power of law in creating truths about nature
and subjectivity, and in so doing, it challenges the common-sense notion
that the law is an arbiter rather than a producer of truth and therefore is
objective rather than powerful. Joel Fortune, in an article about the role
of history in shaping the outcome of an Aboriginal rights case, writes that
though philosophers of history (and many historians) "have long recognized that making 'history' is a problematic activity," Canadian courts
have usually understood history as "simply a set of external facts that, once
presented in the courtroom, will lead the way to an objective evaluation
of the past."[91] But telling stories about the past is a complex activity because
it necessarily involves present-day interpretations of past objects, events,
and peoples, all of which are ultimately inaccessible: they cannot speak
for themselves, except through "the vehicle of human perception."[92] What
distinguishes "the facts of history from other facts about the past" is that
the "facts speak only when the historian calls on them." History becomes
history, then, only through the selection of some facts, not others, and
notably, through the interpretation of those facts.[93] History thus depends
on people in the present as much as it does on people, objects, and events
in the past. Fortune suggests that recognizing this is essential, especially
given the key role that history can play in law and particularly in Aboriginal
rights cases, where "a legal outcome may rest on a question of historical
interpretation."[94] Otherwise, the law can become an avenue for the en-
trenchment of inequities. Bear Island is a case in point.

The arguments of the Teme-Augama Anishnabai and Ontario regarding
the Robinson-Huron Treaty had differing legal implications, yet they relied
on many of the same historical documents and even agreed on certain
facts. For example, both parties agreed that Nebenegwune, who was chief
of the Temagami band in 1850, does not appear on the list of signatories
to the treaty. In the spy mission arranged by Ontario in 1894 and described
in Chapter 2, Chief Dokis of Lake Nipissing told the province's scout that
Nebenegwune had not signed the treaty, because he had not been invited

and did not learn of the treaty process until after it was over.[95] The province and the First Nation also agreed that although Nebenegwune did not sign the treaty, he did receive a payment from the government shortly after it was concluded. A few days after the treaty's signing, William Robinson, who negotiated it on behalf of the British Crown, arrived at Manitoulin Island, where a large number of Indians were gathered for the annual distribution of imperial presents. Members of the Temagami band had attended this annual present-giving event prior to 1850, and Nebenegwune and at least two other band members were in attendance that year as well. Robinson, whose appearance at this event was unexpected, paid money pursuant to the Robinson-Huron Treaty to a number of Indians, including Nebenegwune. Temagami band members attended the present giving until 1855, when it stopped.[96]

The Teme-Augama Anishnabai and Ontario interpreted these events differently. According to the former, the fact that Nebenegwune did not sign the treaty meant that their ancestors had not surrendered their lands by the treaty. The fact that he received money in 1850, which he did not know was pursuant to the treaty, became historically insignificant. But according to Ontario, Nebenegwune's receipt of treaty money at Manitoulin was so important as to make his lack of participation in the treaty an insignificant detail. Nebenegwune was given the money on the same day and in the same location as the chiefs who had signed the treaty. He was paid as a chief, and he knew that the payment was in respect to his band's participation in the treaty.[97] For Ontario, it did not matter that his name did not appear on the treaty, for Tawgawanene, who was not a Temagami band member, had signed it on behalf of Nebenegwune and the band.[98] As evidence that Tawgawanene had acted as a proxy, Ontario cited the fact that his name appeared with Nebenegwune's on DIA records concerning payments pursuant to the 1850 treaty.[99] On one occasion, Tawgawanene signed a requisition under the treaty, apparently on behalf of Nebenegwune.[100]

The legal outcome of the Bear Island case could have rested on historical interpretation. If Nebenegwune participated in the treaty on behalf of the band by receiving money from Robinson on Manitoulin Island in 1850, the current band had no Aboriginal title. If he did not, it did. Similarly, if Tawgawanene signed the treaty on behalf of the band, it had no Aboriginal title. If he did not, it did. It is perhaps trite to say that history is always for the present and future; certainly, it cannot affect the past. But to say that history matters seems an understatement when it comes to Aboriginal law, given the close association between legal truths and material reality. What Nebenegwune was thinking when he received twenty-five dollars in 1850 may be a matter of interpretation, but the interpretation that gains status as truth in law has the power to dictate present and future relationships between people and land. Law certainly is a story with teeth.

JUDGMENT DAYS

On 11 December 1984, in a judgment that commentators have called "antediluvian" and "an example of a conservative, archaic approach to the interpretation of history in the context of Aboriginal rights litigation," Justice Donald Steele decided in favour of Ontario.[101] With this ruling, the territory in question became, in Canadian law at least, public land under the Public Lands Act. Though the Teme-Augama Anishnabai continued to know the region as n'Daki Menan, Ontario received the right to convey or dispose of it without their consent and regardless of whether they objected. In fact, they were denied any right, title, or interest in the territory and were perpetually barred from asserting any such right, title, or interest and from contesting Ontario's right to dispose of it.

In his reasons for judgment, Steele agreed with almost all the arguments put forward by Ontario, which thus came to carry with them the force of law (at least until the Teme-Augama Anishnabai appealed his ruling). Steele's judgment and reasons, then, had the effect of producing nature and subjects by granting Ontario the right to enact its understanding of the lands onto the lands themselves, and so the area became part of an undifferentiated provincial and national space, a site of nature where various activities could occur, all under the authorization of the provincial government. By the same token, the Teme-Augama Anishnabai were created as objects rather than subjects in law: not only did they have no rights to n'Daki Menan, but it did not exist in Canadian law. Although Ontario and the band called into being certain constructions of nature and subjectivity in presenting their claims, it was the judgment, not the arguments in and of themselves, that carried with it the legal authority to make these representations come to life.

Because Justice Steele's reasons concurred so closely with Ontario's argument, I will not discuss each one in detail but instead will highlight a few central ways in which Steele relied upon and reconstituted racialized and gendered categories in the service of making nature Canadian. The lands became national in part through Steele's inscription of a racialized conception of landownership. From the beginning of his judgment, he telegraphed this perspective by explaining the "basic dispute" before the court as "whether Ontario is the owner of certain lands, free of any aboriginal rights claim by the Indians, or whether the band or registered band has aboriginal rights in the lands that prevent Ontario from dealing with the lands *until* those rights are properly extinguished."[102] Certainly, the Teme-Augama Anishnabai did not understand the dispute in this way, particularly given their hope that, by going to court, they would see their rights vindicated and would have their ownership of n'Daki Menan recognized in Canadian law. The question according to Steele, however, was not who owned the territory, but rather whether Ontario owned it outright or had to extinguish Aboriginal rights before doing so. Either way, he left no doubt that Ontario owned the lands, regardless of whether the Teme-Augama Anishnabai had any Aboriginal rights in them.

Justice Steele substantiated his foundational decision that an "aboriginal rights claim is not a claim to the legal title to land" by endorsing as a starting point the stance that the Royal Proclamation of 1763 was the source of whatever Aboriginal rights the Teme-Augama Anishnabai might have.[103] He interpreted the proclamation, as well as the Privy Council's analysis of its effect as articulated in the St. Catherine's Milling case, to mean that "aboriginal title is personal and usufructuary only, and exists solely at the pleasure of the Crown." As such, it "is not akin to a fee simple interest."[104] Steele held that Aboriginal people could not own land, because, in 1763, King George III "did not grant ownership of vast tracts of lands to Indian bands ... when a war had just been fought to acquire those lands." He found this possibility "inconceivable" because at that time "Europeans did not consider Indians to be equal to themselves," and so George III would not "have made such vast grants to undefined bands, thus restricting his European subjects from occupying these lands in the future except at great expense."[105] The land belonged to Ontario, then, because George III would not have had it any other way: Europeans could own land; Aboriginal people could not. Yet even as Justice Steele denied the Teme-Augama Anishnabai the possibility of landownership by relying on racializing reasoning, he simultaneously distanced himself from that very reasoning. As he commented, the fact that Indians had no proprietary interest in lands might not have been "proper law or a proper view," but it *was* the view of Europeans at the time of the proclamation and afterwards, a fact that "*must* be borne in mind in interpreting any legislation or contracts or treaties made at that time."[106] By blaming racism present on racism past,

Steele found himself able to racialize landownership and thus re-entrench the construction of aboriginality as inferior to Europeanness while simultaneously passing it off as a straightforward application of the law.[107]

After establishing that Aboriginal rights did not constitute a proprietary interest in lands, Steele moved on to find that the Teme-Augama Anishnabai had not shown sufficiently that they had Aboriginal rights in n'Daki Menan.[108] He did this in part through refashioning the Baker Lake test and, on the basis of this new test, deciding that the band had not proven its aboriginality. Dara Culhane has called judges' practice of changing the legal tests for Aboriginal rights after the fact (in their reasons for judgment) "a practice that speaks to the uniquely autocratic prerogative of law." Parties usually come prepared to meet a test articulated in a previous case, but judges sometimes change their criteria in response to evidence presented for the first time in the case at hand and then evaluate the evidence based on their new criteria.[109] Justice Steele did exactly that. Though he concluded in his reasons that the Teme-Augama Anishnabai must satisfy the Baker Lake test, he added that they must also indicate the nature of the rights they had enjoyed in 1763, supply proof of an organized landholding system and set of rules and customs distinct to them, and establish their continuity of exclusive occupation from 1763 to the date of the legal action (1973).[110]

In relying on this modified test, Steele took a route that differed slightly from Ontario's, but he arrived at the same conclusion regarding the Aboriginal rights of the Teme-Augama Anishnabai. He agreed with the province that no organized band existed in the region until at least 1850.[111] In so doing, he followed Ontario in constituting the ancestors of the band as inauthentic Indians, against an imagined true form of aboriginality. For example, he commented that the Temagami ancestors "regularly breached" what he considered was the "general rule for Indians" of tracing their ancestry through the male line.[112] And, he added, "in the past even white men have been accepted as members of the band" as had "adopted children, whether Indian or non-Indian," children whose fathers were non-Native, and illegitimate children.[113] The supposedly arbitrary character of band membership, based (through gender and race) on its distance from the practice of an "authentic" band, was proof for Steele, as it was for Ontario, that the Temagami band was not a band at all.

Whereas Ontario's argument depended on the idea that n'Daki Menan was uninhabited in 1763, and that a few people began to trickle into it only during the 1790s, Justice Steele did not concur. He determined that no evidence supported anthropologist Charles Bishop's speculation that the area was vacant until the late eighteenth century, concluding instead that "persons in the families set out in Charts 1, 2, 3, 5, 6, 7, 8, and 14" of the genealogy charts submitted as an exhibit by the Teme-Augama Anishnabai "were Indians who probably resided on the Land Claim Area in or about the time 1800, or even earlier." Given anthropologist Edward Rogers' "evidence of work done elsewhere in Ontario, and the fact that the fur trade was well established in the area in question by 1763," Steele accepted "that the families represented on the named charts probably resided in the area prior to 1800, and as early as 1763."[114]

In so concluding, Steele gave legal authority to the Teme-Augama Anishnabai's assertion that their ancestors had lived in n'Daki Menan for a long time. Whereas Ontario envisioned empty lands populated later by a few individuals, Steele found lands substantially inhabited by ancestors of the current Teme-Augama Anishnabai, and it thus became impossible for him to agree with Ontario's claim that they had not been organized due to low numbers of people.[115] Instead, he found other ways to show that they had no Aboriginal rights. For instance, he determined that they had no "strong ... spiritual attachment to the lands." Evidence showed that some had left the area, such as former chief Tonene, who married into another band, and Joseph Mattias, who left but later returned and hunted on his wife's lands rather than those of his own family.[116] Steele addressed the issue of land and spiritual attachment in a section of his reasons called "The Entitlement to Aboriginal Rights in the Land Claim Area," which signalled that he thought the subject essential in determining whether or not the Teme-Augama Anishnabai were entitled to Aboriginal rights, a consideration dependent on the idea of an authentic aboriginality: real Indians (who felt a spiritual connection to their lands) did not leave home.

His position also depended on gendered definitions of aboriginality. Every example that Steele cited as evidence that the Teme-Augama Anishnabai ancestors felt no great attachment to their lands was one in which a man left the territory. Aboriginality remained intact, it seems, as long as women rather than men left home. This logic complements another of Steele's findings in favour of Ontario, that the Temagami band was not quite normal, because women did not always leave the area when they married, and land did not always pass down the paternal line.

Steele's demand that the Teme-Augama Anishnabai needed to prove continuity of exclusive occupation until 1973 allowed him to push forward in time his finding that their ancestors did not love their lands. In schedules at the back of his reasons, he included lists of registered and unregistered Temagami Indians. Beside the names of adults not living in the land claim

area, he placed the letters "NR" and explained that, at the commencement of the court action, "exactly one-half" of registered Indians and
many more than that percentage of non-registered Indians did not reside
in the disputed region.[117] Those who did lived on the Bear Island reserve,
having "abandoned or moved from the balance of the area."[118] From this
information, he determined that "since approximately 1950, the defendants
reside either outside the Land Claim Area, or within the Land Claim Area,
on Bear Island or in established white settlements such as the Town of
Temagami." As a result, he found that Aboriginal title "was in fact extinguished because the Indians have abandoned their traditional use and
occupation of the Land Claim Area."[119] Steele thus relied on ideas of authenticity in aboriginality to displace history onto culture.[120] It was not
the railway passing through their territory, the tourist invasion and purchase
of islands in Lake Temagami, the forestry and mining, the policing of their
activities, their forced relocation to Bear Island, their loss of Indian status
through marrying the wrong people, or the few economic opportunities
available to them that led Teme-Augama Anishnabai to move elsewhere
over the years. Instead, they left because of their lack of authenticity as
Aboriginal people. They simply did not love the land.

By holding the Teme-Augama Anishnabai up to a particular understanding of aboriginality, Justice Steele created them as not properly Aboriginal,
and he therefore denied them rights in law. The flip side of this is that he
legally constituted a version of aboriginality against which the Teme-
Augama Anishnabai could be (negatively) evaluated. For instance, he
inscribed the version of aboriginality discussed above, one that included
certain "spiritual and mythological connections to the land" but did not
entail a proprietary interest in it.[121] He also, as Tony Hall states, gave "precise
legal expression to the theory that sees true Indianness as a way of life fixed
forever in the past."[122] Indeed, Steele determined that Aboriginal rights
included "only the right to continue using the lands for the purposes and
in the manner enjoyed in 1763" and then proceeded to give a detailed
summary of the evidence presented in court regarding the character of
those rights.[123] He concluded that, in 1763, Aboriginal rights in the disputed
area included hunting all animals for food, clothing, and personal use and
adornment; trapping fur-bearers and selling the furs; fishing; using natural
products for food, medicines, and dyes; using minerals for tools but not
extensive mining; and using trees and bark for housing, fires, canoes,
sleighs, and snowshoes but not lumbering.[124] In defining Aboriginal rights
in this way, Steele created the potential for other courts to reproduce his

definition, thus fixing aboriginality firmly in the past and decidedly away from any modern right to resource extraction.

In his analysis of the Teme-Augama Anishnabai's evidence, Justice Steele configured aboriginality, whiteness, and racial mixing to support his contention that the band did not really have a case. Ontario had asserted that Chief Potts' evidence was questionable because he was not an "authentic" Indian and had also challenged the reliability of non-Native witness testimonies. But Steele went further than this. For example, he stated that Craig Macdonald, Thor Conway, and James Morrison, white witnesses who appeared for the band, "were typical of persons who have worked closely with Indians for so many years that they have lost their objectivity when giving opinion evidence."[125] He added that these witnesses were "emotionally involved," "tainted with ... partisanship," and "biased and unreliable."[126] As Tony Hall observes, "If non-Indians who have lived with Indians thereby lose their 'objectivity,' one wonders how Steele views the capacity of Indians themselves for 'objectivity.' Objectivity, he would have us believe, lies more or less exclusively in the realm of non-Indians who have not lived among Indians."[127] Thus, white people who have had too much contact with Aboriginal people become less objective, and it seems they also become racially marked, or less white, if one defines whiteness by its proximity to objectivity.[128] The presumably racial characteristic of subjectivity in Indians can apparently rub off onto white researchers who spend too much time with them. Justice Steele seemed to think that these particular white witnesses had had so much contact with Aboriginal people that they had lost not only objectivity, but also their expertise and had become willing to invent a case on the Teme-Augama Anishnabai's behalf. As the judge stated, "I believe that a small, dedicated and well-meaning group of white people, in order to meet the aspirations of the current Indian defendants, has pieced together a history from written documents, archaeology and analogy to other bands, and then added to that history a study of physical features and other items, together with limited pieces of oral tradition."[129]

Steele went on to say how "disappointed [he] was that there was so little evidence given by the Indians themselves"; throughout the trial, he had had "an uncomfortable feeling" that "the defendants, in presenting their case, did not want the evidence of the Indians themselves to be given, except through the mouth of Chief Potts."[130] Later, he explained that this uncomfortable feeling sprang from his strong suspicion that "it is not the Indians themselves who first thought that they did not sign the treaty, but rather that it is the wishful thinking of a few well-meaning white people."[131] Whereas racially tainted white witnesses were willing to fabricate a case and lie on the stand, real Indians, it appears, would only have told their (subjective but authentic) truth – that their ancestors signed the treaty. The absence of a performance of authentic aboriginality, then, along with too much evidence presented by witnesses who had lost their objectivity, served to convince the judge that the Teme-Augama Anishnabai had no real claim.

This left only the evidence of Gary Potts, which Steele discounted in much the same way as did Ontario, stating, for instance, that Potts "has a white mother and a father who is not of pure Indian ancestry."[132] To Ontario's argument that Potts could not present oral history since he was not an authentic Indian, Steele added that his "evidence must also be considered in light of his admitted statement that he considers government bureaucrats as imbeciles and that he does not trust anyone at the Department of Indian Affairs, because, in his words, 'There is a war going on.'"[133] Like the evidence of non-Native witnesses, Potts' testimony was discounted by Steele because of the racial contamination of its bearer. Just as Conway, Morrison, and Macdonald were not white enough to give objective (white) evidence, Potts was not Indian enough to give subjective (Indian) evidence. In this way, Steele reinforced the idea that aboriginality existed in a pure form. But, unlike the non-Native witnesses, Potts did not appear as "well-meaning" as a result of his racial impurities: instead, he was a threat to the judicial process (though one might think that falsifying a case might be a greater felony than distrusting DIA officials). In discounting Potts' evidence, Steele also supported the idea that racial mixing was very dangerous. It was one thing for white people to spend time among Indians, and thus to confuse racial boundaries slightly, but another thing entirely to explode those boundaries completely, thereby challenging the biological distinction between whiteness and Indianness, and revealing both as categories imbued with history and power.

The Teme-Augama Anishnabai appealed Justice Steele's decision, and in 1989 the Ontario Court of Appeal found against them. But unlike Steele, the judges at the higher court did not go through each line of reasoning advanced by Ontario. Instead, they held that they were "prepared to assume, without deciding, that the Temagami Indians in 1850 enjoyed aboriginal rights to at least some part of the Land Claim Area and that these rights extended to the use and occupation of the lands in the traditional ways of a band."[134] They found it unnecessary, however, to deal with many of the issues put before the trial judge, because they were satisfied that any rights enjoyed by the Teme-Augama Anishnabai were extinguished by the Robinson-Huron Treaty due to their participation in it or their adherence to it by receiving treaty annuities and a reserve. Even if they had not signed or adhered to the treaty, their Aboriginal rights had been extinguished because the treaty was a unilateral act of extinguishment by the sovereign authority.[135]

Thus, the Teme-Augama Anishnabai gained and lost their Aboriginal rights over the course of a few sentences. By stating that Aboriginal rights extended only to traditional uses, the Court of Appeal, like Justice Steele, inscribed in law a definition of aboriginality that held First Nations in the past. Similarly, the court's understanding that the Crown had the unilateral power to extinguish Aboriginal rights reinforced a racialized definition of landownership, where Aboriginal people never owned lands and so the Crown could extinguish Aboriginal rights at its pleasure. But these arguments have already been made, and it is unnecessary to go over them again. It is, however, striking that the conclusions reached at one level of court can be overridden by a higher level of court, when the case argued at the various levels is comprised of the same basic "facts." In this case, the Court of Appeal judges seemed particularly swayed by the argument for Tawgawanene's participation in the Robinson-Huron Treaty on behalf of the Temagami band, since they spent a large portion of their reasons for judgment on this topic.

When the case was finally decided by the Supreme Court of Canada in 1991, the judges offered no comment on "the situation upon the signing of the Robinson-Huron Treaty," deciding instead that the Teme-Augama Anishnabai's Aboriginal rights were "surrendered by arrangements subsequent to that treaty by which the Indians adhered to the treaty in exchange for treaty annuities and a reserve."[136] Whereas Justice Steele found that the ancestors of the Teme-Augama Anishnabai never had any Aboriginal rights in the lands, and the Court of Appeal declined to consider the matter, the Supreme Court decided "that on the facts found by the trial judge the Indians exercised sufficient occupation of the lands in question throughout the relevant period to establish an aboriginal right."[137] That this case, which according to the Supreme Court, raised "essentially factual issues," could be decided by different judges in different ways supports Fortune's observation that the outcome of court cases can be based on differing interpretations of history. The facts are not obvious until they become the law. In addition to finding that "the aboriginal right has been extinguished," the court "conceded that the Crown has failed to comply with some of its obligations under this agreement [the Robinson-Huron Treaty], and thereby breached its fiduciary obligations to the Indians."[138] Thus, in 1991, the Teme-Augama Anishnabai discovered that they had become treaty Indians in Canadian law, treaty Indians who were owed certain unfulfilled obligations (namely, some money and a bigger reserve). They could take their claim no further in the legal system, for the Supreme Court of Canada is the highest court in the country. Thus, the unfulfilled treaty obligations have been the subject of negotiations between the band and the province ever since.

THE POWER OF THE (LEGAL) TRUTH

On 11 November 1989, the Teme-Augama Anishnabai set up their second logging road blockade in n'Daki Menan. One month later, two hundred had been arrested. Ontario gained the authority to make these arrests via an injunction that prevented the band from interfering with road construction. Justice Dennis Francis O'Leary at the Ontario High Court of Justice stated that he granted the injunction on the basis of certain "relevant facts about which there can be no dispute." Central among these facts was that the "defendant Indian bands are not the owners of and have no aboriginal rights in the land on which the extension to the Red Squirrel Rd. is being built. That fact was determined by the judgment of Mr. Justice Steele [and] upheld by the Court of Appeal." O'Leary added that the "defendants have no right to interfere with the construction of the road yet they are doing just that. Only at its peril will our society allow anyone to flout the law. The Attorney-General as protector of public rights and the custodian of the public interest is entitled to seek an injunction against those flouting the law."[139] There could hardly be a more clear example of the power of the law to construct nature and subjects. Not only was Ontario legally authorized to remake the land as a site of industrial logging, but this was done in the name of the public interest. The public did not include the Teme-Augama Anishnabai, who became criminals for attempting to assert their rights to land, rights that had been denied in law. Another Ontario judge, Justice Warren K. Winkler (later chief justice of Ontario), subsequently quashed the cautions filed in 1973 by the Teme-Augama Anishnabai. The judgment of the Supreme Court of Canada in the Bear Island case led Winkler to conclude that the band had no interest in the cautioned lands, and so there was no reason for the cautions to remain in effect.[140]

I am not sure how to conclude this story, except to say that it has not yet ended. As I describe in the next chapter, the Teme-Augama Anishnabai continue to struggle for control over their territory. Yet the terms of this struggle have been indelibly marked by the Bear Island case. Community members and government officials negotiate under differing assumptions about who, in fact, "owns the bottom of the lake."[141] But government officials have the weight of Canadian law on their side, whereas the Teme-Augama Anishnabai have only their convictions.

CONCLUSION

A Return to n'Daki Menan

European imperialism was an enterprise that involved acquiring and transforming non-European lands. It was also and simultaneously a project of racialization, gendering, and the social construction of nature. In n'Daki Menan/Temagami, as elsewhere, the imperial processes of land acquisition and the fashioning of race, gender, and nature cannot be separated from one another. Together, they worked not only to appropriate and often to degrade Native lands, but also to make those lands appear self-evidently natural and, eventually, national. One result is the wilderness of Temagami, Ontario, Canada. As this book has shown, the Temagami wilderness is a cultural rather than a natural phenomenon, the product of struggles over meaning, identity, and ultimately, land. Although the Teme-Augama Anishnabai have consistently maintained and enacted their claim to their traditional territory, most non-Aboriginal Canadians have come to see it as part of the Canadian wilderness. This has occurred through its feminization as virgin territory and also by the racialization of the Teme-Augama Anishnabai, both as "authentically Indian" (part of the fading wilderness and too uncivilized to count as settlers) and as "inauthentically Indian" (not Indian enough to have legal entitlement to land in the present). The band's long battle for control over land, then, has also been a struggle over race and gender, in which it has had to contest colonial constructions of both land and subjectivity.

Although French, British, and Canadian authorities claimed n'Daki Menan before the twentieth century, it was the 1901 creation of the Tema-gami Forest Reserve that brought it within the direct sphere of British and

Canadian control. This appropriation of indigenous lands by a colonial government depended not only on a legal regime backed by state power, but also on discourses of gender, race, and nature that commodified the region as a source of timber for the benefit of the nation and empire. For the Teme-Augama Anishnabai to articulate their claim to their territory and to press their requirement for land, they had to contest both the idea of the forest reserve as the "nature" of the region and the racialized perception that they inhabited but had no claim to the territory. Similarly, tourism signalled another kind of appropriation of n'Daki Menan – vacationers came to enjoy the vanishing wilderness, not usually to harvest its trees – but it too relied upon the image of a feminized Canadian wilderness created by nature for (male) tourists. The Teme-Augama Anishnabai made their living in part by facilitating tourist visits, but this led to their racialization, especially in travel writing, as a component of the wilderness that sightseers travelled to encounter. Even as band members helped visitors negotiate n'Daki Menan, they were subject to tourist representations of nature and race. In the rent controversy of the 1930s and in the Bear Island case, the Teme-Augama Anishnabai were unable to seek control of their territory without fighting a battle over racialized and gendered definitions of Aboriginal identity and the meaning of the land itself.

Yet even today, when imperialism and its racial logic are widely discredited, the racialized and racializing dimensions of concepts such as "the Canadian wilderness" remain largely unquestioned and mask even as they reproduce the colonial relations that created them. As the well-known anti-racist writer M. Nourbese Philip and her colleagues remind us, these colonial relations include not only Aboriginal dispossession, but also the exclusion of non-European people from a mythic wilderness created primarily by and for Euro-Canadian men.[1] Although the Teme-Augama Anishnabai and their "Welcome to N'Daki Menan" road sign tell a different story, n'Daki Menan exists for many Canadians as "the vast Temagami wilderness."[2] Formulating policy consistent with such a vision, the Ontario government manages the region as a natural space to be exploited for timber and wilderness tourism. A recent management plan for five provincial parks and eight conservation reserves in the region as well as a recreation management plan for its Crown lands (see the map on p. 3) assume that these lands are Ontario parks, conservation reserves, and regular Crown lands, and focus on what activities can take place within them.[3] Likewise, the most recent forest management plan for Temagami, which took effect in 2009, includes the goal of increasing yearly harvesting levels.[4]

Not surprisingly, maximizing wood supply is the province's key management objective. But in a political climate in which it is no longer publicly acceptable to manage forests solely as timber producers, the management plan also aims to protect wildlife habitat and maintain old-growth characteristics, as long as these objectives do not limit the wood supply.[5] As in the parks plan, the Teme-Augama Anishnabai are largely ignored in a forest management plan that posits an external Temagami nature to be managed with the most up-to-date science and computer-modelling techniques.

Part of the reason that Ontario considers itself authorized to manage Temagami nature is the Supreme Court of Canada's decision that gave it control of the region. This decision has not diminished the Teme-Augama Anishnabai's sense of ownership of their territory. It has, though, profoundly shaped the terms of the discussion now taking place between them and the provincial government. Ontario is prepared to turn approximately 130 square miles of land on the east side of Lake Temagami into a reserve for the First Nation (see the map on the following page). This commitment reflects the Supreme Court's determination that the Crown failed to comply with some of its obligations under the Robinson-Huron Treaty, including the duty to provide the Teme-Augama Anishnabai with a reserve selected by the band. One result of the Bear Island case is that Ontario is now legally bound to create the reserve that the band began petitioning for in the 1870s.

As they have explained to government officials for several generations, the Teme-Augama Anishnabai need a land base much larger than Bear Island if they are to survive and thrive in n'Daki Menan in ways of their choosing. Whether they decide to become significant players in the forestry and mining sectors, to focus their energies on running lodges and information centres for visitors, or to incorporate all of these and other activities, a land base significantly greater than Bear Island would better equip them for self-determination. At the same time, negotiations between the Teme-Augama Anishnabai and Ontario are premised upon the idea that the former lost such Aboriginal rights as they once enjoyed in n'Daki Menan through their adherence to the Robinson-Huron Treaty. Although Ontario is willing to countenance a bigger reserve, it is unwilling to grant the band contemporary rights and responsibilities that would challenge its own authority across n'Daki Menan. Many Teme-Augama Anishnabai are incredulous at this. They believe that they should have an important voice in all activities in n'Daki Menan and insist that, as they never participated in a treaty, they could not have lost their territory.

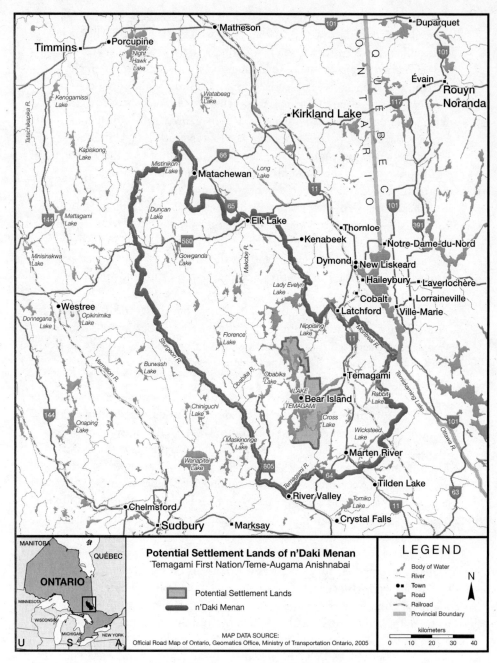

Potential settlement lands of n'Daki Menan.

Other futures, which are anti-colonial rather than recolonizing, are possible. One of these is Teme-Augama Anishnabai self-determination in n'Daki Menan. I am struck by the consistency with which the band has expressed its desire and its right to live on its land in ways that it determines. Control over land and identity is central to self-determination for the band and for other First Nations. My hope is that by understanding how n'Daki Menan transitioned from the Teme-Augama Anishnabai homeland to a part of the Canadian wilderness, non-Aboriginal Canadians will be willing to support rather than impede or remain silent about Aboriginal struggles for self-determination. Recognizing that Canadian wilderness is a created category, a powerful category, and a colonial category reveals the assumptions embedded in terms that seem innocuous but that function to restrict the ability of Aboriginal individuals and communities to move forward as simultaneously Native and modern. When we fail to recognize the created and contested character of wilderness, we risk naturalizing the territorial appropriations and racializing and gendering colonial logic within the national wilderness. Challenging wilderness means contesting the logic that allows it to appear self-evident. To the extent that this book demonstrates that wilderness and nations are made – through history, through law, through discourse, and through struggle – rather than discovered, and that the making of wilderness has had profound implications for people and land, it provides an opening rather than a closing. If we find neither wilderness nor nation to be self-evident, perhaps we are better equipped to tackle the complex questions and demands that result from the history of colonialism, exclusionary nationalism, and environmental exploitation that brought us here in the first place.

Notes

INTRODUCTION

1 "Teme-Augama Anishnabai" (pronounced Tem-eee-awg-ama A-nish-nah-bay) is the term now used by members of the First Nation to describe themselves. Those who have status under the Indian Act make up the Temagami First Nation, the entity that is recognized by Canadian governments. Today, the First Nation is represented by two councils, the Teme-Augama Anishnabai Council and the Temagami First Nation Council, which together form the Joint Council. The nation is currently working on a new membership code to enable all Teme-Augama Anishnabai to be recognized under the Indian Act. Throughout the book, I prefer the term "Teme-Augama Anishnabai" over the various designations used by federal and provincial government officials. Where appropriate, however, I employ the colonial terminology given in the archival documents that I discuss. Often these documents refer to the Teme-Augama Anishnabai as "Temagami Indians" or simply "Indians." Following accepted current-day practice, I rely as much as possible on the terms "Aboriginal people," "Aboriginal peoples," and "First Nations" rather than "Indians" when discussing Aboriginal individuals and nations. See Canada, *Report of the Royal Commission on Aboriginal Peoples*, vol. 1, *Looking Forward, Looking Back* (Ottawa: Canada Communications Group, 1996), xiv-xv.

2 Frank G. Speck, *Family Hunting Territories and Social Life of Various Algonkian Bands of the Ottawa Valley*, Memoir 70, no. 8, Anthropological Series (Ottawa: Department of Mines, Geological Survey of Canada, 1915); Trails in Time, "Traditional Land Use and Resource Management Philosophies and Practices of the Temagami Aboriginal People: Teme-Augama Anishnabai, Temagami First Nation, Ontario Native Affairs Secretariat Joint Project," Land Use and Resource Management Research Box 1, A-o (Temagami First Nation Band Office, 2001), 47-48.

3 The final chapter of this book, however, discusses ongoing negotiations between the Teme-Augama Anishnabai and the Ontario government to create a larger reserve.

4 TemagamiVacation.com, "Experience Temagami: Canoeing," http://www.temagami vacation.com/; "Great Ontario Outdoor Adventures: Signature Landscapes," http://www. ontariooutdoor.com.

5 David T. McNab, *No Place for Fairness: Indigenous Land Rights and Policy in the Bear Island Case and Beyond* (Montreal/Kingston: McGill-Queen's University Press, 2009), III. For details on the controversy surrounding the extension of the logging road, see also Matt Bray and Ashley Thomson, eds., *Temagami: A Debate on Wilderness* (Toronto: Dundurn Press, 1990); Bruce W. Hodgins and Jamie Benidickson, *The Temagami Experience: Recreation, Resources, and Aboriginal Rights in the Northern Ontario Wilderness* (Toronto: University of Toronto Press, 1989), 281-84; Gerald Killan, *Protected Places: A History of Ontario's Provincial Parks System* (Toronto: Dundurn Press, 1993); and Jocelyn Thorpe, "Temagami's Tangled Wild: Race, Gender and the Making of Canadian Nature" (PhD diss., York University, 2008), 13-26.

6 Interestingly, though, according to his autobiography, Rae decided to sit on the logging road not to save the wilderness per se, but to protect Aboriginal rights to land. He discusses a meeting with Teme-Augama Anishnabai chief Gary Potts, who convinced him that his presence would provide the attention and support the First Nation needed in protecting a stand of pine that was central to its land claim. See Bob Rae, *From Protest to Power: Personal Reflections on a Life in Politics* (Toronto: McClelland and Stewart, 2006), 129-31.

7 Gene Allen, "Ministry Wants Freeze on Temagami Logging," *Toronto Globe and Mail,* 21 November 1989, A1, A2.

8 See Olive Patricia Dickason, *Canada's First Nations: A History of Founding Peoples from Earliest Times* (New York: Oxford University Press, 2002), especially Chapter 4, "Canada When Europeans Arrived," 44-64.

9 Here, I am thinking of "justice" in terms of environmental justice as discussed in the recent collection by Julian Agyeman et al., eds., *Speaking for Ourselves: Environmental Justice in Canada* (Vancouver: UBC Press, 2009). In it, the authors consider the loss of Aboriginal lands and title as well as the devastation of traditional Aboriginal territories to be examples of environmental injustice or environmental racism, in which social inequities related to colonialism cannot be separated from the physical and cultural environments in which they occur. I concur with the editors of *Speaking for Ourselves,* who write that "justice is broader than the liberal understanding of distributive equity" and must include a critical examination of the structures through which social differences are constituted. I am also cognisant of the fact that for far too long non-indigenous scholars have attempted, using their own terms and definitions, to speak for Aboriginal individuals and communities on issues that profoundly affect those communities. Randolph Haluza-DeLay, Pat O'Riley, Peter Cole, and Julian Agyeman, "Speaking for Ourselves, Speaking Together: Environmental Justice in Canada," in ibid., 9, 5-6. It is not my intention to speak on behalf of anyone but myself, though I do hope that this book will serve in part to encourage non-Aboriginal Canadians to listen to the words of Aboriginal scholars and community members who have been speaking and writing eloquently for a very long time, often about their relationships with their lands. In the words of Jeannette Armstrong's character Slash in her novel of the same name, "It's hard to show just how much our pride, our culture and our lives all have their roots in the land. It's not easy to explain that to protect and attempt to regain control over it is really the way to protect our own lives as Indian people. It was not easily apparent that it is really the only means we have. I began to see that more and more clearly." Jeannette Armstrong, *Slash* (Penticton, BC: Theytus Books, 1985), 116-17.

10 Our experience was certainly not unique. For a discussion of the history of summer camps in Ontario, which remain popular, see Sharon Wall, *The Nurture of Nature: Childhood, Antimodernism, and Ontario Summer Camps, 1920-55* (Vancouver: UBC Press, 2009).

11 This court case is the topic of Chapter 5.

12 John Temple, "Temagami: One Big Family's Quarrel," *Toronto Star*, 5 May 1988, A24. For a discussion of the differing perspectives of the Teme-Augama Anishnabai and environmentalists on the blockades, see also McNab, *No Place for Fairness*.

13 Tom Spears, "Temagami Indians Told to End Blockade," *Toronto Star*, 9 December 1988, A7. According to David McNab, who offers a view on the road controversy from inside the Ontario government, because the Teme-Augama Anishnabai were blockading not a road per se, but a right of way where the road would be built, they were not arrested in 1988 for their roadblocks. The province was also concerned about possible public outcry if the police were to arrest Aboriginal people whose land claim was before the courts. See McNab, *No Place for Fairness*, 123.

14 See Bruce W. Hodgins, Ute Lischke, and David T. McNab, eds., *Blockades and Resistance: Studies in Actions of Peace and the Temagami Blockades of 1988-89* (Waterloo: Wilfrid Laurier University Press, 2003), in which Teme-Augama Anishnabai and non-Teme-Augama Anishnabai individuals recall the 1988 and 1989 blockades from differing perspectives.

15 For example, the criticism is voiced in William Cronon, "The Trouble with Wilderness: Or, Getting Back to the Wrong Nature," in William Cronon, *Uncommon Ground: Rethinking the Human Place in Nature* (New York: Norton, 1996), 69-90, which is now more than ten years old. In 1989, Ramachandra Guha made a similarly powerful argument about the imperialism of importing Western ideas of wilderness into non-Western contexts. See Ramachandra Guha, "Radical American Environmentalism: A Third World Critique," *Environmental Ethics* 11 (1989): 71-83.

CHAPTER 1: TANGLED WILD

1 For an excellent collection of critical thinking on race, see Philomena Essed and David Theo Goldberg, eds., *Race Critical Theories: Text and Context* (Malden, MA: Blackwell, 2002).

2 In the context of the Pacific Northwest around the turn of the twentieth century, Paige Raibmon similarly argues that non-Aboriginal definitions of aboriginality functioned to restrict the ability of Aboriginal people to access land, resources, and sovereignty. She also discusses how Aboriginal people mobilized ideas of authentic Indianness to survive under colonial rule. See Paige Raibmon, *Authentic Indians: Episodes of Encounter from the Late-Nineteenth-Century Northwest Coast* (Durham: Duke University Press, 2005).

3 Edward Said, *Orientalism* (New York: Pantheon, 1978).

4 Renisa Mawani has argued that the dynamics of race in colonialism can be more thoroughly understood by attending to the multiple forms of racialization that took place within the same spaces at the same times and that shaped colonial ideas about race. She reveals that in the British Columbia context, racial "truths" emerged not through a simplistic construction of a European self against an Aboriginal other, but through a shifting field of interactions among colonial authorities, Aboriginal peoples, immigrant groups from Europe and Asia, and mixed-race populations that resulted from colonial encounters. Although the racial categories that emerged worked to sustain British imperial rule, they did not do so in a straightforward fashion, and Mawani's analysis amply demonstrates the complex

and mutable character of race. See Renisa Mawani, *Colonial Proximities: Crossracial Encounters and Juridical Truths in British Columbia, 1871-1921* (Vancouver: UBC Press, 2009).

5 Mary Louise Pratt, *Imperial Eyes: Travel Writing and Transculturation* (London: Routledge, 1992), 32.

6 Anne McClintock, *Imperial Leather: Gender, Race and Sexuality in the Colonial Contest* (New York: Routledge, 1995), 37.

7 Ibid., 38-39.

8 Ibid., 45.

9 See, for example, Antoinette Burton, *Burdens of History: British Feminists, Indian Women, and Imperial Culture, 1865-1915* (Chapel Hill: University of North Carolina Press, 1994); Sarah Carter, "Transnational Perspectives on the History of Great Plains Women: Gender, Race, Nations, and the Forty-Ninth Parallel," *American Review of Canadian Studies* 33,4 (Winter 2003): 565-96; Anna Davin, "Imperialism and Motherhood," *History Workshop Journal* 5 (Spring 1978): 9-65; Inderpal Grewal, *Home and Harem: Nation, Gender, Empire and the Cultures of Travel* (Durham, NC: Duke University Press, 1996); McClintock, *Imperial Leather;* Adele Perry, *On the Edge of Empire: Gender, Race, and the Making of British Columbia, 1849-1871* (Toronto: University of Toronto Press, 2001); Ruth Roach Pierson and Nupur Chaudhuri, eds., *Nation, Empire, Colony: Historicizing Gender and Race* (Bloomington: Indiana University Press, 1998); Pratt, *Imperial Eyes;* and Ann Laura Stoler, *Race and the Education of Desire: Foucault's History of Sexuality and the Colonial Order of Things* (Durham, NC: Duke University Press, 1995). For excellent critical examinations of sex and gender, see Judith Butler, *Bodies That Matter: On the Discursive Limits of "Sex"* (New York: Routledge, 1993); Donna J. Haraway, *Simians, Cyborgs and Women: The Reinvention of Nature* (New York: Routledge, 1991); and Joan Wallach Scott, ed., *Feminism and History* (Oxford: Oxford University Press, 1996).

10 Carter, "Transnational Perspectives," 576-77; Louis Montrose, "The Work of Gender in the Discourse of Discovery," *Representations* 33 (1991): 3.

11 Donna J. Haraway, *Primate Visions: Gender, Race, and Nation in the World of Modern Science* (New York: Routledge, 1989), 15. Scholarly attention to the social construction of nature has come from a number of fields, including feminist theory, environmental history, geography, anthropology, and political ecology. Texts that particularly shape my thinking on this topic are Kay Anderson, "Culture and Nature at the Adelaide Zoo: At the Frontiers of 'Human' Geography," *Transactions of the Institute of British Geographers* 20,3 (1995): 275-94; Bruce Braun, *The Intemperate Rainforest: Nature, Culture, and Power on Canada's West Coast* (Minneapolis: University of Minnesota Press, 2002); William Cronon, ed., *Uncommon Ground: Rethinking the Human Place in Nature* (New York: Norton, 1996); Haraway, *Primate Visions;* Haraway, *Simians, Cyborgs and Women;* Donna J. Haraway, "The Promises of Monsters: A Regenerative Politics for Inappropriate/d Others," in *Cultural Studies,* ed. Lawrence Grossberg, Cary Nelson, and Paula Treichler (London: Routledge, 1992), 295-337; and Donald S. Moore, Jake Kosek, and Anand Pandian, eds., *Race, Nature, and the Politics of Difference* (Durham, NC: Duke University Press, 2003). In recent years, geographers in particular have contributed a great deal to the literature on social nature. Sarah Whatmore suggests that, perhaps because the discipline of geography straddles the interface between nature and society, the turn to questions of nature has held a specific resonance for geographers. See Sarah Whatmore, *Hybrid Geographies: Natures,*

Cultures, Spaces (London: Sage, 2002). For a survey of geographical work on social nature, see Noel Castree and Bruce Braun, eds., *Social Nature: Theory, Practice, and Politics* (Oxford: Blackwell, 2001).

12 Braun, *The Intemperate Rainforest*, ix-x.

13 See Michael E. Soulé and Gary Lease, eds., *Reinventing Nature? Responses to Postmodern Deconstruction* (Washington, DC: Island Press, 1995).

14 See Braun, *The Intemperate Rainforest;* William Cronon, "The Trouble with Wilderness: Or, Getting Back to the Wrong Nature," in William Cronon, *Uncommon Ground: Rethinking the Human Place in Nature* (New York: Norton, 1996), 69-90; Bruce Braun and Noel Castree, eds., *Remaking Reality* (London: Routledge, 1998); Haraway, "The Promises of Monsters"; and Catriona Sandilands, "Between the Local and the Global: Clayoquot Sound and Simulacral Politics," in *A Political Space: Reading the Global through Clayoquot Sound*, ed. Warren Magnusson and Karena Shaw (Minneapolis: University of Minnesota Press, 2003), 139-67.

15 Cronon, "The Trouble with Wilderness," 85.

16 This is the title of Alexander Wilson's book on the topic. See Alexander Wilson, *The Culture of Nature: North American Landscape from Disney to the Exxon Valdez* (Toronto: Between the Lines, 1991).

17 Haraway, *Primate Visions,* 15.

18 Cronon, "The Trouble with Wilderness," especially 78-79.

19 See Alfred W. Crosby, *Ecological Imperialism: The Biological Expansion of Europe, 900-1900* (Cambridge: Cambridge University Press, 2004).

20 Kay Anderson, *Race and the Crisis of Humanism* (London: Routledge, 2007). See also Moore, Kosek, and Pandian, *Race, Nature, and the Politics of Difference.*

21 Brian Back, "Endangered Ecosystem: Wakimika Triangle, World's Largest Old Growth Red and White Pine Stand," http://www.ottertooth.com/; Braun, *The Intemperate Rainforest,* 68.

22 Gerald Killan, "The Development of a Wilderness Park System in Ontario, 1967-1990: Temagami in Context," in *Temagami: A Debate on Wilderness,* ed. Matt Bray and Ashley Thomson (Toronto: Dundurn Press, 1990), 113.

23 Peter A. Quinby, "Temagami Old Growth Studies (1989-1992)," Ancient Forest Exploration and Research, http://www.ancientforest.org/; Gene Allen, "Ministry Wants Freeze on Temagami Logging," *Toronto Globe and Mail,* 21 November 1989, A1, A2.

24 See Edward Said, *Culture and Imperialism* (New York: Knopf, 1993).

25 Cole Harris, *Making Native Space: Colonialism, Resistance, and Reserves in British Columbia* (Vancouver: UBC Press, 2002), xvii.

26 Benedict Anderson, *Imagined Communities: Reflections on the Origin and Spread of Nationalism* (1983; repr., London: Verso, 1991), 5.

27 Ibid., 6, 7.

28 Carl Berger, *The Sense of Power: Studies in the Ideas of Canadian Imperialism, 1867-1914* (Toronto: University of Toronto Press, 1970).

29 Anderson, *Imagined Communities,* 98.

30 Robert Miles and Malcolm Brown, *Racism* (London: Routledge, 1989), 142.

31 Ibid., 144-46.

32 Etienne Balibar, "The Nation Form: History and Ideology," in Essed and Goldberg, *Race Critical Theories,* 220-30.

33 Ibid., 227, 221.

34 Ibid., 228.
35 Mary Layoun, *Wedded to the Land? Gender, Boundaries, and Nationalism-in-Crisis* (Durham, NC: Duke University Press, 2000).
36 Ibid., 14.
37 McClintock, *Imperial Leather,* 359. On the relationships between gender and the nation, see also Nira Yuval-Davis, *Gender and Nation* (London: Sage, 1997).
38 Davin, "Imperialism and Motherhood."
39 Quoted in John Temple, "Temagami: One Big Family's Quarrel," *Toronto Star,* 5 May 1988, A24.
40 See, for example, Frances Abele and Daiva Stasiulis, "Canada as a 'White Settler Colony': What about Natives and Immigrants?" in *The New Canadian Political Economy,* ed. Wallace Clement and Glen Williams (Montreal/Kingston: McGill-Queen's University Press, 1989), 240-77; Constance Backhouse, *Colour-Coded: A Legal History of Racism in Canada, 1900-1950* (Toronto: Osgoode Society for Canadian Legal History and University of Toronto Press, 1999); Constance Backhouse, *Petticoats and Prejudice: Women and the Law in 19th Century Canada* (Toronto: Women's Press, 1991); Himani Bannerji, "Geography Lessons: On Being an Insider/Outsider to the Canadian Nation," in *Dangerous Territories: Struggles for Difference and Equality,* ed. Leslie Roman and Linda Eyre (New York: Routledge, 1997), 23-41; Enakshi Dua, "Racializing Imperial Canada: Indian Women and the Making of Ethnic Communities," in *Gender, Sexuality and Colonial Modernities,* ed. Antoinette Burton (London: Routledge, 1999), 119-33; Enakshi Dua and Angela Robertson, eds., *Scratching the Surface: Canadian Anti-Racist Feminist Thought* (Toronto: Women's Press, 1999); Elizabeth Furniss, *The Burden of History: Colonialism and the Frontier Myth in a Rural Canadian Community* (Vancouver: UBC Press, 1999); Eva Mackey, *The House of Difference: Cultural Politics and National Identity in Canada* (London: Routledge, 1999); Mawani, *Colonial Proximities;* Perry, *On the Edge of Empire;* Sherene Razack, *Looking White People in the Eye: Gender, Race, and Culture in Courtrooms and Classrooms* (Toronto: University of Toronto Press, 1998); Sherene Razack, "'Simple Logic': Race, the Identity Documents Rule and the Story of a Nation Besieged and Betrayed," *Journal of Law and Social Policy* 15 (2000): 183-211; Daiva Stasiulis and Radha Jhappan, "The Fractious Politics of a Settler Society: Canada," in *Unsettling Settler Societies: Articulations of Gender, Race, Ethnicity and Class,* ed. Daiva Stasiulis and Nira Yuval-Davis (London: Sage, 1995), 95-131; and Sunera Thobani, *Exalted Subjects: Studies of the Making of Race and Nation in Canada* (Toronto: University of Toronto Press, 2007).
41 Dua, "Racializing Imperial Canada."
42 Mackey, *The House of Difference.*
43 Robert Haliburton, speech to the Montreal Literary Club, 1869, quoted in Berger, *The Sense of Power,* 53.
44 Ibid., 66.
45 Mackey, *The House of Difference,* 30.
46 William Foster, "Canada First: Or Our New Nationality," quoted in Berger, *The Sense of Power,* 62-63.
47 See Homi Bhabha, "DissemiNation: Time, Narrative, and the Margins of the Modern Nation," in Homi Bhabha, *Nation and Narration* (London: Routledge, 1990), 297.
48 For the reserves, see Harris, *Making Native Space.* For Asian and black immigrants, see B. Singh Bolaria and Peter S. Li, *Racial Oppression in Canada* (Toronto: Garamond Press,

1985); and Vic Satzewich and Nikolaos Liodakis, *Race and Ethnicity in Canada: A Critical Introduction* (Toronto: Oxford University Press, 2007).

49 See James Youngblood Henderson, *Treaty Rights in the Constitution of Canada* (Toronto: Thomson/Carswell, 2007); Kim Anderson and Bonita Lawrence, eds., *Strong Women Stories: Native Vision and Community Survival* (Toronto: Sumach Press, 2003); Bonita Lawrence, *"Real" Indians and Others: Mixed-Blood Urban Native Peoples and Indigenous Nationhood* (Vancouver: UBC Press, 2004); and Rolf Knight, *Indians at Work: An Informal History of Native Indian Labour in British Columbia* (Vancouver: New Star Books, 1996).

50 Abele and Stasiulis, "Canada as a 'White Settler Colony,'" 241.

51 Dua, "Racializing Imperial Canada," 121.

52 Thobani, *Exalted Subjects,* 84-86, 92-93.

53 Unfortunately, however, middle- and upper-class white women as well as working-class white men historically made their claims for inclusion into the Canadian nation by supporting a racist nation-building project. See ibid., 84-85.

54 Eric Kaufmann, "'Naturalizing the Nation': The Rise of Naturalistic Nationalism in the United States and Canada," *Comparative Studies in Society and History* 40,4 (1998): 666-67.

55 Ibid., 667.

56 Ibid., 667-68.

57 Carl Berger, "The True North Strong and Free," in *Nationalism in Canada,* ed. Peter Russell (Toronto: McGraw Hill, 1966), 3-26. See also Berger, *The Sense of Power.*

58 Berger, "The True North," 6.

59 Ibid., 9-11; Berger, *The Sense of Power,* 53.

60 Susan Smith, "Immigration and Nation-Building in Canada and the United Kingdom," in *Constructions of Race, Place and Nation,* ed. Peter Jackson and Jan Penrose (Minneapolis: University of Minnesota Press, 1993), 55.

61 Mackey, *The House of Difference;* Eva Mackey, "Death by Landscape: Race, Nature, and Gender in Canadian Nationalist Mythology," *Canadian Woman Studies* 20,2 (2000): 125-30.

62 Its members included Lawren Harris, J.E.H. MacDonald, Arthur Lismer, Frederick Varley, Frank Johnston, Franklin Carmichael, and A.Y. Jackson. Tom Thomson, whose name and artwork are often associated with the Group, was not a member, because he died before it was established. For further information about the Group of Seven, see the McMichael Canadian Art Collection website, http://www.mcmichael.com. The McMichael Gallery, located in Kleinburg, Ontario, houses many Group of Seven works.

63 For a collection of multiple views on Emily Carr and her work, see Marnie Butvin and Denise Sirois, eds., *Emily Carr: New Perspectives on a Canadian Icon* (Vancouver: National Gallery of Canada, Vancouver Art Gallery, and Douglas and McIntyre, 2006).

64 Claire Campbell states that in order to provide Canada with impressive national symbols, artists sought out and depicted places that seemed particularly Canadian. Campbell argues that this process served to elevate regional landscapes, transforming them into national art. See Claire Elizabeth Campbell, *Shaped by the West Wind: Nature and History in Georgian Bay* (Vancouver: UBC Press, 2005), 145.

65 Ghassan Hage, *White Nation: Fantasies of White Supremacy in a Multicultural Society* (Annandale, Australia: Pluto Press, 1998).

66 Lauren Berlant, *The Anatomy of National Fantasy: Hawthorne, Utopia, and Everyday Life* (Chicago: University of Chicago Press, 1991), 5.

67 Catriona Sandilands, "Ecological Integrity and National Narrative: Cleaning Up Canada's National Parks," *Canadian Woman Studies* 20,2 (2000): 138.

68 It is also true, however, that the presence of First Nations is sometimes recognized within the concept of wilderness. For example, some 1980s news reports about Temagami acknowledged the Teme-Augama Anishnabai presence on the land, but they often emphasized the *historical* character of Teme-Augama Anishnabai land use, thus rendering invisible contemporary relationships between the First Nation and n'Daki Menan. That it is possible for the Temagami region to appear simultaneously as a wilderness space and a place that contains Aboriginal history also reveals how Aboriginal people become collapsed into nature, a point to which I will return in later chapters. Bruce Braun similarly discusses how an environmentalist publication about Clayoquot Sound positions Aboriginal people as part of nature, and as part of the past. See Bruce Braun, "'Saving Clayoquot': Wilderness and the Politics of Indigeneity," in Braun, *The Intemperate Rainforest,* 66-108.

69 See Jonathan Bordo, "Jack Pine: Wilderness Sublime or the Erasure of the Aboriginal Presence from the Landscape," *Journal of Canadian Studies* 27,4 (1992): 98-128; Bruce Braun, "BC Seeing/Seeing BC: Vision and Visuality on Canada's West Coast," in Braun, *The Intemperate Rainforest,* 156-212; Marcia Crosby, "Construction of the Imaginary Indian," in *Vancouver Anthology,* ed. Stan Douglas (Vancouver: Talonbooks, 1991), 267-91; Gerta Moray, *Unsettling Encounters: First Nations Imagery in the Art of Emily Carr* (Vancouver: UBC Press, 2006). Emily Carr and the Group have not erased Aboriginal peoples in similar ways, however. Although Carr is best-known for her paintings of wilderness landscapes, which sometimes incorporate stylized carved Native figures, she also painted many First Nations villages and totem poles. She is criticized, though, for representing Native culture as static and dying, and in this way participating in the cultural production that was part and parcel of colonial rule. Members of the Group of Seven, on the other hand, played a role in colonialism by ignoring First Nations peoples and cultures in their work.

70 There are exceptions, of course. See Berger, "The True North"; Mackey, "Death by Landscape"; Renisa Mawani, "Genealogies of the Land: Aboriginality, Law, and Territory in Vancouver's Stanley Park," *Social and Legal Studies* 14,3 (2005): 315-40; Catriona Sandilands, "Where the Mountain Men Meet the Lesbian Rangers: Gender, Nation, and Nature in the Rocky Mountain National Parks," in *This Elusive Land: Women and the Canadian Environment,* ed. Melody Hessing, Rebecca Raglon, and Catriona Sandilands (Vancouver: UBC Press, 2005), 142-62; and Thobani, *Exalted Subjects.*

71 Bonita Lawrence and Enakshi Dua, "Decolonizing Antiracism," *Social Justice* 32,4 (2005): 120-43. For a related critique of post-colonial theory, see Jace Weaver, "From I-Hermeneutics to We-Hermeneutics: Native Americans and the Post-Colonial," in Jace Weaver, *Native American Religious Identity: Unforgotten Gods* (Maryknoll, NY: Orbis Books, 1998), 1-25.

72 Michel Foucault, "Nietzsche, Genealogy, History," in *The Foucault Reader,* ed. Paul Rabinow (New York: Pantheon Books, 1984), 76-100; Sara Mills, *Michel Foucault* (London: Routledge, 2003), 25.

73 Michel Foucault, *The Archaeology of Knowledge* (London: Tavistock, 1972), 49.

74 Sara Mills, *Discourse* (1997; repr., London: Routledge, 2004), 54-55.

75 Michel Foucault, "The Discourse on Language," in Michel Foucault, *The Archaeology of Knowledge and the Discourse on Language* (New York: Pantheon, 1972), 219-20.

76 During my time in n'Daki Menan, I conducted two formal interviews with Teme-Augama Anishnabai members on the general theme of tourism. I also had the opportunity to listen to interviews with elders that were recorded during the 1970s. Some of what I learned from these interviews appears in Chapter 3.

77 See Julie Cruikshank, *Do Glaciers Listen? Local Knowledge, Colonial Encounters, and Social Imagination* (Vancouver: UBC Press, 2005). Cruikshank shows that within Athapaskan and Tlingit oral traditions, relationships between people and a changing landscape figure more prominently than do encounters between local peoples and European explorers. In explorers' narratives, on the other hand, much emphasis is placed on descriptions of local people.

78 See, for example, Teme-Augama Anishnabai, "The Native Dimension: Key Dates," in Bray and Thomson, *Temagami*, 147-51. At the National Aboriginal Day of Action in June of 2007, which I attended in Temagami, Teme-Augama Anishnabai members distributed information brochures that featured a very similar timeline. The Day of Action also included an information session about the history of their claim, and the important dates discussed were the same as those in the brochures.

79 Bruce W. Hodgins and Jamie Benidickson, *The Temagami Experience: Recreation, Resources, and Aboriginal Rights in the Northern Ontario Wilderness* (Toronto: University of Toronto Press, 1989). David McNab has also written about the history of Temagami. Like me, he is centrally concerned with the dispossession of the Teme-Augama Anishnabai, but he emphasizes the culpability of particular individuals and governments, whereas my own study focuses more on the cultural processes through which dispossession became possible. I agree wholeheartedly with McNab, though, when he says that the Teme-Augama Anishnabai have found "no place for fairness" in the Canadian court system. His work also offers insight into his involvement in Temagami as a land claims researcher for the Ontario government in the 1980s, when the Teme-Augama Anishnabai case was going through the courts. See David T. McNab, *No Place for Fairness: Indigenous Land Rights and Policy in the Bear Island Case and Beyond* (Montreal/Kingston: McGill-Queen's University Press, 2009); David T. McNab, "'We Hardly Have Any Idea of Such Bargains': Teme-Augama Anishnabai Title and Land Rights," in David T. McNab, *Circles of Time: Aboriginal Land Rights and Resistance in Ontario* (Waterloo: Wilfrid Laurier University Press, 1999), 45-74.

80 Hodgins and Benidickson, *The Temagami Experience*, 4.

81 For a similar treatment of the more recent Temagami conflicts, see Bray and Thomson, *Temagami*. Others have also focused on the more recent history of Temagami. See Bruce W. Hodgins, Shawn Heard, and John S. Milloy, eds., *Co-Existence? Studies in Ontario-First Nations Relations* (Peterborough, ON: Frost Centre for Canadian Heritage and Development Studies, 1992); Bruce W. Hodgins, Ute Lischke, and David T. McNab, *Blockades and Resistance: Studies in Actions of Peace and the Temagami Blockades of 1988-89* (Waterloo: Wilfrid Laurier University Press, 2003); James Lawson, "Environmental Interests and the Forest Products Industry in Temagami and Algonquin Park" (PhD diss., York University, 2001); and Jamie Lawson, "Nastawgan or Not? First Nations' Land Management in Temagami and Algonquin Park," in *Sustainability, the Challenge: People, Power and the Environment*, ed. L. Anders Sandberg and Sverker Sörlin (Montreal: Black Rose Books, 1998), 189-201.

82 Madeline Katt Theriault, *Moose to Moccasins: The Story of Ka Kita Wa Pa No Kwe* (Toronto: Natural Heritage/Natural History, 1992).

83 Trails in Time, "Traditional Land Use and Resource Management Philosophies and Practices of the Temagami Aboriginal People: Teme-Augama Anishnabai, Temagami First Nation, Ontario Native Affairs Secretariat Joint Project," Land Use and Resource Management Research Box 1, A-0 (Temagami First Nation Band Office, 2001), 80-89.

84 Craig Macdonald will reappear in Chapter 5. Drawing from the knowledge he gained during his years of making the map, he testified on behalf of the Teme-Augama Anishnabai

in their land claim case, stating that they had fully utilized n'Daki Menan for hundreds of years.

85 D'Arcy Jenish, "Mapman of Temagami," *Legion Magazine,* 1 May 2006, http://www. legionmagazine.com.

86 Ibid.

87 *The Silent Enemy: An Epic of the American Indian,* directed by H.P. Carver, produced by W. Douglas Burden and William C. Chanler, written by W. Douglas Burden (N.p.: Burden-Chanler Productions, 1930).

88 Theriault, *Moose to Moccasins,* 69.

89 Ibid., 70.

90 Although arresting, such an irony is by no means unique to *The Silent Enemy.* In the early twentieth century, for example, Edward Curtis travelled around North America photographing Aboriginal people. If his subjects were not quite "Indian" enough to fulfill Euro-American romantic expectations of noble (and dying) Indians, he improvised by providing props for them. See Thomas King, "You're Not the Indian I Had in Mind," in Thomas King, *The Truth about Stories: A Native Narrative* (Toronto: House of Anansi, 2003), 31-60. For a refreshing take on the portrayal of North American Natives in Hollywood films, see *Reel Injun,* a recent documentary that examines how, four thousand films about Native people later, Hollywood has helped to define how "Injuns" are seen by the world. *Reel Injun: On the Trail of the Hollywood Indian,* directed by Neil Diamond (Outremount, QC: Rezolution Pictures, 2009).

91 Mary Laronde, "Co-Management of Lands and Resources in n'Daki Menan," in *Rebirth: Political, Economic, and Social Development in First Nations,* ed. Anne-Marie Mawhiney (Toronto: Dundurn Press, 1993), 93. The co-management endeavour – the Wendaban Stewardship Authority (WSA) – was established in 1991 to manage the area over which the road controversy took place. It included six Teme-Augama Anishnabai representatives, six Ontario-appointed members, and a jointly appointed chair. Laronde says that, through its meetings, she saw the emergence of a shared land ethic, and she felt glad that people residing in n'Daki Menan could succeed in co-managing the land. Her only fear was that the Ministry of Natural Resources (MNR) would be unable to relinquish its power over n'Daki Menan and would therefore work against the WSA. See ibid., 101-2. Her fears appear to have been well founded: Bruce Hodgins, an Ontario-appointed representative on the WSA, comments that MNR bureaucracy continuously frustrated WSA efforts. Before this occurred, he was similarly optimistic about the potential of the WSA. See Bruce Hodgins, "The Temagami Blockades of 1989: Personal Reflections," in Hodgins, Lischke, and McNab, *Blockades and Resistance,* 27-28.

92 Gary Potts, "Last-Ditch Defence of a Priceless Homeland," in *Drumbeat: Anger and Renewal in Indian Country,* ed. Boyce Richardson (Toronto: Summerhill Press, 1989), 203-30. Potts employed the language of sustainable development popular at the time to explain the Teme-Augama Anishnabai's land-use philosophy.

CHAPTER 2: TIMBER NATURE

1 See, for example, Karl Jacoby, *Crimes against Nature: Squatters, Poachers, Thieves, and the Hidden History of American Conservation* (Berkeley: University of California Press, 2001); Tina Loo, *States of Nature: Conserving Canada's Wildlife in the Twentieth Century* (Vancouver: UBC Press, 2006); Bill Parenteau and James Kenny, "Survival, Resistance, and the Canadian State: The Transformation of New Brunswick's Native Economy, 1867-1930," *Journal of the*

Canadian Historical Association 13,1 (2002): 49-71; and John Sandlos, *Hunters at the Margin: Native People and Wildlife Conservation in the Northwest Territories* (Vancouver: UBC Press, 2007). This argument differs from other accounts of forest conservation in Ontario, which tend both to evaluate conservationist measures insofar as they measure up to conservationist goals and to assume that the early struggle for forest conservation was a noble pursuit whose ultimate failure was a disappointment. See R. Peter Gillis and Thomas R. Roach, *Lost Initiatives: Canada's Forest Industries, Forest Policy, and Forest Conservation* (New York: Greenwood, 1986); Bruce W. Hodgins and Jamie Benidickson, *The Temagami Experience: Recreation, Resources, and Aboriginal Rights in the Northern Ontario Wilderness* (Toronto: University of Toronto Press, 1989), 68-107, 153-76; Bruce W. Hodgins, R. Peter Gillis, and Jamie Benidickson, "The Ontario Experiments in Forest Reserves," in *Changing Parks: The History, Future and Cultural Context of Parks and Heritage Landscapes,* ed. John S. Marsh and Bruce W. Hodgins (Toronto: Natural Heritage, 1998), 77-93; and H.V. Nelles, *The Politics of Development: Forests, Mines and Hydro-Electric Power in Ontario, 1849-1941* (Toronto: Macmillan, 1974), 182-214. As these authors make clear, Ontario's forest reserve system failed in its goal of producing timber according to a rational scientific model. Management decisions were made on an ad hoc basis from the beginning, and by the 1950s, there was next to no difference between management activities and regulations within and outside of forest reserves. In 1964, the provincial government abolished what little was left of the reserve system. To be fair, though, I should note that Hodgins and Benidickson do show that the creation of the Temagami Forest Reserve and provincial regulations under the Forest Reserves Act had negative effects on the Teme-Augama Anishnabai, including restrictions on their movement through the TFR and their ability to access game and other resources. See Hodgins and Benidickson, *The Temagami Experience,* 136-52. But for the most part in their account, forest conservation in Temagami appears as a laudable, though ultimately unrealized, goal. Because the establishment of the reserve and its impact on the Teme-Augama Anishnabai are examined in separate chapters of their book, it is difficult for the reader to gain a complete picture of the relationships between forest conservation and the First Nation. Thus, it appears that the two are remotely rather than inextricably connected, a representation that makes it possible for forest conservation to appear an innocent and benevolent activity.

2 Hodgins and Benidickson, *The Temagami Experience,* 27. For the development of this argument, see 27-67.

3 Ibid., 13.

4 Trails in Time, "Traditional Land Use and Resource Management Philosophies and Practices of the Temagami Aboriginal People: Teme-Augama Anishnabai, Temagami First Nation, Ontario Native Affairs Secretariat Joint Project," Land Use and Resource Management Research Box 1, A-0 (Temagami First Nation Band Office, 2001).

5 Indeed, as part of both these processes, Teme-Augama Anishnabai have written and commissioned histories of pre-contact Teme-Augama Anishnabai life. See "Appellants' Factum, vol. 3, History of the Teme-Agama Anishnabay and Land Use" (draft), Dernoi Research Box 3 (Temagami First Nation Band Office, undated); Trails in Time, "Traditional Land Use"; Gary Potts, "Last-Ditch Defence of a Priceless Homeland," in *Drumbeat: Anger and Renewal in Indian Country,* ed. Boyce Richardson (Toronto: Summerhill Press, 1989), 203-30; and Mary Laronde, "Co-Management of Lands and Resources in n'Daki Menan," in *Rebirth: Political, Economic, and Social Development in First Nations,* ed. Anne-Marie Mawhiney (Toronto: Dundurn Press, 1993), 93-106.

6   See Bonita Lawrence, *"Real" Indians and Others: Mixed-Blood Urban Native Peoples and Indigenous Nationhood* (Vancouver: UBC Press, 2004).
7   Mary Louise Pratt, *Imperial Eyes: Travel Writing and Transculturation* (London: Routledge, 1992), 7.
8   Hodgins and Benidickson, *The Temagami Experience*, 14-19.
9   Chief Cana Chintz to D. Laird, 9 September 1876, Library and Archives Canada (LAC), Ottawa, RG 10, vol. 1998, file 7208 (reel C-11131).
10 Hodgins and Benidickson, *The Temagami Experience*, 29-30, 35-40.
11 See Temagamingue Post, Ontario, Archives of Ontario (AO), Toronto, Fur Trade Collection, · F 431; and Ontario, Department of Crown Lands, *Report of the Survey and Exploration of Northern Ontario, 1900* (Toronto: L.K. Cameron, 1901), vii, viii, 86.
12 Hodgins and Benidickson, *The Temagami Experience*, 50-51.
13 Ontario, *Report of the Survey and Exploration*, v (emphasis in original); *Toronto Daily Star,* "The Exploration of Northern Ontario," 16 May 1900, 3.
14 C. Skene to L. Vankoughnet, 1 March 1880, LAC, RG 10, vol. 7757, file 27043-9.
15 Canada, "Copy of the Robinson Treaty Made in the Year 1850 with the Ojibewa Indians of Lake Huron Conveying Certain Lands to the Crown," http://www.ainc-inac.gc.ca.
16 Report of the Vidal Anderson Commission, 5 December 1849, LAC, RG 10, vol. 266 (reel C-12652), 163121-26.
17 C. Skene to L. Vankoughnet, 3 May 1880, LAC, RG 10, vol. 7757, file 27043-9; C. Skene to L. Vankoughnet, 28 February 1881, LAC, RG 10, vol. 7757, file 27043-9; C. Skene to L. Vankoughnet (enclosure), 28 February 1881, LAC, RG 10, vol. 7757, file 27043-9; C. Skene to J.A. Macdonald, 26 May 1881, LAC, RG 10, vol. 7757, file 27043-9.
18 C. Rankin to C. Skene, 22 April 1880, LAC, RG 10, vol. 7757, file 27043-9, forwarded in C. Skene to L. Vankoughnet, 6 May 1880, LAC, RG 10, vol. 7757, file 27043-9; C. Skene to L. Vankoughnet, 14 August 1880, LAC, RG 10, vol. 7757, file 27043-9.
19 L. Vankoughnet to C. Skene, 18 May 1880, LAC, RG 10, vol. 7757, file 27043-9.
20 C. Skene to Chief Tonene, 11 June 1881, LAC, RG 10, vol. 7757, file 27043-9; Chief Tonene to C. Skene, 19 August 1881, LAC, RG 10, vol. 7757, file 27043-9.
21 T. Walton to Superintendent General of Indian Affairs (SGIA), 5 September 1884, LAC, RG 10, vol. 7757, file 27043-9; G.B. Abrey to SGIA, 12 February 1885, LAC, RG 10, vol. 7757, file 27043-9; T. Walton to SGIA, 28 September 1885, LAC, RG 10, vol. 7757, file 27043-9.
22 L. Vankoughnet to C. Skene, 6 June 1881, LAC, RG 10, vol. 7757, file 27043-9; J.C. Phipps to C. Skene, 26 August 1882, LAC, RG 10, vol. 7757, file 27043-9; L. Vankoughnet to C. Skene, 16 June 1883, LAC, RG 10, vol. 7757, file 27043-9.
23 I do not mean to suggest that obtaining a reserve was the ideal solution to their problems. Instead, the historical record indicates that they pressured the government to set aside some lands for them so that they could make the best of their (less than ideal) situation.
24 L. Vankoughnet to T. Walton, 16 October 1885, LAC, RG 10, vol. 7757, file 27043-9.
25 Deputy Superintendent General of Indian Affairs to J.C. Phipps, 28 April 1883, LAC, RG 10, vol. 10267, file 411/30-8-6 (reel T-7558); G.B. Abrey to SGIA, 12 February 1885, LAC, RG 10, vol. 7757, file 27043-9.
26 Secretary of State, Canada, to Lieutenant Governor of Ontario, 13 May 1885, Ontario Ministry of Aboriginal Affairs Archives (ONAS), Toronto, file 186217 (fiche 1); Secretary of State, Canada, to Lieutenant Governor of Ontario, 27 February 1886, ONAS, file 186217 (fiche 1); Secretary of State, Canada, to Lieutenant Governor of Ontario, 8 July 1886, ONAS, file 186217 (fiche 1); G. Powell to Lieutenant Governor of Ontario, 24 November

1886, ONAS, file 186217 (fiche 1); G. Powell to Lieutenant Governor of Ontario, 18 June 1887, ONAS, file 186217 (fiche 1); G. Powell to Lieutenant Governor of Ontario, 27 October 1888, ONAS, file 186217 (fiche 1); G. Powell to Lieutenant Governor of Ontario, 27 March 1890, ONAS, file 186217 (fiche 1); D.C. Scott to A. White, 15 May 1896, LAC, RG 10, vol. 7757, file 27043-9; H. Reed to A. White, 28 September 1896, LAC, RG 10, vol. 7757, file 27043-9; C. Sifton to J.M. Gibson, 20 March 1897, LAC, RG 10, vol. 7757, file 27043-9.

27 Lieutenant Governor of Ontario to G. Powell, 26 November 1886, ONAS, file 186217 (fiche 1); Lieutenant Governor of Ontario to G. Powell, 20 May 1887, ONAS, file 186217 (fiche 1).

28 L. Vankoughnet to R. Sedgewick, 23 May 1889, LAC, RG 10, vol. 7757, file 27043-9; R. Sedgewick to L. Vankoughnet, 28 February 1890, LAC, RG 10, vol. 7757, file 27043-9; W.D. Hogg, statement of Dominion's case in the arbitration, 10 March 1894, LAC, RG 10, vol. 7757, file 27043-9; O'Connor and Hogg to H. Reed, 11 May 1896, LAC, RG 10, vol. 7757, file 27043-9; D.C. Scott to A. White, 15 May 1896, LAC, RG 10, vol. 7757, file 27043-9; H. Reed to A. White, 28 September 1896, LAC, RG 10, vol. 7757, file 27043-9; C. Sifton to J.M. Gibson, 20 March 1897, LAC, RG 10, vol. 7757, file 27043-9.

29 A. White to D.F. MacDonald, 10 April 1894, ONAS, file 186217 (fiche 1).

30 Of the eleven-page report by MacDonald, six pages are taken up with Chief Dokis' story, which begins with his description of a letter in which Walton attempted to convince him to sell the pine timber on his band's reserve (the entire letter from Walton is transcribed into MacDonald's report). When Dokis ignored the letter, Walton became very angry and told him that the government would sell the timber in spite of him. Alarmed at this prospect, the chief wrote to the Department of Indian Affairs and was reassured that the timber would not be sold without the band's permission. Walton again expressed anger toward Dokis, this time for having written a letter to the DIA without sending it through the proper channels (Walton himself), and Dokis replied that he did not consider it necessary to consult the Indian agent in all matters, particularly since he thought that Walton was either helpless or negligent in his duties. Dokis concluded his story by stating that he and his band "will never surrender our right to our timber as long as I live." This incident reveals both the determination of the chief to maintain control of his band's lands and his ability to manipulate a government mission to serve his own interests. It also shows the power that an individual Indian agent had in shaping the lives of the Aboriginal people he "supervised." After Dokis refused to sell the timber, Walton would not visit Lake Nipissing to deliver treaty annuities to the band. In 1908, after the death of Dokis, the Dokis First Nation was forced to sell its timber. See James T. Angus, "How the Dokis Indians Protected Their Timber," *Ontario History* 81,3 (1989): 181-99.

31 D.F. MacDonald to A. White, 18 September 1894, ONAS, file 186217 (fiche 1).

32 T. Walton to SGIA, annual report, 31 December 1884, DIA, Victoria University, E.J. Pratt Library, Toronto, microfilm .C1595a, 8-9.

33 G.B. Abrey to SGIA, 12 February 1885, LAC, RG 10, vol. 7757, file 27043-9; T. Walton to SGIA, annual report, 31 December 1885, DIA, Victoria University, E.J. Pratt Library, microfilm .C1595a, 8-9; T. Walton to SGIA, annual report, 31 December 1886, DIA, Victoria University, E.J. Pratt Library, microfilm .C1595a, 8-9; J. Turner to T. Walton, 31 May 1887, LAC, RG 10, vol. 7757, file 27043-9; W.B. Maclean to SGIA, annual report, 30 June 1897, DIA, Victoria University, E.J. Pratt Library, microfilm .C1595a, 30-34.

34 Cole Harris, *Making Native Space: Colonialism, Resistance, and Reserves in British Columbia* (Vancouver: UBC Press, 2002).

35 Chief Tonene to T. Walton, 11 February 1890, LAC, RG 10, vol. 7757, file 27043-9.

36 T. Walton to SGIA, annual report, 30 June 1894, DIA, Victoria University, E.J. Pratt Library, microfilm .C1595a, 7-9.

37 This was part of Paradis' (failed) colonization scheme to bring French Canadians to settle in northeastern Ontario. For more details about Paradis, who was a strange and controversial figure, see Hodgins and Benidickson, *The Temagami Experience*, 56-61; and Bruce Hodgins, *Paradis of Temagami: The Story of Charles Paradis, 1848-1926, Northern Priest, Colonizer and Rebel* (Cobalt, ON: Highway Book Shop, 1976).

38 Hodgins and Benidickson, *The Temagami Experience*, 72.

39 *Toronto Globe*, "Means Millions: Eastern Outlet from Temiscamingue for Ottawa Lumbermen," 13 June 1899, 4.

40 Recorded in Clerk of Forestry, annual report, 1900-01, AO, film B97 (reel 75), 12-13.

41 *Forest Reserves Act*, Clerk of Forestry, annual report, 1898, AO, film B97 (reel 64), 7.

42 A. White, memorandum, 7 January 1901, AO, RG 1-545-1-2, 3.

43 Clerk of Forestry, annual report, 1900-01, AO, film B97 (reel 75), 11.

44 A. White, memorandum, 7 January 1901, AO, RG 1-545-1-2, 3.

45 "Forestry," *Rod and Gun* 2,9 (February 1901): 454.

46 Clerk of Forestry, annual report, 1900-01, AO, film B97 (reel 75), 12.

47 Richard S. Lambert and Paul Pross, *Renewing Nature's Wealth: A Centennial History of the Public Management of Lands, Forests and Wildlife in Ontario, 1763-1967* ([Toronto?]: Hunter Rose Company for the Ontario Department of Lands and Forests, 1967), 167-73.

48 *Algonquin National Park Act*, 56 Vict., c. 8 (1893), quoted in ibid., 173.

49 Hodgins and Benidickson, *The Temagami Experience*, 68-89.

50 Nelles, *Politics of Development*, 184, 188. On the popularization of the forest conservation movement, see also Joanna M. Beyers and L. Anders Sandberg, "Canadian Federal Forest Policy: Present Initiatives and Historical Constraints," in *Sustainability, the Challenge: People, Power, and the Environment*, ed. L. Anders Sandberg and Sverker Sörlin (Montreal: Black Rose Books, 1998), 99-107; R. Peter Gillis, "The Ottawa Lumber Barons and the Conservation Movement, 1880-1914," *Journal of Canadian Studies* 9,1 (February 1974): 14-29; Gillis and Roach, *Lost Initiatives;* Lambert and Pross, *Renewing Nature's Wealth;* Jamie Lawson, Marcelo Levy, and L. Anders Sandberg, "'Perpetual Revenues and the Delights of the Primitive': Change, Continuity, and Forest Policy Regimes in Ontario," in *Canadian Forest Policy: Adapting to Change*, ed. Michael Howlett (Toronto: University of Toronto Press, 2001), 279-315; Donald Mackay, *Heritage Lost: The Crisis in Canada's Forests* (Toronto: Macmillan of Canada, 1985); and Jamie Swift, *Cut and Run: The Assault on Canada's Forests* (Toronto: Between the Lines, 1983). The authors generally agree that though the *idea* of forest conservation became popular in the early twentieth century, forestry *practices* in line with conservationist principles did not quickly follow.

51 A.R.M. Lower, *Settlement and the Forest Frontier in Eastern Canada* (Toronto: Macmillan of Canada, 1936).

52 Nelles, *Politics of Development*, 184.

53 Swift, *Cut and Run*, 51-52.

54 Nelles, *Politics of Development*, 184.

55 See Mark Kuhlberg, *One Hundred Rings and Counting: Forestry Education and Forestry in Toronto and Canada, 1907-2007* (Toronto: University of Toronto Press, 2009); and Andrew Denny Rodgers, *Bernhard Eduard Fernow: A Story of North American Forestry* (Princeton: Princeton University Press, 1951). For a critical analysis of the implementation of a state-driven forestry regime in eighteenth- and nineteenth-century Germany, see James C. Scott,

"Nature and Space," in James C. Scott, *Seeing Like a State: How Certain Schemes to Improve the Human Condition Have Failed* (New Haven: Yale University Press, 1998), 11-52.

56 Hodgins and Benidickson, *The Temagami Experience,* 69; Lambert and Pross, *Renewing Nature's Wealth,* 156-62, 177-201; Swift, *Cut and Run,* 52-53.

57 Nelles, *Politics of Development,* 202.

58 Hodgins and Benidickson agree with this statement and add that this commitment was "fleeting." Hodgins and Benidickson, *The Temagami Experience,* 68.

59 Clerk of Forestry, annual report, 1899, AO, film B97 (reel 68), 6.

60 Clerk of Forestry, annual report, 1896, AO, film B97 (reel 56), 27.

61 Lambert and Pross, *Renewing Nature's Wealth,* 179. Delegates also concluded that, before these tasks could be accomplished, the public must be educated about forest conservation. In addition, they determined that they would advocate for forest fire suppression, the implementation of less wasteful cutting practices, the planting of trees on farms, and the employment of trained forestry experts. See ibid., 163, 179-81. When it was established in 1900, the Canadian Forestry Association pursued similar objectives, which were to educate the public about the results of forest destruction and to teach the younger generation of the value of the forest; to recommend that some portion of the country become a permanent timber reserve and that the public domain be divided into agricultural, timber, and mineral lands; and to promote tree planting, especially in cities, along highways, and in the prairies. See Canadian Forestry Association, *Report of the First Annual Meeting of the Canadian Forestry Association* (Ottawa: Government Printing Bureau, 1900), 10.

62 "The Canadian Forestry Association," *Canadian Forestry Journal* 1,1 (January 1905): 5; Lambert and Pross, *Renewing Nature's Wealth,* 163; Clerk of Forestry, annual report, 1899, AO, film B97 (reel 68), 130-33.

63 Clerk of Forestry, annual report, 1900-01, AO, film B97 (reel 75), 9-11.

64 Hodgins and Benidickson, *The Temagami Experience,* 68-69.

65 A. White, memorandum, 7 January 1901, AO, RG 1-545-1-2, 3.

66 "Forestry," *Rod and Gun* 2,11 (April 1901): 503; "Forestry" (February 1901): 454.

67 Ibid., 454-55.

68 Ibid., 455.

69 Nelles, *Politics of Development,* 187-88.

70 Bernhard Fernow, "The Forest as a Resource," 1903, Department of Crown Lands, AO, film B97 (reel 85), 13; Clerk of Forestry, annual report, 1900-01, AO, film B97 (reel 75), 12; "Northern Ontario's Timber Resources," *Canadian Forestry Journal* 9,12 (December 1913): 181-83; J.R. Dickson, "Our Forest Reserve Problem," *Canadian Forestry Journal* 8,3 (May-June 1912): 66-71; "Forestry," *Rod and Gun* 2,3 (August 1900): 300-4; Clerk of Forestry, annual report, 1896, AO, film B97 (reel 56).

71 Fernow, "The Forest as a Resource," 1903, Department of Crown Lands, AO, film B97 (reel 85), 11.

72 See Anne McClintock, *Imperial Leather: Gender, Race and Sexuality in the Colonial Contest* (New York: Routledge, 1995), 30, which states that, within colonial narratives, the myth of the virgin land "effects a territorial appropriation, for if this land is virgin, colonized peoples cannot claim aboriginal territorial rights."

73 W.F. Shaw, "The Forest Wealth of Ontario: A Scheme for Its Perpetuation," *Rod and Gun* 7,8 (January 1906): 856; "The Canadian Forestry Association," 8.

74 Elihu Stewart, "The Approaching Timber Famine," *Canadian Magazine* 22,1 (November 1903): 22.

75 A. White, memorandum, 7 January 1901, AO, RG 1-545-1-2, 6; Clerk of Forestry, annual report, 1900-01, AO, film B97 (reel 75), 13, 15.

76 See Harris, *Making Native Space;* and John C. Weaver, *The Great Land Rush and the Making of the Modern World, 1650-1900* (Montreal/Kingston: McGill-Queen's University Press, 2003).

77 Clerk of Forestry, annual report, 1900-01, AO, film B97 (reel 75), 15.

78 Ibid., 13.

79 A. White, memorandum, 7 January 1901, AO, RG 1-545-1-2, 6-7.

80 A. White to J.D. McLean, 22 June 1910, LAC, RG 10, vol. 7757, file 27043-9.

81 A. White to J.D. McLean, 28 June 1911, LAC, RG 10, vol. 7757, file 27043-9.

82 A. White to J.D. McLean, 22 June 1910, LAC, RG 10, vol. 7757, file 27043-9.

83 Chief François Whitebear to DIA, 21 May 1910, LAC, RG 10, vol. 7757, file 27043-9; Chief Alexander Paul to F. Pedley, c. 1 July 1912, LAC, RG 10, vol. 7757, file 27043-9.

84 J.D. McLean to A. White, 18 January 1906, LAC, RG 10, vol. 7757, file 27043-9; Temagami Band to G.P. Cockburn, 23 February 1907, LAC, RG 10, vol. 7757, file 27043-9; S. Stewart to A. White, 11 January 1910, LAC, RG 10, vol. 7757, file 27043-9; Chief François Whitebear to DIA, 21 May 1910, LAC, RG 10, vol. 7757, file 27043-9; G.P. Cockburn to J.D. McLean, 24 July 1911, LAC, RG 10, vol. 7757, file 27043-9; Chief Alexander Paul to F. Pedley, c. 1 July 1912, LAC, RG 10, vol. 7757, file 27043-9.

85 Temagami Band to G.P. Cockburn, 23 February 1907, LAC, RG 10, vol. 7757, file 27043-9. The reserves to which the petition refers were those negotiated under the James Bay Treaty, or Treaty No. 9, in 1905 and 1906.

86 A. White, memorandum, 7 January 1901, AO, RG 1-545-1-2, 4.

87 Clerk of Forestry, annual report, 1900-01, AO, film B97 (reel 75), 13.

88 Donald McKenzie, recorded interview, Land Use and Resource Management Research Box 3, C-10, Temagami First Nation Band Office, 17 December 1973.

89 E.J. Davis, recommended regulations for forest reserves, 11 December 1902, AO, RG 1-545-1-3, 22.

90 "Ontario Forest Reserves," *Rod and Gun* 4,9 (February 1903): 331.

91 Hodgins and Benidickson, *The Temagami Experience,* 82.

92 Grand Trunk Railway, *The Eldorado of New Ontario: Cobalt, the Rich New Silver District* (Toronto: Mail Job Print, 1907), 3.

93 *Toronto Daily Star,* "Enthusiastic over Lake Temagami," 7 June 1906, 11; Hodgins and Benidickson, *The Temagami Experience,* 94.

94 Canadian Forestry Association, "Ontario's Forest Policy," *Rod and Gun* 5,6 (November 1903): 254. Nelles argues that conservationist reasons for selling timber in the TFR at this time were merely the pretext under which the province "held its usual pre-election timber limit auction." Nelles, *Politics of Development,* 205.

95 Hodgins and Benidickson, *The Temagami Experience,* 83; F. Cochrane, notice, c. 1905, AO, RG 1-549-0-3, 49.

96 A. White, memorandum, 2 December 1903, AO, RG 1-545-1-4; Clerk of Forestry, annual report, 1904, AO, film B97 (reel 85), 11.

97 Ontario, notices of sale of damaged pine timber, 5 February 1909, 17 August 1909, AO, RG 1-549-0-3, 73, 79; A. White, memorandum, 28 November 1904, AO, RG 1-68-0-2 (box 1); A. White, memorandum, 28 February 1910, AO, RG 1-68-0-3 (box 2); A. White, draft memorandum, c. 1910, AO, RG 1-68-0-3 (box 2); A. White, memorandum, 9 September 1912, AO, RG 1-68-0-4 (box 3); W. Hearst, recommendations to sell timber, 27 February

1912, 10 February 1914, AO, RG 1-545-1-4, 166-68, 391-95; A. White, memorandum, 23 March 1914, AO, RG 1-545-1-4, 413-15; Deputy Minister to Chief Forest Ranger, 24 September 1910, AO, RG 1-273-3-29 (box 7).

98 *Toronto Globe,* "Two Townships Less in Forest Reserve," 1 March 1912, 9; *Toronto Globe,* "New Ontario Prepares Its Program," 20 May 1912, 10; A. White, memorandum, 7 June 1910, AO, RG 1-68-0-3 (box 2); Deputy Minister to Chief Forest Ranger, 24 September 1910, AO, RG 1-273-3-29 (box 7).

99 *Toronto Globe,* "Survey of Temagami Islands," 18 February 1904, 8; Lease 1, 8 December 1905, AO, RG 1-165-1.

100 A. White, memorandum, 9 February 1910, AO, RG 1-68-0-3 (box 2); A. White, draft report, 1910, AO, RG 1-68-0-3 (box 2).

101 D.C. Scott to A. White, 15 May 1896, LAC, RG 10, vol. 7757, file 27043-9; H. Reed to A. White, 28 September 1896, LAC, RG 10, vol. 7757, file 27043-9; A. White to H. Reed, 3 February 1897, LAC, RG 10, vol. 7757, file 27043-9.

102 A. White, memorandum, 7 January 1901, AO, RG 1-545-1-2, 6.

103 J.D. McLean to A. White, 18 January 1906, LAC, RG 10, vol. 7757, file 27043-9; A. White to J.D. McLean, 25 January 1906, LAC, RG 10, vol. 7757, file 27043-9.

104 F. Pedley to A. White, 6 February 1906, LAC, RG 10, vol. 7757, file 27043-9; J.D. McLean to A. White, 8 February 1907, ONAS, file 186217 (fiche 1).

105 A. White to S. Stewart, 20 January 1910, LAC, RG 10, vol. 7757, file 27043-9.

106 J.D. McLean to A. White, 7 February 1910, LAC, RG 10, vol. 7757, file 27043-9.

107 A. White to J.D. McLean, 14 June 1910, LAC, RG 10, vol. 7757, file 27043-9.

108 J.D. McLean to Chief François Whitebear, 17 June 1910, LAC, RG 10, vol. 7757, file 27043-9.

109 G.P. Cockburn to J.D. McLean, 19 June 1911, LAC, RG 10, vol. 7757, file 27043-9; A. White to J.D. McLean, 28 June 1911, LAC, RG 10, vol. 7757, file 27043-9.

110 G.P. Cockburn to J.D. McLean, 24 July 1911, LAC, RG 10, vol. 7757, file 27043-9; J.D. McLean to A. White, 26 July 1911, LAC, RG 10, vol. 7757, file 27043-9.

111 Chief Alexander Paul to F. Pedley, c. 1 July 1912, LAC, RG 10, vol. 7757, file 27043-9.

112 J.D. McLean to A. White, 4 October 1912, LAC, RG 10, vol. 7757, file 27043-9.

113 Clerk of Forestry, annual report, 1900-01, AO, film B97 (reel 75), 13.

114 A. White to J.D. McLean, 22 June 1910, LAC, RG 10, vol. 7757, file 27043-9.

115 E.J. Davis, annexed regulations, 11 December 1902, AO, RG 1-545-1-3, 22-25.

116 Aleck Paul, speech recorded by Frank Speck, Land Use and Resource Management Research Box 3, C-17 (Temagami First Nation Band Office, 1913).

117 Chief Alexander Paul to SGIA, 3 September 1917, LAC, RG 10, vol. 7757, file 27043-9.

CHAPTER 3: VIRGIN TERRITORY FOR THE SPORTSMAN

1 W.M. Jones, *Sport and Pleasure in the Virgin Wilds of Canada on Lakes Temiskaming, Temagaming* (Ottawa: Mortimer, 1899), 3; "The 'Bobs' on Temagami," *Rod and Gun* 7,4 (September 1905): 425; J.M. Norris, "Fishing in Beautiful Temagami District: An Earthly Paradise," *Rod and Gun* 10,8 (January 1909): 696; *Toronto Daily Star,* "Enthusiastic over Lake Temagami," 7 June 1906, 11; T.J.T., "Two Weeks in Temagami," *Outdoor Canada* 6,1 (February 1910): 18.

2 See William Cronon, "A Place for Stories: Nature, History, and Narrative," *Journal of American History* 78,4 (March, 1992): 1347-76.

3 Patricia Jasen, *Wild Things: Nature, Culture, and Tourism in Ontario, 1790-1914* (Toronto: University of Toronto Press, 1995), 13.

4 Ibid., 13, 16-17.

5 See, for example, Alison Blunt, *Travel, Gender, and Imperialism: Mary Kingsley and West Africa* (New York: Guilford Press, 1994); Inderpal Grewal, *Home and Harem: Nation, Gender, Empire and the Cultures of Travel* (Durham, NC: Duke University Press, 1996); Patrick Holland and Graham Huggan, *Tourists with Typewriters: Critical Reflections on Contemporary Travel Writing* (Ann Arbor: University of Michigan Press, 1998); Nigel Leask, *Curiosity and the Aesthetics of Travel Writing* (Oxford: Oxford University Press, 2002); Mary Louise Pratt, *Imperial Eyes: Travel Writing and Transculturation* (London: Routledge, 1992); and David Spurr, *The Rhetoric of Empire: Colonial Discourse in Journalism, Travel Writing, and Imperial Administration* (Durham, NC: Duke University Press, 1993).

6 Pratt, *Imperial Eyes*, 6.

7 Jasen, *Wild Things*, 20-21.

8 Bruce W. Hodgins and Jamie Benidickson, *The Temagami Experience: Recreation, Resources, and Aboriginal Rights in the Northern Ontario Wilderness* (Toronto: University of Toronto Press, 1989), 112-14.

9 Sharon Wall, *The Nurture of Nature: Childhood, Antimodernism, and Ontario Summer Camps, 1920-55* (Vancouver: UBC Press, 2009), 18. Clarke worked at the Gunnery School in Connecticut and Cochrane at Upper Canada College in Toronto.

10 *Toronto Globe*, "To Temagami in through Pullman Sleeper Daily," Grand Trunk Railway advertisement, 10 July 1905, 7; Jasen, *Wild Things*, 21.

11 *New Liskeard Speaker*, "Oddfellows Have Glorious Trip," 3 August 1906, 1. At the turn of the twentieth century, the Independent Order of Odd Fellows (I.O.O.F.), a fraternal organization of working-class men, was the largest social society in Canada and the United States. A volunteer group of mutual-aid members gave time and money to help one another through illnesses; it had its origins in similar organizations that began in England during the early nineteenth century. See George Emery, *A Young Man's Benefit: The Independent Order of Odd Fellows and Sickness Insurances in the United States and Canada, 1860-1929* (Montreal/Kingston: McGill-Queen's University Press, 1999). The I.O.O.F. exists in modified form today. See the Sovereign Grand Lodge: Independent Order of Odd Fellows, http://www.ioof.org.

12 Jasen, *Wild Things*, 24. See also Sara Mills, *Discourses of Difference: An Analysis of Women's Travel Writing and Colonialism* (London: Routledge, 1991).

13 Tina Loo, *States of Nature: Conserving Canada's Wildlife in the Twentieth Century* (Vancouver: UBC Press, 2006), 34. *Rod and Gun* was published under a variety of names (for example, *Rod and Gun in Canada* and *Rod and Gun and Motor Sports in Canada*) from 1899 until the 1970s. By 1913, it had a circulation of approximately eighteen thousand.

14 For the development of these arguments in the American context, see Philip J. Deloria, "Natural Indians and Identities of Modernity," in Philip J. Deloria, *Playing Indian* (New Haven: Yale University Press, 1998), 95-127; in the Canadian context, see Kristopher Churchill, "Learning about Manhood: Gender Ideals and 'Manly Camping,'" in *Using Wilderness: Essays on the Evolution of Youth Camping in Ontario,* ed. Bruce W. Hodgins and Bernadine Dodge (Peterborough, ON: Frost Centre for Canadian Heritage and Development Studies, 1992), 5-27; Sharon Wall, "Totem Poles, Tepees, and Token Traditions: 'Playing Indian' at Camp," in Wall, *The Nurture of Nature*, 216-50.

15 Pratt, *Imperial Eyes*, 155; Jasen, *Wild Things*, 22.

16 Mrs. A.G. Adams, "A Lady's Hunting Trip," *Rod and Gun* 11,5 (October 1909): 400.

17 Anne McClintock, *Imperial Leather: Gender, Race and Sexuality in the Colonial Contest* (New York: Routledge, 1995), 24.

18 "Canada and the Tourist," *Canadian Magazine* 15,1 (May 1900): 4.

19 C.C. Farr, "A Trip to Matachuan," part 2, *Rod and Gun* 3,8 (January 1902): 1.

20 Mills, *Discourses of Difference,* shows that white women struggled against external constraints to create travel writing that would be published and read.

21 Ella Walton, "A Woman's Views on Camping Out," *Rod and Gun* 1,4 (September 1899): 72.

22 Jasen, *Wild Things,* 114-15.

23 Joseph R. Johnson, "Some Delights of Camping Out," *Busy Man's Magazine* 16,3 (July 1908): 128.

24 Myrle Cameron, "A Day's Journey in the Wilds," *Rod and Gun* 12,8 (January 1911): 1021.

25 Jasen, *Wild Things,* 114-15. For a Temagami example, see Anna C. Ruddy, "A Gentleman of Temagami," *Canadian Magazine* 29,6 (October 1907): 544-47.

26 Chief François Whitebear to Department of Indian Affairs (DIA), 21 May 1910, Library and Archives Canada (LAC), Ottawa, RG 10, vol. 7757, file 27043-9; Donald McKenzie, recorded interview, Land Use and Resource Management Research Box 3, C-10, Temagami First Nation Band Office, 22 November 1973.

27 Teme-Augama Anishnabai member, pers. comm., July 2006.

28 G.P. Cockburn to Superintendent General of Indian Affairs (SGIA), annual report, 30 June 1904, DIA, Victoria University, E.J. Pratt Library, Toronto, microfilm .C1595a; G.P. Cockburn to SGIA, annual report, 30 June 1905, DIA, Victoria University, E.J. Pratt Library, microfilm .C1595a; G.P. Cockburn to SGIA, annual report, 31 March 1911, DIA, Victoria University, E.J. Pratt Library, microfilm .C1595a; M.R. Lovell, "Penn Professor's Discovery Confounds Indian 'History,'" *Philadelphia Public Ledger,* 23 November 1913, mag. sec.; Teme-Augama Anishnabai member, pers. comm., July 2006.

29 Jasen, *Wild Things,* 26.

30 G.P. Cockburn to SGIA, annual report, 30 June 1905, DIA, Victoria University, E.J. Pratt Library, microfilm .C1595a; R.E. Schubart, "A Moose Hunt at Wabigoon, Ontario," *Rod and Gun* 13,3 (August 1911): 289; *Toronto Globe,* "Northland Notes of Summer Travel," 19 August 2005, 16.

31 Commissioner to Lieutenant Governor of Ontario, recommendation, 20 July 1906, Archives of Ontario (AO), Toronto, RG 1-545-1-3, 248; G.P. Cockburn to SGIA, annual report, 31 March 1911, DIA, Victoria University, E.J. Pratt Library, microfilm .C1595a; L.V. Rorke to A.F. MacKenzie, 12 July 1929, LAC, RG 10, vol. 7757, file 27043-9.

32 Teme-Augama Anishnabai members, pers. comm., July 2006; A. W. C., "A Cruise in the Ojibway Paradise," part 2, *Forest and Stream,* 2 May 1903, 344; "The 'Bobs' on Temagami"; Frank Carrell, "Our Fishing and Hunting Trip in Northern Ontario," part 1, *Rod and Gun* 8,11 (April 1907): 937; Madeline Katt Theriault, *Moose to Moccasins: The Story of Ka Kita Wa Pa No Kwe* (Toronto: Natural Heritage/Natural History, 1992).

33 *Toronto Globe,* "Scotch Indians of Temagami," 10 October 1903, 15; W.C. Caldwell, diary, AO, MU 839; George P. Beswick, "After Fish in Temagami," *Rod and Gun* 7,3 (August 1905): 316-19; Frank Yeigh, "Touring in Temagami Land," *Rod and Gun* 8,5 (October 1906): 324-27; Carrell, "Our Fishing and Hunting Trip," part 1.

34 See Thomas King, "You're Not the Indian I Had in Mind," in Thomas King, *The Truth about Stories: A Native Narrative* (Toronto: House of Anansi, 2003), 31-60.

35 Teme-Augama Anishnabai member, pers. comm., July 2006; Tina Loo, "Of Moose and Men: Hunting for Masculinities in British Columbia, 1880-1939," *Western Historical Quarterly* 32 (Autumn 2001): 296-319. Loo brings an interesting perspective to this discussion, though one that equally reflects the class base of wilderness tourists. In this article, she suggests that the attempt by sport hunters to control their guides in the bush was related to their sense of entitlement as bosses and managers at home. They expected obedience from their Aboriginal guides partly because they were used to receiving it from their employees. Loo further contends that, for big-game hunters, a successful hunt depended on their abilities to manage their guides. In this way, they not only attempted to bring into the bush the urban class-based system from which they benefited in their daily lives, but also masked their dependence on their guides by constructing them as obstacles to a hunt (since, according to sportsmen, they had to be managed and controlled to ensure that they did their job). Loo also indicates how guides subverted such attempts at management – for example, by leading tourists through the bush at breakneck speeds.
36 Engineer, "South of Abitibi," *Rod and Gun* 4,8 (January 1903): 274.
37 An Eye Witness, "In Temagami's Tangled Wild," *Rod and Gun* 8,1 (June 1906): 36-42.
38 "Fields and Pastures New," *Forest and Stream,* 2 April 1904, 266.
39 G.P. Cockburn to SGIA, annual report, 30 June 1905, DIA, Victoria University, E.J. Pratt Library, microfilm .C1595a.
40 O.E. Fischer, "Canoe Cruises in Canadian Reserves," part 2, *Forest and Stream,* 24 September 1910, 506; Fraser Raney, "Canoe Trips in Temagami," *Rod and Gun* 12,2 (July 1910): 191.
41 Dixmont, "Moose Hunting in Temagami," *Forest and Stream,* 9 December 1911, 835; Me, "Biff and Hec and Me," *Rod and Gun* 16,6 (November 1914): 570.
42 "Timagami, Mississagua, French River and That Sort of Thing," *Rod and Gun* 6,11 (April 1905): 589; Grey Owl, *Pilgrims of the Wild* (London: Lovat Dickson and Thompson, 1935), 12-13; Lovat Dickson, *Wilderness Man: The Strange Story of Grey Owl* (Toronto: Macmillan, 1973), especially 50-82; Donald B. Smith, *From the Land of the Shadows: The Making of Grey Owl* (Saskatoon: Western Producer Prairie Books, 1990).
43 W.R. Wadsworth, "With Rifle and Rod in the Moose Lands of Northern Ontario," part 1, *Canadian Magazine* 13,2 (June 1899): 151; *Toronto Daily Star,* "Ontario: A Field for the Settler, the Miner, the Lumberman, and Tourist," 23 June 1905, 28; Camp Temagami, *Camp Temagami: A Summer Camp for Men and Boys, Established 1900, Conducted by Arthur L. Cochrane,* camp brochure, 1915, 7.
44 Jas. W. Barry, "Timagami, a Region Organized by Nature for Real Sport," *Rod and Gun* 7,2 (July 1905): 168.
45 Wadsworth, "With Rifle and Rod," 149; *Toronto Globe,* "Primeval Beauty at Lake Temagami," 12 June 1906, 10.
46 For regulations of and controversies over damming lakes in the Temagami region, see AO, RG 1-273-3-29, box 7, and RG 1-273-3-30, box 7. The regulations ensuring that tourists did not encounter dead trees or logged areas were not unique to Temagami. See Gerald Killan, *Protected Places: A History of Ontario's Provincial Parks System* (Toronto: Dundurn Press, 1993).
47 Jasen, *Wild Things,* 29.
48 Ibid., 7.
49 Ibid., 8-9, 12, 13.
50 A. W. C., "A Cruise in the Ojibway Paradise," 343; Yeigh, "Touring in Temagami Land," 324.

51 See William Cronon, "The Trouble with Wilderness: Or, Getting Back to the Wrong Nature," in William Cronon, *Uncommon Ground: Rethinking the Human Place in Nature* (New York: Norton, 1996), 75.

52 Frank Carrell, "Our Fishing and Hunting Trip in Northern Ontario," part 3, *Rod and Gun* 9,1 (June 1907): 50; Frank J. Clowes, "August Days in Temagami," *Rod and Gun* 8,10 (March 1907): 837.

53 Jasen, *Wild Things*, 82-83.

54 Grand Trunk Railway, *Temagami: A Peerless Region for the Sportsman, Canoeist, Camper* (Montreal: Grand Trunk Railway, 1908), 1.

55 For a discussion of the tourist gaze, see John Urry, *The Tourist Gaze: Leisure and Travel in Contemporary Societies* (London: Sage, 1990).

56 S.E. Sangster, "The Woods Indian," *Busy Man's Magazine* 24,4 (August 1912): 124; Farr, "A Trip to Matachuan," 2; *Toronto Globe*, "The Wonderland of the Dominion," 3 August 1907, 4.

57 *Toronto Globe*, "Temagami," 13 June 1905, 9.

58 Louis Oliver Armstrong, *A Canoe Trip through Temagaming the Peerless in the Land of Hiawatha* (N.p.: Canadian Pacific Railway, 1900); Me, "Biff and Hec and Me," 569. See also Claire Elizabeth Campbell, *Shaped by the West Wind: Nature and History in Georgian Bay* (Vancouver: UBC Press, 2005), 98, 101. Campbell makes a similar observation about Georgian Bay travel literature, stating that it often described Aboriginal peoples alongside other "natural" elements such as geological formations and lake conditions. She also notes that the reputed savagery of the Georgian Bay Iroquois and Ojibwa reinforced for non-Natives the idea of the region as wilderness, while at the same time the character of Georgian Bay made its Aboriginal inhabitants appear particularly wild.

59 Yeigh, "Touring in Temagami Land," 326; "Our Medicine Bag," *Rod and Gun* 4,11 (April 1903): 409.

60 The Chief, "Away 'Up North,'" part 3, *Forest and Stream*, 12 May 1894, 412; C.C. Farr, "In the Woods with Indian Guides," *Rod and Gun* 8,5 (October 1906): 327-28; St. Croix, "Second Sight and the Indian," *Rod and Gun* 4,3 (August 1902): 103.

61 Carrell, "Our Fishing and Hunting Trip," part 1, 936.

62 Frank Carrell, "Our Fishing and Hunting Trip in Northern Ontario," part 4, *Rod and Gun* 9,2 (July 1907): 146.

63 St. Croix, "An Exploration to the Height of Land," part 3, *Rod and Gun* 3,7 (December 1901): 8.

64 Carrell, "Our Fishing and Hunting Trip," part 4, 138; Cameron, "A Day's Journey in the Wilds," 1020.

65 Armstrong, *A Canoe Trip through Temagaming*, 6.

66 See, for instance, Peter Boag, "Thinking Like Mount Rushmore: Sexuality and Gender in the Republican Landscape," in *Seeing Nature through Gender*, ed. Virginia J. Scharff (Lawrence: University Press of Kansas, 2003), 40-59; Churchill, "Learning about Manhood"; Jasen, *Wild Things*, 106-7, 140; and Loo, *States of Nature*, 29-35.

67 Louis Oliver Armstrong, "Down the Mississaga," *Rod and Gun* 6,2 (July 1904): 60-61; Louis Oliver Armstrong, "Out of Doors," *Rod and Gun* 6,1 (June 1904): 15.

68 "Why We Take to the Woods," *Rod and Gun* 13,5 (October 1911): 560; Another Wet Bob, "Temagaming," *Rod and Gun* 1,3 (August 1899): 53.

69 E. and S.W., "John Green, Guide," *Rod and Gun* 10,1 (June 1908): 10.

70 Raney, "Canoe Trips in Temagami," 191.

71 Matthew Parkinson, "Lake Timagami: A Northern Ontario Playground," *Canadian Magazine* 43,2 (June 1914): 167.

72 Jasen, *Wild Things*, 16.

73 *Toronto Daily Star*, "Temagami, Mecca of Sportsmen," 23 June 1905, 29.

74 Ibid.; "The Ontario Government and the Lake Temagami Islands," *Rod and Gun* 7,4 (September 1905): 406; "Canada and the Tourist," 4; Robert Wilson, "A Land of Enchantment," *Rod and Gun* 13, 11 (April 1912): 1297; Frank E. Dorchester, "Physical Culture: A Nation's Need," part 10, *Rod and Gun* 11,4 (September 1909): 347.

75 Raymond Gummer, "The Still Small Voice," *Rod and Gun* 10,8 (January 1909): 710; "Timagami, Mississagua, French River," 585; W.H. Thurston, "Two Weeks in Paradise: Being a True Narrative of a Visit Paid Thereto by Three Worthy and Care-Free Mortals," *Rod and Gun* 11,12 (May 1910): 1133.

76 W.T. Robson, "The Value of the Tourist Sportsman as a Means of Publicity for Undeveloped Country," *Rod and Gun* 12,11 (April 1911): 1466-67. See also Campbell, *Shaped by the West Wind*, 83. Campbell observes that although "we tend to think of the romantic wilderness seeker and the profit-minded logger as ideological opposites and political foes competing for the environment," wilderness appreciation and resource extraction in Canada have historically not been mutually exclusive. In the 1880s, for example, company owners vacationed in the same Georgian Bay region where their companies extracted timber. Today, the Canadian economy remains dependent on the export of raw natural resources even as national narratives emphasize the wilderness character of Canada. There has, however, been a cultural shift. Although Georgian Bay cottagers of the 1880s may not have minded watching logs float past their cottage windows, tourists no longer find it acceptable to encounter signs of resource extraction on their wilderness vacations. In Temagami, for instance, one contemporary environmentalist concern is that the new forest management plan, discussed in the Conclusion, allows for the possibility that clearcuts will be visible from Maple Mountain, an iconic tourist destination (and also a sacred site for the Teme-Augama Anishnabai). See Earthroots, "How You Can Help Protect Temagami," http:// www.earthroots.org.

77 "Our Medicine Bag," *Rod and Gun* 9,2 (July 1907): 202-3; *Toronto Daily Star*, "Rail Mill in New Ontario," 4 March 1904, 1.

78 Hodgins and Benidickson, *The Temagami Experience*, 57, 81; C.C. Farr, *The Dominion of Canada as a Field for Emigration: Its Advantages and Disadvantages: The Temiscamingue District in Particular* (Ipswich, UK: East Anglia Printing Works, 1896), 3, 15; Jasen, *Wild Things*, 149.

79 See also note 1 in Chapter 2.

80 Hodgins and Benidickson, *The Temagami Experience*, 109.

81 Ibid., 128. For their story of the dam controversy, see 124-35.

82 "Our Medicine Bag," *Rod and Gun* 13,6 (November 1911): 736 (emphasis added); Hodgins and Benidickson, *The Temagami Experience*, 126.

83 Hodgins and Benidickson, *The Temagami Experience*, 124.

84 As Bruce Braun argues about contemporary ecotourism in British Columbia, the tourist gaze imposes a particular view of nature onto the landscape, which then comes to appear as *the* perspective of nature and thereby masks other understandings of the region. See Bruce Braun, *The Intemperate Rainforest: Nature, Culture, and Power on Canada's West Coast* (Minneapolis: University of Minnesota Press, 2002), 109-55.

85 Pratt, *Imperial Eyes,* 7.
86 Norris, "Fishing in Beautiful Temagami District," 698, 703; Barry, "Timagami, a Region Organized by Nature"; Beswick, "After Fish in Temagami," 316; *Toronto Daily Star,* "One Hundred Miles in a Canoe," 19 August 1904, 5.
87 Pratt, *Imperial Eyes,* 31.
88 K. K. K., "Spring's Unrest," *Rod and Gun* 7,12 (May 1906): 1380; The Guide, "The Lure of Northern Ontario: A Canoe Trip in Temagami," *Rod and Gun* 16,12 (May 1915): 1207.
89 Walton, "A Woman's Views on Camping Out"; Edward Angus, "Temagami," *Rod and Gun* 9,9 (February 1908): 864 (emphasis added).
90 McClintock, *Imperial Leather,* 26.
91 Commissioner to Lieutenant Governor of Ontario, recommendation, 20 July 1906, AO, RG 1-545-1-3, 248.
92 See King, "You're Not the Indian I Had in Mind," 48.
93 Carrell, "Our Fishing and Hunting Trip," part 4, 146; Carrell, "Our Fishing and Hunting Trip," part 1, 939-40.

CHAPTER 4: A ROCKY RESERVE

1 W.C. Cain to Pete Misabi, 12 June 1929, Library and Archives Canada (LAC), Ottawa, RG 10, vol. 7757, file 27043-9; W.C. Cain to John Katt, 15 June 1929, LAC, RG 10, vol. 7757, file 27043-9; W.C. Cain to W. Pishabo, 15 June 1929, LAC, RG 10, vol. 7757, file 27043-9; W.C. Cain to A. Mattias, 17 June 1929, LAC, RG 10, vol. 7757, file 27043-9; L.V. Rorke to A.F. MacKenzie, 12 July 1929, LAC, RG 10, vol. 7757, file 27043-9.
2 See Jamie Benidickson, "Idleness, Water, and a Canoe: Canadian Recreational Paddling between the Wars," in *Nastawgan: The Canadian North by Canoe and Snowshoe,* ed. Bruce W. Hodgins and Margaret Hobbs (Toronto: Betelgeuse, 1985), 163-82; Claire Elizabeth Campbell, *Shaped by the West Wind: Nature and History in Georgian Bay* (Vancouver: UBC Press, 2005), 107, 113-14, 145-47; and Bruce W. Hodgins and Jamie Benidickson, *The Temagami Experience: Recreation, Resources, and Aboriginal Rights in the Northern Ontario Wilderness* (Toronto: University of Toronto Press, 1989), 184.
3 Hodgins and Benidickson, *The Temagami Experience,* 178; *Toronto Globe,* "North Road Reveals Fine Scenic Glories of Forest Reserve," 7 June 1927, 11. For a detailed look at tourism in Temagami from the 1920s to the 1960s, see Bruce W. Hodgins and Jamie Benidickson, "Recreation and the Temagami Wilderness," in Hodgins and Benidickson, *The Temagami Experience,* 177-209.
4 Sunera Thobani, *Exalted Subjects: Studies of the Making of Race and Nation in Canada* (Toronto: University of Toronto Press, 2007), 92; Eva Mackey, *The House of Difference: Cultural Politics and National Identity in Canada* (London: Routledge, 1999), 33.
5 William Milne, quoted in Hodgins and Benidickson, *The Temagami Experience,* 160; see also 83, 160-61.
6 For a list of other licences granted, see Hodgins and Benidickson, *The Temagami Experience,* 165-69.
7 Quoted in ibid., 165; see also 166; H.V. Nelles, *The Politics of Development: Forests, Mines and Hydro-Electric Power in Ontario, 1849-1941* (Toronto: Macmillan, 1974), 182-214. The Department of Lands and Forests was the 1920-72 equivalent of the Department of Crown Lands discussed in Chapter 2. In 1972, it became the Ministry of Natural Resources, a name that stands today.

8   G. Friday to Department of Indian Affairs (DIA), 6 June 1927, LAC, RG 10, vol. 8007, file 411/20-7-6-0 (reel C-9486); G.P. Cockburn to J.D. McLean, 27 June 1927, LAC, RG 10, vol. 8007, file 411/20-7-6-0 (reel C-9486).

9   Hodgins and Benidickson, *The Temagami Experience,* 178-82, 195. After the Depression, more camps appeared, including the first girls' camp, Cayuga, which opened in 1940.

10   Ibid., 185-88.

11   Ibid., 188.

12   George W. Lee, "Ontario's Railway, Owned by Province, Run by Commission," *Toronto Globe,* 3 January 1928, 27; *Toronto Globe,* "Anglers Enjoy Timagami," 15 June 1934, 13; *Toronto Globe,* "Attractions of Temagami Never Lose Their Charm for Eager Vacationists," 2 July 1934, 11.

13   *Toronto Globe,* "Temiskaming and Northern Ontario Railway," advertisement, 3 January 1929, 27; *Toronto Globe,* "A World Apart," advertisement, 12 August 1929, 5.

14   *Toronto Globe,* "A World Apart"; Hodgins and Benidickson, *The Temagami Experience,* 221; *Toronto Globe,* "Attractions of Temagami."

15   *Toronto Globe,* "Lost from Civilization in 3 Million Acres of Forest," advertisement, 16 June 1928, 19.

16   Hodgins and Benidickson, *The Temagami Experience,* 190; Pamela Sinclair, *Temagami Lakes Association: An Historical Perspective* (Temagami: Temagami Lakes Association, 1992), 25.

17   Sinclair, *Temagami Lakes Association,* 25.

18   Quoted in ibid. (emphasis added). In 1934, at the age of sixty-one, Robert Newcomb murdered his wife, Faith, and then killed himself. Ibid., 28. In a rather bizarre repetition of this gendered violence, the Temagami Association dedicated a memorial plaque to him, which remains at the site of the old HBC post on Bear Island. The plaque, which does not mention Faith, reads, "In memory of Robert Burton Newcomb, 1872-1934, first president of the Temagami Association. This tablet has been erected by a great number of his Canadian and American friends and associates."

19   Sinclair, *Temagami Lakes Association,* 25.

20   Joe Friday to DIA, 29 July 1940, LAC, RG 10, vol. 7757, file 27043-9.

21   J.A. Marleau to T.R.L. MacInnes, 3 August 1940, LAC, RG 10, vol. 7757, file 27043-9.

22   The association was not unique in this. During this period, those who campaigned to conserve Ontario wilderness emphasized a primary goal as preserving scenic shorelines for canoeists. See George M. Warecki, *Protecting Ontario's Wilderness: A History of Changing Ideas and Preservation Politics, 1927-1973* (New York: Peter Lang, 2000), 17, 28-29.

23   Quoted in Hodgins and Benidickson, *The Temagami Experience,* 191.

24   Ibid., 172.

25   Hodgins and Benidickson, *The Temagami Experience,* 172.

26   Ibid., 184-85.

27   G.P. Cockburn to Secretary, DIA, 1 July 1929, LAC, RG 10, vol. 7757, file 27043-9; T. McGookin to H.W. McGill, 13 September 1938, LAC, RG 10, vol. 7757, file 27043-9.

28   A.F. MacKenzie to W.C. Cain, 10 July 1929, LAC, RG 10, vol. 7757, file 27043-9; L.V. Rorke to A.F. MacKenzie, 12 July 1929, LAC, RG 10, vol. 7757, file 27043-9; L.V. Rorke to A.F. MacKenzie, 17 June 1930, LAC, RG 10, vol. 7757, file 27043-9.

29   L.V. Rorke to A.F. MacKenzie, 12 July 1929, LAC, RG 10, vol. 7757, file 27043-9.

30   Chief William Pishabo to G.P. Cockburn, 25 January 1932, LAC, RG 10, vol. 7757, file 27043-9.

31   T. McGookin to H.W. McGill, 13 September 1938, LAC, RG 10, vol. 7757, file 27043-9.

32 Chief William Pishabo, A. Mattias, J. Mattias, A. Paul, T. Potts, J. Katt, J. Paul, B. McKenzie, G. Pishabo, C. Potts, D. McKenzie, J. Twain, H. Twain, C. Moore Jr., C. Paul, M. Katt, D. Potts, J. Pishabo, P. McKenzie, and J. Aguna to DIA, 1 October 1935, LAC, RG 10, vol. 7757, file 27043-9; Bear Island Indians and L. Wittig to A. Levesque, 24 August 1936, LAC, RG 10, vol. 10708, file 30-6.

33 W.C. Cain to A.F. MacKenzie, 18 November 1936, LAC, RG 10, vol. 7757, file 27043-9; A.F. MacKenzie to A. Levesque, 25 November 1936, LAC, RG 10, vol. 7757, file 27043-9; J.C. Caldwell to T.R.L. MacInnes, 29 August 1938, LAC, RG 10, vol. 7757, file 27043-9.

34 H.W. McGill to W.C. Cain, 1 September 1933, LAC, RG 10, vol. 7757, file 27043-9; H.W. McGill to W.C. Cain, 23 May 1938, LAC, RG 10, vol. 7757, file 27043-9.

35 W.C. Cain to A.F. MacKenzie, 23 July 1934, LAC, RG 10, vol. 7757, file 27043-9; W.C. Cain to H.W. McGill, 29 June 1938, LAC, RG 10, vol. 7757, file 27043-9.

36 J.P. Marchildon to J.A. Marleau, 5 September 1939, LAC, RG 10, vol. 7757, file 27043-9.

37 Ibid.

38 R.H. Bliss to J.P. Marchildon, 15 September 1939, Ontario Ministry of Aboriginal Affairs Archives (ONAS), Toronto, file 7970 (vol. 1).

39 R.S. Hyslop to Department of Lands and Forests, 15 September 1939, ONAS, file 7970 (vol. 1). The clearings referred to in this report were made by the Teme-Augama Anishnabai beginning in the late nineteenth century. See T. Walton to L. Vankoughnet, 10 February 1890, LAC, RG 10, vol. 7757, file 27043-9.

40 W.C. Cain to D.J. Allan, 20 October 1939, LAC, RG 10, vol. 7757, file 27043-9.

41 J.A. Marleau to DIA, c. 31 October 1939, LAC, RG 10, vol. 7757, file 27043-9.

42 D.J. Allan to H.W. McGill, 23 October 1939, LAC, RG 10, vol. 7757, file 27043-9; H.W. McGill to W.C. Cain, 25 October 1939, LAC, RG 10, vol. 7757, file 27043-9.

43 J.A. Marleau to J.P. Marchildon, 28 September 1939, LAC, RG 10, vol. 10708, file 30-6.

44 Chief John Twain to W. Little, 8 July 1940, LAC, RG 10, vol. 7757, file 27043-9. See also J.A. Marleau to DIA, c. 31 October 1939, LAC, RG 10, vol. 7757, file 27043-9; Chief John Twain to W. Little, 28 May 1941, LAC, RG 10, vol. 7757, file 27043-9; Chief John Twain to H.W. McGill, 16 June 1941, LAC, RG 10, vol. 7757, file 27043-9; Chief John Twain to W. Little, 8 March 1943, LAC, RG 10, vol. 7757, file 27043-9; Chief John Twain to W. Little, 26 June 1943, LAC, RG 10, vol. 7757, file 27043-9.

45 Minister, Department of Mines and Resources, to F.A. MacDougall, 15 April 1943, LAC, RG 10, vol. 7757, file 27043-9; Department of Lands and Forests to Department of Mines and Resources, receipt, 26 April 1943, LAC, RG 10, vol. 7757, file 27043-9; H.C. Nixon and C.F. Bulmer, order-in-council, 15 June 1943, LAC, RG 10, vol. 7757, file 27043-9.

46 Minister, Department of Lands and Forests, to Lieutenant-Governor in Council, draft recommendation, 18 May 1943, RG 10, vol. 7757, file 27043-9.

47 Ibid.

48 Ibid.

49 Quoted in H.W. McGill to Deputy Minister, Department of Mines and Resources, 25 May 1943, LAC, RG 10, vol. 7757, file 27043-9.

50 C.N. Jackson to F.A. MacDougall, 20 February 1943, LAC, RG 10, vol. 7757, file 27043-9.

51 H.W. Crosbie to C.N. Jackson, 3 March 1943, LAC, RG 10, vol. 7757, file 27043-9.

52 Ibid. No-cut areas along shorelines were established elsewhere in Ontario during this time, as, for example, in Algonquin Park. See Warecki, Protecting Ontario's Wilderness, 28.

53 Director, Indian Affairs Branch, to W. Little, 10 July 1943, LAC, RG 10, vol. 7757, file 27043-9.

54 H.W. McGill to Deputy Minister, Department of Mines and Resources, 25 May 1943, LAC, RG 10, vol. 7757, file 27043-9.

55 T. McGookin to H.W. McGill, 13 September 1938, LAC, RG 10, vol. 7757, file 27043-9.

56 J.A. Marleau to Grade 3 class, 28 March 1939, LAC, RG 10, vol. 7757, file 27043-9.

57 John Turner to J.P. Marchildon, 5 July 1943, LAC, RG 10, vol. 7757, file 27043-9; J.P. Lanoie to undisclosed recipient (J.P. Marchildon), 6 July 1943, LAC, RG 10, vol. 7757, file 27043-9.

58 H.S. Shannon to H.W. McGill, 17 December 1943, LAC, RG 10, vol. 7757, file 27043-9.

59 Claire Campbell observes that similar dynamics were at work on Georgian Bay, where cottagers appreciated Natives' historic association with the bay but were displeased when they made claims in and to the present by camping or picking blueberries close to cottages. See Campbell, *Shaped by the West Wind*, 102-3.

60 D.J. Allan to H.W. Crosbie, 21 July 1943, LAC, RG 10, vol. 7757, file 27043-9.

61 For a discussion of the legal construction of Aboriginal spaces and bodies as degenerate, see Sherene Razack, "Gendered Racial Violence and Spatialized Justice: The Murder of Pamela George," *Canadian Journal of Law and Society* 15,2 (2000): 91-130.

62 Joe Friday to Department of Lands, c. August 1942, ONAS, file 7970 (vol. 1).

63 Ontario to DIA, 18 August 1942, ONAS, file 7970 (vol. 1).

64 Chief John Twain to W. Little, 26 June 1943, LAC, RG 10, vol. 7757, file 27043-9; R.D. Cumming to DIA, 1 July 1943, LAC, RG 10, vol. 7757, file 27043-9; E.J. Young to Department of Mines and Resources, 16 October 1945, Indian and Northern Affairs Canada (INAC), Ottawa, file 411/30-6-0 (vol. 1); A. Paull to R.A. Hoey, 4 September 1946, INAC, file 411/30-6-0; Temagami Band Council, resolution, 22 January 1947, INAC, file 411/30-6-0 (vol. 1).

65 W.C. Bethune to F. Matters, 26 May 1960, INAC, file 411/30-6-0 (vol. 1); W.C. Bethune to Regional Supervisor, 26 May 1960, LAC, RG 10, vol. 10708, file 30-6; Chief John Twain to Nipissing Indian Agency, 2 June 1960, LAC, RG 10, vol. 10708, file 30-6; F. Matters to W.C. Bethune, 7 June 1960, INAC, file 411/30-6-0 (vol. 1); F. Matters to W.C. Bethune, 27 June 1960, INAC, file 411/30-6-0 (vol. 1).

66 Temagami Band Council, resolution, 10 January 1961, INAC, file 411/30-6-0 (vol. 1); Temagami Band Council Resolution, 3 February 1964, INAC, file 411/30-6-0 (vol. 1).

67 Amended Reply to Statement of Defence to Counterclaim and Joinder of Issue, 29 January 1979, para. 7.

68 Ontario, order-in-council, 17 November 1970, ONAS, file 7970 (vol. 2); Canada, order-in-council, 8 June 1971, ONAS, file 7970 (vol. 2).

69 Director of Legal Services, Ministry of Natural Resources (MNR), to Minister, MNR, 11 September 1973, INAC, file 411/30-1 (vol. 2); *Attorney-General for Ontario v. Bear Island Foundation et al., Potts et al. v. Attorney-General for Ontario*, [1984] O.J. No. 3432, para. 5.

CHAPTER 5: LEGAL LANDSCAPES

1 Gary Potts, "Last-Ditch Defence of a Priceless Homeland," in *Drumbeat: Anger and Renewal in Indian Country*, ed. Boyce Richardson (Toronto: Summerhill Press, 1989), 206.

2 Teme-Augama Anishnabai, "Teme-Augama Anishnabai, Deep Water People," 1980-1995 Land Claim Negotiations Box (Temagami First Nation Band Office, 1989).

3 For analyses of the Supreme Court of Ontario decision, see Bruce Clark, *Indian Title in Canada* (Toronto: Carswell, 1987); Bruce Clark, *Justice in Paradise* (Montreal/Kingston:

McGill-Queen's University Press, 1999); Dara Culhane, *The Pleasure of the Crown: Anthropology, Law and First Nations* (Vancouver: Talon Books, 1998), 97-100; Tony Hall, "Where Justice Lies: Aboriginal Rights and Wrongs in Temagami," in *Temagami: A Debate on Wilderness,* ed. Matt Bray and Ashley Thomson (Toronto: Dundurn Press, 1990), 223-53; David T. McNab, *No Place for Fairness: Indigenous Land Rights and Policy in the Bear Island Case and Beyond* (Montreal/Kingston: McGill-Queen's University Press, 2009), 75-83; and Potts, "Last-Ditch Defence." For the Ontario Court of Appeal decision, see Kent McNeil, "The Temagami Indian Land Claim: Loosening the Judicial Strait-Jacket," in Bray and Thomson, *Temagami,* 185-221. For the Supreme Court of Canada decision, see Kent McNeil, "The High Cost of Accepting Benefits from the Crown: A Comment on the Temagami Indian Land Case," *Canadian Native Law Reporter* 1 (1992): 40-69.

4 Freda Hawkins, *Critical Years in Immigration: Canada and Australia Compared* (Montreal/Kingston: McGill-Queen's University Press, 1989); Lisa Marie Jakubowski, *Immigration and the Legalization of Racism* (Halifax: Fernwood, 1997).

5 Sunera Thobani, *Exalted Subjects: Studies of the Making of Race and Nation in Canada* (Toronto: University of Toronto Press, 2007), 146.

6 Ibid., 150-52.

7 Ibid., 95-96.

8 Ibid., 150.

9 See Himani Bannerji, *The Dark Side of the Nation: Essays on Multiculturalism, Nationalism and Gender* (Toronto: Canadian Scholar's Press, 2000); Eva Mackey, *The House of Difference: Cultural Politics and National Identity in Canada* (London: Routledge, 1999); and Thobani, *Exalted Subjects,* 143-75. For similar arguments about Australian multiculturalism, see Sara Ahmed, *Strange Encounters: Embodied Others in Post-Coloniality* (London: Routledge, 2000); and Ghassan Hage, *White Nation: Fantasies of White Supremacy in a Multicultural Society* (Annandale, Australia: Pluto Press, 1998).

10 In *The Dark Side of the Nation,* Himani Bannerji notes that political alliances between racialized groups are made difficult by multiculturalism because it divides these groups along cultural lines rather than highlighting their shared experiences of discrimination within the nation. Wendy Brown moves beyond the Canadian context to explore the complex ways in which the tolerance discourse works to construct powerful groups as normal and to present marginalized groups, both within and outside of the United States, as deviant or barbaric. See Wendy Brown, *Regulating Aversion: Tolerance in the Age of Identity and Empire* (Princeton: Princeton University Press, 2006).

11 Thobani, *Exalted Subjects,* 217-47. Of course, this treatment was not limited to Canada. In the US context, Wendy Brown points out that, following the events of 11 September, the state-driven violence both at home and abroad seemingly opposed but in fact depended upon government calls for "Americans" to treat "Arab Americans" with respect and tolerance. See Brown, *Regulating Aversion,* 99-101.

12 *Calder v. Attorney-General of British Columbia,* [1973] S.C.R. 313.

13 On the Nisga'a case and subsequent treaty, see Culhane, *The Pleasure of the Crown,* 79-83; and Indian and Northern Affairs Canada, "Fact Sheet: The Nisga'a Treaty," http://www.ainc-inac.gc.ca. On the white paper, see Culhane, *The Pleasure of the Crown,* 83-84; and Olive Patricia Dickason, *Canada's First Nations: A History of Founding Peoples from Earliest Times* (New York: Oxford University Press, 2002), 377-81.

14 Culhane, *The Pleasure of the Crown,* 91. For a discussion of Aboriginal rights and the Constitution Act, 1982, see Michael Asch, *Home and Native Land: Aboriginal Rights and*

the *Canadian Constitution* (Scarborough: Nelson Canada, 1988); Patrick Macklem, *Indigenous Difference and the Constitution of Canada* (Toronto: University of Toronto Press, 2001); and James Youngblood Henderson, *Treaty Rights in the Constitution of Canada* (Toronto: Thomson/Carswell, 2007). For commentary on cases related to Aboriginal rights, see Catherine Bell, "New Directions in the Law of Aboriginal Rights," *Canadian Bar Review* 77,1 and 2 (1998): 36-72. The legal literature on this topic is vast. Commentators tend to agree that though the courts may be useful for furthering Aboriginal rights up to a point, the work of negotiating co-existence between First Nations and newcomers must take place in the political rather than the legal arena. See also Cole Harris, *Making Native Space: Colonialism, Resistance, and Reserves in British Columbia* (Vancouver: UBC Press, 2002), 296-97.

15 Susan S. Siley, "Making a Place for Cultural Analyses of Law," *Law and Social Inquiry* 17,1 (1992): 41. See also Judith Butler, "Sexual Inversions," in *Feminist Interpretations of Michel Foucault*, ed. Susan J. Hekman (University Park: Pennsylvania State University Press, 1996), 59-75; David Delaney, "Making Nature/Marking Humans: Law as a Site of (Cultural) Production," *Annals of the Association of American Geographers* 91,3 (2001): 487-503; Alan Hunt, "Foucault's Expulsion of Law: Toward a Retrieval," *Law and Social Inquiry* 17,1 (1992): 1-38; Nicos Poulantzas, *State, Power, Socialism* (London: New Left Books, 1978); and Alan Hunt and Gary Wickham, *Foucault and Law: Toward a New Sociology of Law as Governance* (Boulder: Westview Press, 1996).

16 Delaney, "Making Nature/Marking Humans," 489.

17 Ibid. (emphasis in original).

18 The literature on this topic is quite large. See Constance Backhouse, *Petticoats and Prejudice: Women and the Law in 19th Century Canada* (Toronto: Women's Press, 1991); Rosemary J. Coombe, "Room for Manoeuver: Toward a Theory of Practice in Critical Legal Studies," *Law and Social Inquiry* 14,1 (1989): 69-121; Culhane, *The Pleasure of the Crown;* Jonathan Hart and Richard W. Bauman, eds., *Explorations in Difference: Law, Culture and Politics* (Toronto: University of Toronto Press, 1996); James Youngblood Henderson, *First Nations Jurisprudence and Aboriginal Rights* (Saskatoon: University of Saskatchewan, Native Law Centre, 2006); Peter Just, "History, Power, Ideology and Culture: Current Directions in the Anthropology of Law," *Law and Society Review* 26,2 (1992): 373-412; Peter Kulchyski, ed., *Unjust Relations: Aboriginal Rights in Canadian Courts* (Toronto: Oxford University Press, 1994); Mindy Lazarus-Black and Susan F. Hirsch, eds., *Contested States: Law, Hegemony and Resistance* (New York: Routledge, 1994); Tina Loo and Lorna R. McLean, eds., *Historical Perspectives on Law and Society in Canada* (Toronto: Copp Clark Longman, 1994); Gerald Rosenberg, *The Hollow Hope: Can Courts Bring about Social Change?* (Chicago: University of Chicago Press, 1991); and Carol Smart, *Feminism and the Power of Law* (London: Routledge, 1994).

19 For an example of the former, see Patricia Monture-Angus, *Journeying Forward: Dreaming First Nations' Independence* (Halifax: Fernwood, 1999). For the latter, see Menno Boldt and J. Anthony Long, eds., *The Quest for Justice: Aboriginal Peoples and Aboriginal Rights* (Toronto: University of Toronto Press, 1985).

20 Delaney, "Making Nature/Marking Humans," 491.

21 Adriel Weaver, "Salmon for Sale, Moose for Meat: Legal Constructions of Nature and Aboriginal Subjectivities" (master's major paper, York University, 2006), 2.

22 Delaney, "Making Nature/Marking Humans," 491, 489.

23 Amended Reply to the Statement of Defence of Gary Potts et al. and Joinder of Issue, 12 January 1979, paras. 2, 4, 5, 9, 10.

24 Statement of Defence of Gary Potts et al., paras. 4, 6, 10; Amended Reply to Statement of Defence to Counterclaim and Joinder of Issue, 29 January 1979, paras. 3, 5, 6.

25 For a discussion of some of the precedents that have shaped contemporary Canadian rulings on Aboriginal rights and title cases, see Dara Culhane, "The Great Chain of Precedent," in Culhane, *The Pleasure of the Crown*, 61-71.

26 For a discussion of the tensions in the common law between maintaining tradition and allowing for change, see Allan C. Hutchinson, *Evolution and the Common Law* (Cambridge: Cambridge University Press, 2005).

27 John A. Yogis, *Canadian Law Dictionary* (1983; repr., New York: Barron's Educational Series, 2003).

28 For a longer discussion of the Baker Lake case, see Culhane, *The Pleasure of the Crown*, 92-97.

29 *Hamlet of Baker Lake et al. v. Minister of Indian Affairs and Northern Development et al.*, [1979] 107 D.L.R. (3d) 513 at para. 542. Kent McNeil discusses what he calls the "serious difficulties" in Mahoney's test. For instance, if the claimants did prove that their Aboriginal system of property ownership existed, what if it did not require that they occupy the lands to the exclusion of other societies? See McNeil, "The Temagami Indian Land Claim," 187.

30 Culhane, *The Pleasure of the Crown*, 72-97.

31 Delaney, "Making Nature/Marking Humans," 491; Trial Transcript for *Attorney-General for Ontario v. Bear Island Foundation et al., Potts et al. v. Attorney-General for Ontario*, cross-examination of Chief Gary Potts, vol. 40, 7032 (BITT).

32 Statement of Defence of Gary Potts et al., para. 4.

33 BITT, examination of Chief Gary Potts, vol. 39, 6737-62.

34 Ibid., 6733.

35 BITT, examinations of Alex Missabi, vol. 35, 6202-4; Michael James Paul Sr., vol. 35, 6211; William Twain, vol. 35, 6231-36; and Chief Gary Potts, vol. 39, 6782-84. Potts offered extensive testimony about the band's oral history, stating that part of his responsibility as chief was to gain knowledge about the oral tradition through listening to the stories of the elders. He explained that he collected many stories over time from a number of elders, many of whom died before the commencement of the trial. BITT, examination of Chief Gary Potts, vol. 38, 6704.

36 BITT, Teme-Augama Anishnabai oral argument, vol. E, 724, 771.

37 This map is a living document. Craig Macdonald continues to speak publicly about both it and the process of its creation. At a gathering of Teme-Augama Anishnabai members that I attended on Bear Island in 2007, he spoke about the map and the experience of interviewing elders as part of his research.

38 Factum Summary, Bear Island Foundation, 1-2; BITT, Teme-Augama Anishnabai oral argument, vol. E, 726.

39 BITT, Teme-Augama Anishnabai oral argument, vol. E, 769, 724; Factum and Written Argument, Bear Island Foundation, part 4, Band Issue, vol. 5, 79-82; BITT, Teme-Augama Anishnabai oral argument, vol. D, 662.

40 Factum Summary, Bear Island Foundation, 1; Factum and Written Argument, Bear Island Foundation, part 4, Band Issue, vol. 5, 51; BITT, Teme-Augama Anishnabai oral argument, vol. E, 725; BITT, examination of Edward Rogers, vol. 16, 2869.

41 Factum and Written Argument, Bear Island Foundation, part 4, Band Issue, vol. 5, 24-25.

42 Ibid., 25-93.

43 Factum and Written Argument, Bear Island Foundation, part 4, Band Issue, vol. 5, 49.

44 BITT, examination of Chief Gary Potts, vol. 37, 6495-96.

45 Ibid., 6520, 6579; ibid., vol. 38, 6657.

46 Ibid., vol. 38, 6650, 6660-61.

47 Ibid., vol. 37, 6611.

48 Ibid., 6931.

49 Statement of Claim of the Attorney General for the Province of Ontario, 8 May 1978, paras. 5, 6; Outline of Plaintiff's Argument, 746.

50 Amended Reply to the Statement of Defence of Gary Potts et al. and Joinder of Issue, 12 January 1979, para. 2; Statement of Claim of the Attorney General for the Province of Ontario, 8 May 1978, para. 6.

51 Amended Reply to the Statement of Defence of Gary Potts et al. and Joinder of Issue, 12 January 1979, para. 3; BITT, Ontario oral argument, vol. C, 414.

52 Factum and Written Argument, Attorney-General, vol. 3, para. 544.

53 Ibid., para. 545.

54 BITT, Ontario oral argument, vol. A, 123.

55 Ibid., 124-25.

56 Ibid., 160.

57 Ibid., 27.

58 Ibid., 17.

59 Ibid., 38.

60 Ibid., 40.

61 Ibid., 15-16.

62 Ibid., 11.

63 Ibid., vol. B, 273.

64 Ibid., 274.

65 Ibid., 274-75.

66 BITT, cross-examination of Chief Gary Potts, vol. 40, 6918-19; BITT, Ontario oral argument, vol. B, 275.

67 BITT, Ontario oral argument, vol. B, 276.

68 Ibid.

69 Ibid., vol. F, 1061.

70 See Bonita Lawrence, *"Real" Indians and Others: Mixed-Blood Urban Native Peoples and Indigenous Nationhood* (Vancouver: UBC Press, 2004), 31; Thobani, *Exalted Subjects,* 277n85.

71 BITT, Ontario oral argument, vol. B, 276.

72 Statement of Defence of Gary Potts et al., paras. 3, 6.

73 "Royal Proclamation of 7 October 1763," in *British Royal Proclamations Relating to America,* ed. Clarence S. Brigham (Worcester, MA: American Antiquarian Society, 1911), 212. For a detailed discussion of the proclamation and its effects, see Brian Slattery, *The Land Rights of Indigenous Canadian Peoples, as Affected by the Crown's Acquisition of Their Territories* (Saskatoon: University of Saskatchewan Native Law Centre, 1979), 191-349.

74 BITT, examination of Chief Gary Potts, vol. 37, 6599.

75 Report to Commissioner for Presentation to Indian and Northern Affairs Canada (INAC) Minister, 28 August 1974, Indian and Northern Affairs Canada, Ottawa, file B-8260-126-5;

Gary Potts, "Report to Band Members on the Land Claim," 1970s Land Claim Box (Temagami First Nation Band Office, c. February 1975).

76 BITT, Teme-Augama Anishnabai oral argument, vol. F, 898, 903.

77 Ibid., 903.

78 Ibid., 897, 899.

79 To complicate matters, however, Chief Potts later indicated that the band considered non-human animals as also having rights. During a CBC Radio interview in 1990, he said that the band wanted to ensure that people respected the fact that "the land itself is a living thing and everything that depends on the land has a place as well. Just because they can't speak English, the moose or the ducks or the fish, that doesn't mean that they don't have rights." See Gary Potts, "The Battle over Temagami," radio interview by Dale Goldhawk, *As It Happens,* Canadian Broadcasting Corporation, 23 April 1990, http://archives.cbc.ca.

80 Index of Plaintiff's Argument, 725-26.

81 BITT, Ontario oral argument, vol. B, 351.

82 Quoted in ibid., 352.

83 BITT, Teme-Augama Anishnabai oral argument, vol. D, 600.

84 BITT, Ontario oral argument, vol. B, 344.

85 Ibid., 397.

86 For legal commentary on the "frozen title" theory of Aboriginal rights, see Bell, "New Directions"; Brian Slattery, "Understanding Aboriginal Rights," *Canadian Bar Review* 66,4 (1987): 727-83; and Brian Slattery, "Making Sense of Aboriginal and Treaty Rights," *Canadian Bar Review* 79,2 (2000): 196-224.

87 BITT, Ontario oral argument, vol. F, 1028.

88 Factum and Written Argument, Attorney-General, vol. 6, paras. 909-14, quotation from 910.

89 Amended Reply to Statement of Defence to Counterclaim and Joinder of Issue, 29 January 1979, para. 6.

90 Amended Reply to the Statement of Defence of Gary Potts et al. and Joinder of Issue, 12 January 1979, para. 9.

91 Joel R. Fortune, "Constructing *Delgamuukw:* Legal Arguments, Historical Argumentation, and the Philosophy of History," *University of Toronto Faculty of Law Review* 51,1 (1993): 83, 86.

92 Ibid., 84.

93 Edward Hallett Carr, *What Is History?* (Harmondsworth, UK: Pelican Books, 1964), 10, 11; Fortune, "Constructing *Delgamuukw,*" 99. For similar discussions about the complexities of telling stories about the past, see William Cronon, "A Place for Stories: Nature, History, and Narrative," *Journal of American History* 78,4 (March 1992): 1347-76. In this article, Cronon also suggests that there are limits to the flexibility of such stories. For example, they cannot contradict known facts about the past, must make ecological sense, and are subjected to processes such as peer review that evaluate their truth claims.

94 Fortune, "Constructing *Delgamuukw,*" 88.

95 BITT, Teme-Augama Anishnabai oral argument, vol. E, 854; Factum of the Appellants, paras. 16, 78.

96 Factum of the Appellants, paras. 17, 18, 86.

97 Factum of the Attorney-General for Ontario, para. 9.

98 BITT, Ontario oral argument, vol. B, 204.

99 Factum of the Attorney-General for Ontario, para. 11.

100 Ibid., para. 55.
101 Sally Weaver, quoted in Hall, "Where Justice Lies," 232; Culhane, *The Pleasure of the Crown*, 98.
102 *Attorney-General for Ontario v. Bear Island Foundation et al., Potts et al. v. Attorney-General for Ontario*, [1984] O.J. No. 3432, para. 3 (emphasis added) *(A-G v. Bear Island)*.
103 Ibid., paras. 20, 64.
104 Ibid., para. 79; *St. Catherine's Milling and Lumber Co. v. The Queen* (1888), 14 A.C. 46 (P.C.).
105 *A-G v. Bear Island*, para. 95.
106 Ibid., paras. 91, 95 (emphasis added).
107 See Culhane, *The Pleasure of the Crown*, 98; Hall, "Where Justice Lies," 237-38. Culhane discusses how, in the 1970s and 1980s, Canadian courts struggled over the interpretation of history in the context of Aboriginal rights cases. The results, she says, were varied and often contradictory. Some judges, such as Justice Hall in the Calder case (*Calder v. Attorney-General of British Columbia*, [1973] S.C.R. 313), spoke about the importance of interpreting historical documents in light of contemporary awareness that Aboriginal peoples were not a "subhuman species," as was held in previous (European) thought. Other judges, such as Justice Steele, reached just the opposite conclusion. In his discussion of Steele's decision, Tony Hall comments that though notions of racial inequality were certainly "ubiquitous and deep-rooted" among colonial officials who dealt with Aboriginal peoples in past centuries, contemporary jurisprudence has no need to legitimize their racist principles.
108 That judges "find" things to be the case based on the evidence presented to them is interesting in light of Fortune's discussion of how legal decisions can come down to a matter of historical interpretation. In such cases, it is particularly clear that judges do not "find" self-evident facts but rather produce truths by deciding what to find as fact. Yet the idea of judicial objectivity is inscribed in the very term "to find" (it was there all along!). It seems, then, that this term constitutes one subtle way in which the objectivity, and thus power-neutrality, of the courts is reinforced.
109 Culhane, *The Pleasure of the Crown*, 99.
110 *A-G v. Bear Island*, para. 35.
111 Ibid., para. 159.
112 Ibid., para. 158.
113 Ibid., para. 126.
114 Ibid., paras. 151, 171. That the fur trade was well established in the area was significant for Steele because it revealed the presence of Indians. No substantial drop had occurred in the region's fur trade prior to or around 1763, so Steele concluded that no mass movement out of the region, as hypothesized by Bishop, had taken place. Also, throughout his reasons, he called the lands in question the "Land Claim Area." Like Ontario, he did not use the name "n'Daki Menan," as he made clear in his statement that "The defendants referred to the land claim area as 'n'Daki Menan.' I refer to it as the 'Land Claim Area.'" Ibid., para. 4.
115 In what was perhaps his most bizarre finding, Steele determined that the "historical facts in this area indicate much stronger individual family control over the hunting territory than band control." He explained that "aboriginal rights in land must be held by a band" and added that "a present-day band whose member families had their ancestral family hunting territories on the same lands as the band holds today can only claim those lands to the extent that their ancestors held the lands in 1763 as a band, not as individual families." See ibid., paras. 159, 22. Steele offered no explanation as to why Aboriginal rights must be

held by a band but suggested that this requirement was related to the fact that the Crown obtained cessions of territories from bands rather than from individual families. According to Steele, then, Teme-Augama Anishnabai ancestors occupied the lands in question in 1763 *as an organized society.* But, as he saw it, Aboriginal rights could be created by the Crown only if the organized society were organized in a way authorized by the Crown.

116 Ibid., para. 166.

117 Ibid., paras. 128, 129.

118 Ibid., para. 167.

119 Ibid., para. 242.

120 See Mary Louise Pratt, *Imperial Eyes: Travel Writing and Transculturation* (London: Routledge, 1992), 31.

121 *A-G v. Bear Island,* para. 115.

122 Hall, "Where Justice Lies," 235.

123 *A-G v. Bear Island,* para. 99. The trial evidence delineating Aboriginal rights in 1763 is at paras. 103-15.

124 Ibid., para. 116. Unlike Steele, Ontario did not give such a detailed description of what constituted Aboriginal rights.

125 Ibid., para. 109.

126 Ibid., paras. 218, 163, 112.

127 Hall, "Where Justice Lies," 233.

128 The Teme-Augama Anishnabai called no woman witnesses, and so it is impossible to comment with certainty on how Justice Steele might have addressed the question of objectivity had women testified. It seems fair to speculate, however, that since objectivity has historically been attributed to white men, he might have found it to exist in white *men* who had not lived among Indians.

129 *A-G v. Bear Island,* para. 51.

130 Ibid., paras. 41, 42.

131 Ibid., para. 287.

132 Ibid., para. 44.

133 Ibid., para. 45.

134 *Ontario (Attorney-General) v. Bear Island Foundation,* [1989] O.J. No. 267, para. 7.

135 Ibid., para. 8.

136 *Ontario (Attorney-General) v. Bear Island Foundation,* [1991] S.C.J. No. 61, para. 7.

137 Ibid., para. 6.

138 Ibid., para. 7.

139 *Ontario (Attorney-General) v. Bear Island Foundation,* [1989] 63 D.L.R. (4th) 756.

140 *Bear Island Foundation v. Ontario,* [1995] O.J. No. 3431.

141 At a 2006 meeting I attended on Bear Island between the Teme-Augama Anishnabai and Ontario Ministry of Natural Resources representatives, a band member stated, "The question is, who owns the bottom of the lake? – and I say the Indians do."

Conclusion: A Return to n'Daki Menan

1 M. Nourbese Philip et al., "Fortress in the Wilderness: A Conversation about Land," *Borderlines* 45 (1997): 20-25.

2 TemagamiVacation.com, "Experience Temagami: Provincial Parks in the Temagami Area," http://www.temagamivacation.com/parks.asp. As an example of the different story told, in June 2007, as part of the National Aboriginal Day of Action, the Teme-Augama

Anishnabai set up stations in the town of Temagami and at an access road popular with cottagers in order to inform passersby about the history and present-day situation of their claim to n'Daki Menan.

3 Ontario, *Temagami Integrated Planning: Background Information* (N.p.: Queen's Printer, 2005); Ontario, *Temagami Integrated Planning: Management Options Workbook* (N.p.: Queen's Printer, 2006).

4 Ontario, *Summary of the Long Term Management Direction, Temagami Crown Management Unit (898), 2009-2019 Forest Management Plan*, 19, http://www.earthroots.org (webpage now discontinued).

5 Ibid., 7.

Bibliography

PRIMARY SOURCES

Court Documents

Bear Island Trial Documents

Amended Reply to Statement of Defence to Counterclaim and Joinder of Issue, 29 January 1979. Copy available at the Court of Appeal for Ontario, court file nos. C22677, C22678, C22682, Joint Appeal Book, vol. 1, 178-86.

Amended Reply to the Statement of Defence of Gary Potts et al. and Joinder of Issue, 12 January 1979. Copy available at the Court of Appeal for Ontario, court file nos. C22677, C22678, C22682, Joint Appeal Book, vol. 1, 169-75.

Factum and Written Argument, Attorney-General, 6 vols. Copy available at the Court of Appeal for Ontario, court file nos. 25196/78, 45/85.

Factum and Written Argument, Bear Island Foundation, 7 vols. Copy available at the Court of Appeal for Ontario, court file nos. 25196/78, 45/85.

Factum of the Appellants. Copy available at the Supreme Court of Canada, file no. 21435.

Factum of the Attorney-General for Ontario, Respondent. Copy available at the Supreme Court of Canada, file no. 21435.

Factum Summary, Bear Island Foundation. Copy available at the Court of Appeal for Ontario, court file nos. 25196/78, 45/85.

Index of Plaintiff's Argument. Copy available at the Court of Appeal for Ontario, court file nos. C22677, C22678, C22682, Joint Appeal Book, vol. 3, 725-26.

Outline of Plaintiff's Argument. Copy available at the Court of Appeal for Ontario, court file nos. C22677, C22678, C22682, Joint Appeal Book, vol. 3, 727-64.

Statement of Claim of the Attorney General for the Province of Ontario, 8 May 1978. Copy available at the Court of Appeal for Ontario, court file nos. C22677, C22678, C22682, Joint Appeal Book, vol. 1, 158-61.

Statement of Defence of Gary Potts et al. Copy available at the Court of Appeal for Ontario, court file nos. C22677, C22678, C22682, Joint Appeal Book, vol. 1, 162-66.
Trial Transcript for *Attorney-General for Ontario v. Bear Island Foundation et al., Potts et al. v. Attorney-General for Ontario*, [1984] O.J. No. 3432. Vols. 1-68 (trial proceedings), A-F (oral arguments). Copy at Temagami First Nation Band Office.

Cases

Attorney-General for Ontario v. Bear Island Foundation et al., Potts et al. v. Attorney-General for Ontario, [1984] O.J. No. 3432.
Bear Island Foundation v. Ontario, [1995] O.J. No. 3431.
Calder v. Attorney-General of British Columbia, [1973] S.C.R. 313.
Hamlet of Baker Lake et al. v. Minister of Indian Affairs and Northern Development et al., [1979] 107 D.L.R. (3d) 513.
Ontario (Attorney-General) v. Bear Island Foundation, [1989] 63 D.L.R. (4th) 756.
Ontario (Attorney-General) v. Bear Island Foundation, [1989] O.J. No. 267.
Ontario (Attorney-General) v. Bear Island Foundation, [1991] S.C.J. No. 61.
St. Catherine's Milling and Lumber Co. v. The Queen (1888), 14 A.C. 46 (P.C.).

Published and Unpublished Sources

A. W. C. "A Cruise in the Ojibway Paradise." Part 2. *Forest and Stream*, 2 May 1903, 343-44.
Adams, Mrs. A.G. "A Lady's Hunting Trip." *Rod and Gun* 11,5 (October 1909): 400-3.
Angus, Edward. "Temagami." *Rod and Gun* 9,9 (February 1908): 864-69.
Another Wet Bob. "Temagaming." *Rod and Gun* 1,3 (August 1899): 53.
"Appellants' Factum, vol. 3, History of the Teme-Agama Anishnabay and Land Use" (draft). Dernoi Research Box 3. Temagami First Nation Band Office, undated.
Armstrong, Louis Oliver. *A Canoe Trip through Temagaming the Peerless in the Land of Hiawatha*. N.p.: Canadian Pacific Railway, 1900.
–. "Down the Mississaga." *Rod and Gun* 6,2 (July 1904): 55-61.
–. "Out of Doors." *Rod and Gun* 6,1 (June 1904): 15-18.
Barry, Jas. W. "Timagami, a Region Organized by Nature for Real Sport." *Rod and Gun* 7,2 (July 1905): 165-68.
Beswick, George P. "After Fish in Temagami." *Rod and Gun* 7,3 (August 1905): 316-19.
"The 'Bobs' on Temagami." *Rod and Gun* 7,4 (September 1905): 424-25.
Caldwell, W.C. Diaries. Archives of Ontario, Toronto, MU 839.
Cameron, Myrle. "A Day's Journey in the Wilds." *Rod and Gun* 12,8 (January 1911): 1018-22.
Camp Temagami. *Camp Temagami: A Summer Camp for Men and Boys, Established 1900, Conducted by Arthur L. Cochrane*. Camp brochure. 1915.
Canada. "Copy of the Robinson Treaty Made in the Year 1850 with the Ojibewa Indians of Lake Huron Conveying Certain Lands to the Crown." http://www.ainc-inac.gc.ca.
–. Department of Indian Affairs. *Annual Reports of the Department of Indian Affairs*. Ottawa, 1880-1936. Victoria University, E.J. Pratt Library, Microfilm .C1595a.
–. Department of Indian Affairs. Library and Archives Canada, Ottawa, RG 10, vols. 266, 1998, 7757, 8007, 10267, 10708.

"Canada and the Tourist." *Canadian Magazine* 15,1 (May 1900): 3-4.

"The Canadian Forestry Association." *Canadian Forestry Journal* 1,1 (January 1905): 1-9.

Canadian Forestry Association. "Ontario's Forest Policy." *Rod and Gun* 5,6 (November 1903): 253-54.

–. *Report of the First Annual Meeting of the Canadian Forestry Association.* Ottawa: Government Printing Bureau, 1900.

Carrell, Frank. "Our Fishing and Hunting Trip in Northern Ontario." Part 1. *Rod and Gun* 8,11 (April 1907): 931-43.

–. "Our Fishing and Hunting Trip in Northern Ontario." Part 3. *Rod and Gun* 9,1 (June 1907): 39-52.

–. "Our Fishing and Hunting Trip in Northern Ontario." Part 4. *Rod and Gun* 9,2 (July 1907): 137-50.

The Chief. "Away 'Up North.'" Part 3. *Forest and Stream,* 12 May 1894, 412.

Clowes, Frank J. "August Days in Temagami." *Rod and Gun* 8,10 (March 1907): 827-38.

Dickson, J.R. "Our Forest Reserve Problem." *Canadian Forestry Journal* 8,3 (May-June 1912): 66-71.

Dixmont. "Moose Hunting in Temagami." *Forest and Stream,* 9 December 1911, 835-37.

Dorchester, Frank E. "Physical Culture: A Nation's Need." Part 10. *Rod and Gun* 11,4 (September 1909): 347-49.

E. and S. W. "John Green, Guide." *Rod and Gun* 10,1 (June 1908): 10-14.

Engineer. "South of Abitibi." *Rod and Gun* 4,8 (January 1903): 273-74.

An Eye Witness. "In Temagami's Tangled Wild." *Rod and Gun* 8,1 (June 1906): 36-42.

Farr, C.C. *The Dominion of Canada as a Field for Emigration: Its Advantages and Disadvantages: The Temiscamingue District in Particular.* Ipswich, UK: East Anglia Printing Works, 1896.

–. "In the Woods with Indian Guides." *Rod and Gun* 8,5 (October 1906): 327-34.

–. "A Trip to Matachuan." Part 2. *Rod and Gun* 3,8 (January 1902): 1-5.

"Fields and Pastures New." *Forest and Stream,* 2 April 1904, 266.

Fischer, O.E. "Canoe Cruises in Canadian Reserves." Part 2. *Forest and Stream,* 24 September 1910, 505-6.

"Forestry." *Rod and Gun* 2,3 (August 1900): 300-4.

"Forestry." *Rod and Gun* 2,9 (February 1901): 454-58.

"Forestry." *Rod and Gun* 2,11 (April 1901): 503-7.

Grand Trunk Railway. *The Eldorado of New Ontario: Cobalt, the Rich New Silver District.* Toronto: Mail Job Print, 1907.

–. *Temagami: A Peerless Region for the Sportsman, Canoeist, Camper.* Montreal: Grand Trunk Railway, 1908.

Grey Owl. *Pilgrims of the Wild.* London: Lovat Dickson and Thompson, 1935.

The Guide. "The Lure of Northern Ontario: A Canoe Trip in Temagami." *Rod and Gun* 16,12 (May 1915): 1207-8.

Gummer, Raymond. "The Still Small Voice." *Rod and Gun* 10,8 (January 1909): 710-11.

Johnson, Joseph R. "Some Delights of Camping Out." *Busy Man's Magazine* 16,3 (July 1908): 124-28.

Jones, W.M. *Sport and Pleasure in the Virgin Wilds of Canada on Lakes Temiskaming, Temagaming.* Ottawa: Mortimer, 1899.

K. K. K. "Spring's Unrest." *Rod and Gun* 7,12 (May 1906): 1380-81.

Lee, George W. "Ontario's Railway, Owned by Province, Run by Commission." *Toronto Globe,* 3 January 1928, 27.

McKenzie, Donald. Recorded Interview. Land Use and Resource Management Research Box 3, C-10. Temagami First Nation Band Office, 22 November 1973 and 17 December 1973.

Me. "Biff and Hec and Me." *Rod and Gun* 16,6 (November 1914): 569-77.

New Liskeard Speaker, "Oddfellows Have Glorious Trip," 3 August 1906, 1.

Norris, J.M. "Fishing in Beautiful Temagami District: An Earthly Paradise." *Rod and Gun* 10,8 (January 1909): 696-703.

"Northern Ontario's Timber Resources." *Canadian Forestry Journal* 9,12 (December 1913): 181-83.

Ontario. Department of Crown Lands. *Annual Reports of the Clerk of Forestry.* Toronto, 1896-1904. Archives of Ontario, Toronto, film B97.

–. Department of Crown Lands. Assistant Commissioner of Crown Lands Memoranda. Archives of Ontario, Toronto, RG 1-68-0.

–. Department of Crown Lands. Crown Lands Survey Correspondence regarding Contentious Survey Projects. Archives of Ontario, Toronto, RG 1-273-3.

–. Department of Crown Lands. Lake Temagami Island Leases. Archives of Ontario, Toronto, RG 1-165-1.

–. Department of Crown Lands. *Report of the Survey and Exploration of Northern Ontario, 1900.* Toronto: L.K. Cameron, 1901.

–. Department of Crown Lands. *Woods and Forests Branch Report Books*, 1851-1936. Archives of Ontario, Toronto, RG 1-545-1.

–. Department of Crown Lands. "Woods and Forests Branch Timber Scrapbooks," 1844-1911. Archives of Ontario, Toronto, RG 1-549-0.

–. Fur Trade Collection. Archives of Ontario, Toronto, F 431.

–. Ministry of Aboriginal Affairs Archives, Toronto, files 186217, 7970.

"Ontario Forest Reserves." *Rod and Gun* 4,9 (February 1903): 331-32.

"The Ontario Government and the Lake Temagami Islands." *Rod and Gun* 7,4 (September 1905): 406.

"Our Medicine Bag." *Rod and Gun* 4,11 (April 1903): 409, 411.

"Our Medicine Bag." *Rod and Gun* 9,2 (July 1907): 202-3.

"Our Medicine Bag." *Rod and Gun* 13,6 (November 1911): 736.

Parkinson, Matthew. "Lake Timagami: A Northern Ontario Playground." *Canadian Magazine* 43,2 (June 1914): 167-72.

Paul, Aleck. Speech recorded by Frank Speck. Land Use and Resource Management Research Box 3, C-17. Temagami First Nation Band Office, 1913.

Potts, Gary. "Report to Band Members on the Land Claim." 1970s Land Claim Box. Temagami First Nation Band Office, c. February 1975.

Raney, Fraser. "Canoe Trips in Temagami." *Rod and Gun* 12,2 (July 1910): 186-93.

Robson, W.T. "The Value of the Tourist Sportsman as a Means of Publicity for Undeveloped Country." *Rod and Gun* 12,11 (April 1911): 1466-67.

"Royal Proclamation of 7 October 1763." In *British Royal Proclamations Relating to America*, ed. Clarence S. Brigham, 212-18. Worcester, MA: American Antiquarian Society, 1911.

Ruddy, Anna C. "A Gentleman of Temagami." *Canadian Magazine* 29,6 (October 1907): 544-47.

Sangster, S.E. "The Woods Indian." *Busy Man's Magazine* 24,4 (August 1912): 122–28.

Schubart, R.E. "A Moose Hunt at Wabigoon, Ontario." *Rod and Gun* 13,3 (August 1911): 289-92.

Shaw, W.F. "The Forest Wealth of Ontario: A Scheme for Its Perpetuation." *Rod and Gun* 7,8 (January 1906): 856-58.

Speck, Frank G. *Family Hunting Territories and Social Life of Various Algonkian Bands of the Ottawa Valley.* Memoir 70, no. 8, Anthropological Series. Ottawa: Department of Mines, Geological Survey of Canada, 1915.

St. Croix. "An Exploration to the Height of Land." Part 3. *Rod and Gun* 3,7 (December 1901): 8-9, 11-13.

–. "Second Sight and the Indian." *Rod and Gun* 4,3 (August 1902): 103-4.

Stewart, Elihu. "The Approaching Timber Famine." Canadian Magazine 22,1 (November 1903): 19-22.

Teme-Augama Anishnabai. "Teme-Augama Anishnabai, Deep Water People." 1980-1995 Land Claim Negotiations Box. Temagami First Nation Band Office, 1989.

Thurston, W.H. "Two Weeks in Paradise: Being a True Narrative of a Visit Paid Thereto by Three Worthy and Care-Free Mortals." *Rod and Gun* 11,12 (May 1910): 1133-36.

"Timagami, Mississagua, French River and That Sort of Thing." *Rod and Gun* 6,11 (April 1905): 585-98.

T. J. T. "Two Weeks in Temagami." *Outdoor Canada* 6,1 (February 1910): 18-20.

Toronto Daily Star, "Enthusiastic over Lake Temagami," 7 June 1906, 11.

–, "The Exploration of Northern Ontario," 16 May 1900, 3.

–, "One Hundred Miles in a Canoe," 19 August 1904, 5.

–, "Ontario: A Field for the Settler, the Miner, the Lumberman, and Tourist," 23 June 1905, 28.

–, "Rail Mill in New Ontario," 4 March 1904, 1.

–, "Temagami, Mecca of Sportsmen," 23 June 1905, 29.

Toronto Globe, "Anglers Enjoy Timagami," 15 June 1934, 13.

–, "Attractions of Temagami Never Lose Their Charm for Eager Vacationists," 2 July 1934, 11.

–, "Lost from Civilization in 3 Million Acres of Forest," advertisement, 16 June 1928, 19.

–, "Means Millions: Eastern Outlet from Temiscamingue for Ottawa Lumbermen," 13 June 1899, 4.

–, "New Ontario Prepares Its Program," 20 May 1912, 10.

–, "North Road Reveals Fine Scenic Glories of Forest Reserve," 7 June 1927, 11.

–, "Northland Notes of Summer Travel," 19 August 1905, 16.

–, "Primeval Beauty at Lake Temagami," 12 June 1906, 10.

–, "Scotch Indians of Temagami," 10 October 1903, 15.

–, "Survey of Temagami Islands," 18 February 1904, 8.

–, "Temagami," 13 June 1905, 9.

–, "Temiskaming and Northern Ontario Railway," advertisement, 3 January 1929, 27.

–, "To Temagami in through Pullman Sleeper Daily," Grand Trunk Railway advertisement, 10 July 1905, 7.

–, "Two Townships Less in Forest Reserve," 1 March 1912, 9.

–, "The Wonderland of the Dominion," 3 August 1907, 4.

–, "A World Apart," advertisement, 12 August 1929, 5.

Trails in Time. "Traditional Land Use and Resource Management Philosophies and Practices of the Temagami Aboriginal People: Teme-Augama Anishnabai, Temagami First Nation, Ontario Native Affairs Secretariat Joint Project." Land Use and Resource Management Research Box 1, A-0. Temagami First Nation Band Office, 2001.

Wadsworth, W.R. "With Rifle and Rod in the Moose Lands of Northern Ontario." Part
    1. *Canadian Magazine* 13,2 (June 1899): 149-57.
Walton, Ella. "A Woman's Views on Camping Out." *Rod and Gun* 1,4 (September 1899):
    72-74.
"Why We Take to the Woods." *Rod and Gun* 13,5 (October 1911): 560.
Wilson, Robert. "A Land of Enchantment." *Rod and Gun* 13,11 (April 1912): 1292-98.
Yeigh, Frank. "Touring in Temagami Land." *Rod and Gun* 8,5 (October 1906): 324-27.

                              SECONDARY SOURCES

Abele, Frances, and Daiva Stasiulis. "Canada as a 'White Settler Colony': What about
    Natives and Immigrants?" In *The New Canadian Political Economy,* ed. Wallace Clement
    and Glen Williams, 240-77. Montreal/Kingston: McGill-Queen's University Press,
    1989.
Agyeman, Julian, Peter Cole, Randolph Haluza-DeLay, and Pat O'Riley, eds. *Speaking for
    Ourselves: Environmental Justice in Canada.* Vancouver: UBC Press, 2009.
Ahmed, Sara. *Strange Encounters: Embodied Others in Post-Coloniality.* London: Routledge,
    2000.
Allen, Gene. "Ministry Wants Freeze on Temagami Logging." *Toronto Globe and Mail,* 21
    November 1989, A1, A2.
Anderson, Benedict. *Imagined Communities: Reflections on the Origin and Spread of
    Nationalism.* 1983. Reprint, London: Verso, 1991.
Anderson, Kay. "Culture and Nature at the Adelaide Zoo: At the Frontiers of 'Human'
    Geography." *Transactions of the Institute of British Geographers* 20,3 (1995): 275-94.
–. *Race and the Crisis of Humanism.* London: Routledge, 2007.
Anderson, Kim, and Bonita Lawrence, eds. *Strong Women Stories: Native Vision and
    Community Survival.* Toronto: Sumach Press, 2003.
Angus, James T. "How the Dokis Indians Protected Their Timber." *Ontario History* 81,3
    (1989): 181-99.
Armstrong, Jeannette. *Slash.* Penticton, BC: Theytus Books, 1985.
Asch, Michael. *Home and Native Land: Aboriginal Rights and the Canadian Constitution.*
    Scarborough: Nelson Canada, 1988.
Back, Brian. "Endangered Ecosystem: Wakimika Triangle, World's Largest Old Growth
    Red and White Pine Stand." http://www.ottertooth.com.
Backhouse, Constance. *Colour-Coded: A Legal History of Racism in Canada, 1900–1950.*
    Toronto: Osgoode Society for Canadian Legal History and University of Toronto Press,
    1999.
–. *Petticoats and Prejudice: Women and the Law in 19th Century Canada.* Toronto: Women's
    Press, 1991.
Balibar, Etienne. "The Nation Form: History and Ideology." In Essed and Goldberg, *Race
    Critical Theories,* 220-30.
Bannerji, Himani. *The Dark Side of the Nation: Essays on Multiculturalism, Nationalism
    and Gender.* Toronto: Canadian Scholar's Press, 2000.
–. "Geography Lessons: On Being an Insider/Outsider to the Canadian Nation." In
    Dangerous Territories: Struggles for Difference and Equality, ed. Leslie Roman and Linda
    Eyre, 23-41. New York: Routledge, 1997.
Bell, Catherine. "New Directions in the Law of Aboriginal Rights." *Canadian Bar Review*
    77,1 and 2 (1998): 36-72.

Benidickson, Jamie. "Idleness, Water, and a Canoe: Canadian Recreational Paddling between the Wars." In *Nastawgan: The Canadian North by Canoe and Snowshoe,* ed. Bruce W. Hodgins and Margaret Hobbs, 163-82. Toronto: Betelgeuse, 1985.

Berger, Carl. *The Sense of Power: Studies in the Ideas of Canadian Imperialism, 1867-1914.* Toronto: University of Toronto Press, 1970.

–. "The True North Strong and Free." In *Nationalism in Canada,* ed. Peter Russell, 3-26. Toronto: McGraw Hill, 1966.

Berlant, Lauren. *The Anatomy of National Fantasy: Hawthorne, Utopia, and Everyday Life.* Chicago: University of Chicago Press, 1991.

Beyers, Joanna M., and L. Anders Sandberg. "Canadian Federal Forest Policy: Present Initiatives and Historical Constraints." In *Sustainability, the Challenge: People, Power, and the Environment,* ed. L. Anders Sandberg and Sverker Sörlin, 99-107. Montreal: Black Rose Books, 1998.

Bhabha, Homi. "DissemiNation: Time, Narrative, and the Margins of the Modern Nation." In Homi Bhabha, *Nation and Narration,* 291-322. London: Routledge, 1990.

Blunt, Alison. *Travel, Gender, and Imperialism: Mary Kingsley and West Africa.* New York: Guilford Press, 1994.

Boag, Peter. "Thinking Like Mount Rushmore: Sexuality and Gender in the Republican Landscape." In *Seeing Nature through Gender,* ed. Virginia J. Scharff, 40-59. Lawrence: University Press of Kansas, 2003.

Bolaria, B. Singh, and Peter S. Li. *Racial Oppression in Canada.* Toronto: Garamond Press, 1985.

Boldt, Menno, and J. Anthony Long, eds. *The Quest for Justice: Aboriginal Peoples and Aboriginal Rights.* Toronto: University of Toronto Press, 1985.

Bordo, Jonathan. "Jack Pine: Wilderness Sublime or the Erasure of the Aboriginal Presence from the Landscape." *Journal of Canadian Studies* 27,4 (1992): 98-128.

Braun, Bruce. "BC Seeing/Seeing BC: Vision and Visuality on Canada's West Coast." In Braun, *The Intemperate Rainforest,* 156-212.

–. *The Intemperate Rainforest: Nature, Culture, and Power on Canada's West Coast.* Minneapolis: University of Minnesota Press, 2002.

–. "'Saving Clayoquot': Wilderness and the Politics of Indigeneity." In Braun, *The Intemperate Rainforest,* 66-108.

Braun, Bruce, and Noel Castree, eds. *Remaking Reality.* London: Routledge, 1998.

Bray, Matt, and Ashley Thomson, eds. *Temagami: A Debate on Wilderness.* Toronto: Dundurn Press, 1990.

Brown, Wendy. *Regulating Aversion: Tolerance in the Age of Identity and Empire.* Princeton: Princeton University Press, 2006.

Burton, Antoinette. *Burdens of History: British Feminists, Indian Women, and Imperial Culture, 1865–1915.* Chapel Hill: University of North Carolina Press, 1994.

Butler, Judith. *Bodies That Matter: On the Discursive Limits of "Sex."* New York: Routledge, 1993.

–. "Sexual Inversions." In *Feminist Interpretations of Michel Foucault,* ed. Susan J. Hekman, 59-75. University Park: Pennsylvania State University Press, 1996.

Butvin, Marnie, and Denise Sirois, eds. *Emily Carr: New Perspectives on a Canadian Icon.* Vancouver: National Gallery of Canada, Vancouver Art Gallery, and Douglas and McIntyre, 2006.

Campbell, Claire Elizabeth. *Shaped by the West Wind: Nature and History in Georgian Bay.* Vancouver: UBC Press, 2005.

Canada. *Report of the Royal Commission on Aboriginal Peoples.* Vol. 1, *Looking Forward, Looking Back.* Ottawa: Canada Communications Group, 1996.

Carr, Edward Hallett. *What Is History?* Harmondsworth, UK: Pelican Books, 1964.

Carter, Sarah. "Transnational Perspectives on the History of Great Plains Women: Gender, Race, Nations, and the Forty-Ninth Parallel." *American Review of Canadian Studies* 33,4 (Winter 2003): 565-96.

Castree, Noel, and Bruce Braun, eds. *Social Nature: Theory, Practice, and Politics.* Oxford: Blackwell, 2001.

Churchill, Kristopher. "Learning about Manhood: Gender Ideals and 'Manly Camping.'" In *Using Wilderness: Essays on the Evolution of Youth Camping in Ontario,* ed. Bruce W. Hodgins and Bernadine Dodge, 5-27. Peterborough, ON: Frost Centre for Canadian Heritage and Development Studies, 1992.

Clark, Bruce. *Indian Title in Canada.* Toronto: Carswell, 1987.

–. *Justice in Paradise.* Montreal/Kingston: McGill-Queen's University Press, 1999.

Coombe, Rosemary J. "Room for Manoeuver: Toward a Theory of Practice in Critical Legal Studies." *Law and Social Inquiry* 14,1 (1989): 69-121.

Cronon, William. "A Place for Stories: Nature, History, and Narrative." *Journal of American History* 78,4 (March 1992): 1347-76.

–. "The Trouble with Wilderness: Or, Getting Back to the Wrong Nature." In Cronon, *Uncommon Ground,* 69-90.

–. *Uncommon Ground: Rethinking the Human Place in Nature.* New York: Norton, 1996.

Crosby, Alfred W. *Ecological Imperialism: The Biological Expansion of Europe, 900-1900.* Cambridge: Cambridge University Press, 2004.

Crosby, Marcia. "Construction of the Imaginary Indian." In *Vancouver Anthology,* ed. Stan Douglas, 267-91. Vancouver: Talonbooks, 1991.

Cruikshank, Julie. *Do Glaciers Listen? Local Knowledge, Colonial Encounters, and Social Imagination.* Vancouver: UBC Press, 2005.

Culhane, Dara. "The Great Chain of Precedent." In Culhane, *The Pleasure of the Crown,* 61-71.

–. *The Pleasure of the Crown: Anthropology, Law and First Nations.* Vancouver: Talon Books, 1998.

Davin, Anna. "Imperialism and Motherhood." *History Workshop Journal* 5 (Spring 1978): 9-65.

Delaney, David. "Making Nature/Marking Humans: Law as a Site of (Cultural) Production." *Annals of the Association of American Geographers* 91,3 (2001): 487-503.

Deloria, Philip J. "Natural Indians and Identities of Modernity." In Philip J. Deloria, *Playing Indian,* 95-127. New Haven: Yale University Press, 1998.

Dickason, Olive Patricia. "Canada When Europeans Arrived." In Dickason, *Canada's First Nations,* 44-64.

–. *Canada's First Nations: A History of Founding Peoples from Earliest Times.* New York: Oxford University Press, 2002.

Dickson, Lovat. *Wilderness Man: The Strange Story of Grey Owl.* Toronto: Macmillan, 1973.

Dua, Enakshi. "Racializing Imperial Canada: Indian Women and the Making of Ethnic Communities." In *Gender, Sexuality and Colonial Modernities,* ed. Antoinette Burton, 119-33. London: Routledge, 1999.

Dua, Enakshi, and Angela Robertson, eds. *Scratching the Surface: Canadian Anti-Racist Feminist Thought.* Toronto: Women's Press, 1999.

Earthroots. "How You Can Help Protect Temagami." http://www.earthroots.org.

Emery, George. *A Young Man's Benefit: The Independent Order of Odd Fellows and Sickness Insurances in the United States and Canada, 1860-1929.* Montreal/Kingston: McGill-Queen's University Press, 1999.

Essed, Philomena, and David Theo Goldberg, eds. *Race Critical Theories: Text and Context.* Malden, MA: Blackwell, 2002.

Fortune, Joel R. "Constructing *Delgamuukw:* Legal Arguments, Historical Argumentation, and the Philosophy of History." *University of Toronto Faculty of Law Review* 51,1 (1993): 80-117.

Foucault, Michel. *The Archaeology of Knowledge.* 1969. Reprint, London: Tavistock, 1972.

–. "The Discourse on Language." In Michel Foucault, *The Archaeology of Knowledge and the Discourse on Language,* 215-37. New York: Pantheon, 1972.

–. "Nietzsche, Genealogy, History." In *The Foucault Reader,* ed. Paul Rabinow, 76-100. New York: Pantheon Books, 1984.

Furniss, Elizabeth. *The Burden of History: Colonialism and the Frontier Myth in a Rural Canadian Community.* Vancouver: UBC Press, 1999.

Gillis, R. Peter. "The Ottawa Lumber Barons and the Conservation Movement, 1880-1914." *Journal of Canadian Studies* 9,1 (February 1974): 14-29.

Gillis, R. Peter, and Thomas R. Roach. *Lost Initiatives: Canada's Forest Industries, Forest Policy, and Forest Conservation.* New York: Greenwood, 1986.

"Great Ontario Outdoor Adventures: Signature Landscapes." http://www.ontariooutdoor.com.

Grewal, Inderpal. *Home and Harem: Nation, Gender, Empire and the Cultures of Travel.* Durham, NC: Duke University Press, 1996.

Guha, Ramachandra. "Radical American Environmentalism: A Third World Critique." *Environmental Ethics* 11 (1989): 71-83.

Hage, Ghassan. *White Nation: Fantasies of White Supremacy in a Multicultural Society.* Annandale, Australia: Pluto Press, 1998.

Hall, Tony. "Where Justice Lies: Aboriginal Rights and Wrongs in Temagami." In Bray and Thomson, *Temagami,* 223-53.

Haraway, Donna J. *Primate Visions: Gender, Race, and Nation in the World of Modern Science.* New York: Routledge, 1989.

–. "The Promises of Monsters: A Regenerative Politics for Inappropriate/d Others." In *Cultural Studies,* ed. Lawrence Grossberg, Cary Nelson, and Paula Treichler, 295-337. London: Routledge, 1992.

–. *Simians, Cyborgs and Women: The Reinvention of Nature.* New York: Routledge, 1991.

Harris, Cole. *Making Native Space: Colonialism, Resistance, and Reserves in British Columbia.* Vancouver: UBC Press, 2002.

Hart, Jonathan, and Richard W. Bauman, eds. *Explorations in Difference: Law, Culture and Politics.* Toronto: University of Toronto Press, 1996.

Hawkins, Freda. *Critical Years in Immigration: Canada and Australia Compared.* Montreal/Kingston: McGill-Queen's University Press, 1989.

Henderson, James Youngblood. *First Nations Jurisprudence and Aboriginal Rights.* Saskatoon: University of Saskatchewan, Native Law Centre, 2006.

–. *Treaty Rights in the Constitution of Canada.* Toronto: Thomson/Carswell, 2007.

Hodgins, Bruce. *Paradis of Temagami: The Story of Charles Paradis, 1848-1926, Northern Priest, Colonizer and Rebel.* Cobalt, ON: Highway Book Shop, 1976.

–. "The Temagami Blockades of 1989: Personal Reflections." In Hodgins, Lischke, and McNab, *Blockades and Resistance*, 23-29.

Hodgins, Bruce W., and Jamie Benidickson. "Recreation and the Temagami Wilderness." In Hodgins and Benidickson, *The Temagami Experience*, 177-209.

–. *The Temagami Experience: Recreation, Resources, and Aboriginal Rights in the Northern Ontario Wilderness.* Toronto: University of Toronto Press, 1989.

Hodgins, Bruce W., R. Peter Gillis, and Jamie Benidickson. "The Ontario Experiments in Forest Reserves." In *Changing Parks: The History, Future and Cultural Context of Parks and Heritage Landscapes*, ed. John S. Marsh and Bruce W. Hodgins, 77-93. Toronto: Natural Heritage, 1998.

Hodgins, Bruce W., Shawn Heard, and John S. Milloy, eds. *Co-Existence? Studies in Ontario-First Nations Relations.* Peterborough, ON: Frost Centre for Canadian Heritage and Development Studies, 1992.

Hodgins, Bruce W., Ute Lischke, and David T. McNab, eds. *Blockades and Resistance: Studies in Actions of Peace and the Temagami Blockades of 1988-89.* Waterloo: Wilfrid Laurier University Press, 2003.

Holland, Patrick, and Graham Huggan. *Tourists with Typewriters: Critical Reflections on Contemporary Travel Writing.* Ann Arbor: University of Michigan Press, 1998.

Hunt, Alan. "Foucault's Expulsion of Law: Toward a Retrieval." *Law and Social Inquiry* 17,1 (1992): 1-38.

Hunt, Alan, and Gary Wickham. *Foucault and Law: Toward a New Sociology of Law as Governance.* Boulder: Westview Press, 1996.

Hutchinson, Allan C. *Evolution and the Common Law.* Cambridge: Cambridge University Press, 2005.

Indian and Northern Affairs Canada, "Fact Sheet: The Nisga'a Treaty." http://www.ainc-inac.gc.ca.

Jacoby, Karl. *Crimes against Nature: Squatters, Poachers, Thieves, and the Hidden History of American Conservation.* Berkeley: University of California Press, 2001.

Jakubowski, Lisa Marie. *Immigration and the Legalization of Racism.* Halifax: Fernwood, 1997.

Jasen, Patricia. *Wild Things: Nature, Culture, and Tourism in Ontario, 1790-1914.* Toronto: University of Toronto Press, 1995.

Jenish, D'Arcy. "Mapman of Temagami." *Legion Magazine*, 1 May 2006. http://www.legionmagazine.com.

Just, Peter. "History, Power, Ideology and Culture: Current Directions in the Anthropology of Law." *Law and Society Review* 26,2 (1992): 373-412.

Kaufmann, Eric. "'Naturalizing the Nation': The Rise of Naturalistic Nationalism in the United States and Canada." *Comparative Studies in Society and History* 40,4 (1998): 666-95.

Killan, Gerald. "The Development of a Wilderness Park System in Ontario, 1967-1990: Temagami in Context." In Bray and Thomson, *Temagami*, 85-120.

–. *Protected Places: A History of Ontario's Provincial Parks System.* Toronto: Dundurn Press, 1993.

King, Thomas. "You're Not the Indian I Had in Mind." In Thomas King, *The Truth about Stories: A Native Narrative*, 31-60. Toronto: House of Anansi, 2003.

Knight, Rolf. *Indians at Work: An Informal History of Native Indian Labour in British Columbia.* Vancouver: New Star Books, 1996.

Kuhlberg, Mark. *One Hundred Rings and Counting: Forestry Education and Forestry in Toronto and Canada, 1907-2007.* Toronto: University of Toronto Press, 2009.

Kulchyski, Peter, ed. *Unjust Relations: Aboriginal Rights in Canadian Courts.* Toronto: Oxford University Press, 1994.

Lambert, Richard S., and Paul Pross. *Renewing Nature's Wealth: A Centennial History of the Public Management of Lands, Forests and Wildlife in Ontario, 1763-1967.* [Toronto?]: Hunter Rose Company for the Ontario Department of Lands and Forests, 1967.

Laronde, Mary. "Co-Management of Lands and Resources in n'Daki Menan." In *Rebirth: Political, Economic, and Social Development in First Nations,* ed. Anne-Marie Mawhiney, 93-106. Toronto: Dundurn Press, 1993.

Lawrence, Bonita. *"Real" Indians and Others: Mixed-Blood Urban Native Peoples and Indigenous Nationhood.* Vancouver: UBC Press, 2004.

Lawrence, Bonita, and Enakshi Dua. "Decolonizing Antiracism." *Social Justice* 32,4 (2005): 120-43.

Lawson, James. "Environmental Interests and the Forest Products Industry in Temagami and Algonquin Park." PhD diss., York University, 2001.

Lawson, Jamie. "Nastawgan or Not? First Nations' Land Management in Temagami and Algonquin Park." In *Sustainability, the Challenge: People, Power and the Environment,* ed. L. Anders Sandberg and Sverker Sörlin, 189-201. Montreal: Black Rose Books, 1998.

Lawson, Jamie, Marcelo Levy, and L. Anders Sandberg. "'Perpetual Revenues and the Delights of the Primitive': Change, Continuity, and Forest Policy Regimes in Ontario." In *Canadian Forest Policy: Adapting to Change,* ed. Michael Howlett, 279-315. Toronto: University of Toronto Press, 2001.

Layoun, Mary. *Wedded to the Land? Gender, Boundaries, and Nationalism-in-Crisis.* Durham, NC: Duke University Press, 2000.

Lazarus-Black, Mindy, and Susan F. Hirsch, eds. *Contested States: Law, Hegemony and Resistance.* New York: Routledge, 1994.

Leask, Nigel. *Curiosity and the Aesthetics of Travel Writing.* Oxford: Oxford University Press, 2002.

Loo, Tina. "Of Moose and Men: Hunting for Masculinities in British Columbia, 1880-1939." *Western Historical Quarterly* 32 (Autumn 2001): 296-319.

–. *States of Nature: Conserving Canada's Wildlife in the Twentieth Century.* Vancouver: UBC Press, 2006.

Loo, Tina, and Lorna R. McLean, eds. *Historical Perspectives on Law and Society in Canada.* Toronto: Copp Clark Longman, 1994.

Lovell, M.R. "Penn Professor's Discovery Confounds Indian 'History.'" *Philadelphia Public Ledger,* 23 November 1913, mag. sec.

Lower, A.R.M. *Settlement and the Forest Frontier in Eastern Canada.* Toronto: Macmillan of Canada, 1936.

Mackay, Donald. *Heritage Lost: The Crisis in Canada's Forests.* Toronto: Macmillan of Canada, 1985.

Mackey, Eva. "Death by Landscape: Race, Nature, and Gender in Canadian Nationalist Mythology." *Canadian Woman Studies* 20,2 (2000): 125-30.

–. *The House of Difference: Cultural Politics and National Identity in Canada.* London: Routledge, 1999.

Macklem, Patrick. *Indigenous Difference and the Constitution of Canada.* Toronto: University of Toronto Press, 2001.

Mawani, Renisa. *Colonial Proximities: Crossracial Encounters and Juridical Truths in British Columbia, 1871-1921.* Vancouver: UBC Press, 2009.

–. "Genealogies of the Land: Aboriginality, Law, and Territory in Vancouver's Stanley Park." *Social and Legal Studies* 14,3 (2005): 315-40.

McClintock, Anne. *Imperial Leather: Gender, Race and Sexuality in the Colonial Contest.* New York: Routledge, 1995.

McNab, David T. *No Place for Fairness: Indigenous Land Rights and Policy in the Bear Island Case and Beyond.* Montreal/Kingston: McGill-Queen's University Press, 2009.

–. "'We Hardly Have Any Idea of Such Bargains': Teme-Augama Anishnabai Title and Land Rights." In David T. McNab, *Circles of Time: Aboriginal Land Rights and Resistance in Ontario,* 45-74. Waterloo: Wilfrid Laurier University Press, 1999.

McNeil, Kent. "The High Cost of Accepting Benefits from the Crown: A Comment on the Temagami Indian Land Case." *Canadian Native Law Reporter* 1 (1992): 40-69.

–. "The Temagami Indian Land Claim: Loosening the Judicial Strait-Jacket." In Bray and Thomson, *Temagami,* 185-221.

Miles, Robert, and Malcolm Brown. *Racism.* London: Routledge, 1989.

Mills, Sara. *Discourse.* 1997. Reprint, London: Routledge, 2004.

–. *Discourses of Difference: An Analysis of Women's Travel Writing and Colonialism.* London: Routledge, 1991.

–. *Michel Foucault.* London: Routledge, 2003.

Montrose, Louis. "The Work of Gender in the Discourse of Discovery." *Representations* 33 (1991): 1-41.

Monture-Angús, Patricia. *Journeying Forward: Dreaming First Nations' Independence.* Halifax: Fernwood, 1999.

Moore, Donald S., Jake Kosek, and Anand Pandian, eds. *Race, Nature, and the Politics of Difference.* Durham, NC: Duke University Press, 2003.

Moray, Gerta. *Unsettling Encounters: First Nations Imagery in the Art of Emily Carr.* Vancouver: UBC Press, 2006.

Nelles, H.V. *The Politics of Development: Forests, Mines and Hydro-Electric Power in Ontario, 1849-1941.* Toronto: Macmillan, 1974.

Ontario. *Summary of the Long Term Management Direction, Temagami Crown Management Unit (898), 2009-2019 Forest Management Plan.* http://www.earthroots.org. Webpage now discontinued.

–. *Temagami Integrated Planning: Background Information.* N.p.: Queen's Printer, 2005.

–. *Temagami Integrated Planning: Management Options Workbook.* N.p.: Queen's Printer, 2006.

Parenteau, Bill, and James Kenny. "Survival, Resistance, and the Canadian State: The Transformation of New Brunswick's Native Economy, 1867-1930." *Journal of the Canadian Historical Association* 13,1 (2002): 49-71.

Perry, Adele. *On the Edge of Empire: Gender, Race, and the Making of British Columbia, 1849-1871.* Toronto: University of Toronto Press, 2001.

Philip, M. Nourbese, Hiren Mistry, Geoffrey Chan, and Kevin Modeste. "Fortress in the Wilderness: A Conversation about Land." *Borderlines* 45 (1997): 20-25.

Pierson, Ruth Roach, and Nupur Chaudhuri, eds. *Nation, Empire, Colony: Historicizing Gender and Race.* Bloomington: Indiana University Press, 1998.

Potts, Gary. "The Battle over Temagami." Radio interview by Dale Goldhawk. *As It Happens,* Canadian Broadcasting Corporation, 23 April 1990. http://archives.cbc.ca.

–. "Last-Ditch Defence of a Priceless Homeland." In *Drumbeat: Anger and Renewal in Indian Country,* ed. Boyce Richardson, 203-30. Toronto: Summerhill Press, 1989.

Poulantzas, Nicos. *State, Power, Socialism.* London: New Left Books, 1978.

Pratt, Mary Louise. *Imperial Eyes: Travel Writing and Transculturation.* London: Routledge, 1992.

Quinby, Peter A. "Temagami Old Growth Studies (1989-1992)." Ancient Forest Exploration and Research. http://www.ancientforest.org.

Rae, Bob. *From Protest to Power: Personal Reflections on a Life in Politics.* Toronto: McClelland and Stewart, 2006.

Raibmon, Paige. *Authentic Indians: Episodes of Encounter from the Late-Nineteenth-Century Northwest Coast.* Durham: Duke University Press, 2005.

Razack, Sherene. "Gendered Racial Violence and Spatialized Justice: The Murder of Pamela George." *Canadian Journal of Law and Society* 15,2 (2000): 91-130.

–. *Looking White People in the Eye: Gender, Race, and Culture in Courtrooms and Classrooms.* Toronto: University of Toronto Press, 1998.

–. "'Simple Logic': Race, the Identity Documents Rule and the Story of a Nation Besieged and Betrayed." *Journal of Law and Social Policy* 15 (2000): 183-211.

Rodgers, Andrew Denny. *Bernhard Eduard Fernow: A Story of North American Forestry.* Princeton: Princeton University Press, 1951.

Rosenberg, Gerald. *The Hollow Hope: Can Courts Bring about Social Change?* Chicago: University of Chicago Press, 1991.

Said, Edward. *Culture and Imperialism.* New York: Knopf, 1993.

–. *Orientalism.* New York: Pantheon, 1978.

Sandilands, Catriona. "Between the Local and the Global: Clayoquot Sound and Simulacral Politics." In *A Political Space: Reading the Global through Clayoquot Sound,* ed. Warren Magnusson and Karena Shaw, 139-67. Minneapolis: University of Minnesota Press, 2003.

–. "Ecological Integrity and National Narrative: Cleaning Up Canada's National Parks." *Canadian Woman Studies* 20,2 (2000): 137-42.

–. "Where the Mountain Men Meet the Lesbian Rangers: Gender, Nation, and Nature in the Rocky Mountain National Parks." In *This Elusive Land: Women and the Canadian Environment,* ed. Melody Hessing, Rebecca Raglon, and Catriona Sandilands, 142-62. Vancouver: UBC Press, 2005.

Sandlos, John. *Hunters at the Margin: Native People and Wildlife Conservation in the Northwest Territories.* Vancouver: UBC Press, 2007.

Satzewich, Vic, and Nikolaos Liodakis. *Race and Ethnicity in Canada: A Critical Introduction.* Toronto: Oxford University Press, 2007.

Scott, James C. "Nature and Space." In James C. Scott, *Seeing Like a State: How Certain Schemes to Improve the Human Condition Have Failed,* 11-52. New Haven: Yale University Press, 1998.

Scott, Joan Wallach, ed. *Feminism and History.* Oxford: Oxford University Press, 1996.

The Silent Enemy: An Epic of the American Indian. Directed by H.P. Carver, produced by W. Douglas Burden and William C. Chanler, written by W. Douglas Burden. N.p.: Burden-Chanler Productions, 1930.

Siley, Susan S. "Making a Place for Cultural Analyses of Law." *Law and Social Inquiry* 17,1 (1992): 39-48.

Sinclair, Pamela. *Temagami Lakes Association: An Historical Perspective.* Temagami: Temagami Lakes Association, 1992.

Slattery, Brian. *The Land Rights of Indigenous Canadian Peoples, as Affected by the Crown's Acquisition of Their Territories.* Saskatoon: University of Saskatchewan Native Law Centre, 1979.

–. "Making Sense of Aboriginal and Treaty Rights." *Canadian Bar Review* 79,2 (2000): 196-224.

–. "Understanding Aboriginal Rights." *Canadian Bar Review* 66,4 (1987): 727-83.

Smart, Carol. *Feminism and the Power of Law.* London: Routledge, 1994.

Smith, Donald B. *From the Land of the Shadows: The Making of Grey Owl.* Saskatoon: Western Producer Prairie Books, 1990.

Smith, Susan. "Immigration and Nation-Building in Canada and the United Kingdom." In *Constructions of Race, Place and Nation,* ed. Peter Jackson and Jan Penrose, 50-77. Minneapolis: University of Minnesota Press, 1993.

Soulé, Michael E., and Gary Lease, eds. *Reinventing Nature? Responses to Postmodern Deconstruction.* Washington, DC: Island Press, 1995.

Spears, Tom. "Temagami Indians Told to End Blockade." *Toronto Star,* 9 December 1988, A7.

Spurr, David. *The Rhetoric of Empire: Colonial Discourse in Journalism, Travel Writing, and Imperial Administration.* Durham, NC: Duke University Press, 1993.

Stasiulis, Daiva, and Radha Jhappan. "The Fractious Politics of a Settler Society: Canada." In *Unsettling Settler Societies: Articulations of Gender, Race, Ethnicity and Class,* ed. Daiva Stasiulis and Nira Yuval-Davis, 95-131. London: Sage, 1995.

Stoler, Ann Laura. *Race and the Education of Desire: Foucault's History of Sexuality and the Colonial Order of Things.* Durham, NC: Duke University Press, 1995.

Swift, Jamie. *Cut and Run: The Assault on Canada's Forests.* Toronto: Between the Lines, 1983.

TemagamiVacation.com. "Experience Temagami: Canoeing." http://www.temagami vacation.com.

–. "Experience Temagami: Provincial Parks in the Temagami Area." http://www.temagami vacation.com.

Teme-Augama Anishnabai. "The Native Dimension: Key Dates." In Bray and Thomson, *Temagami,* 147-51.

Temple, John. "Temagami: One Big Family's Quarrel." *Toronto Star,* 5 May 1988, A24.

Theriault, Madeline Katt. *Moose to Moccasins: The Story of Ka Kita Wa Pa No Kwe.* Toronto: Natural Heritage/Natural History, 1992.

Thobani, Sunera. *Exalted Subjects: Studies of the Making of Race and Nation in Canada.* Toronto: University of Toronto Press, 2007.

Thorpe, Jocelyn. "Temagami's Tangled Wild: Race, Gender and the Making of Canadian Nature." PhD diss., York University, 2008.

Urry, John. *The Tourist Gaze: Leisure and Travel in Contemporary Societies.* London: Sage, 1990.

Wall, Sharon. *The Nurture of Nature: Childhood, Antimodernism, and Ontario Summer Camps, 1920-55.* Vancouver: UBC Press, 2009.

–. "Totem Poles, Tepees, and Token Traditions: 'Playing Indian' at Camp." In Wall, *The Nurture of Nature,* 216-50.

Warecki, George M. *Protecting Ontario's Wilderness: A History of Changing Ideas and Preservation Politics, 1927-1973.* New York: Peter Lang, 2000.

Weaver, Adriel. "Salmon for Sale, Moose for Meat: Legal Constructions of Nature and
    Aboriginal Subjectivities." Master's major paper, York University, 2006.
Weaver, Jace. "From I-Hermeneutics to We-Hermeneutics: Native Americans and the
    Post-Colonial." In Jace Weaver, *Native American Religious Identity: Unforgotten Gods*,
    1-25. Maryknoll, NY: Orbis Books, 1998.
Weaver, John C. *The Great Land Rush and the Making of the Modern World, 1650-1900.*
    Montreal/Kingston: McGill-Queen's University Press, 2003.
Whatmore, Sarah. *Hybrid Geographies: Natures, Cultures, Spaces.* London: Sage, 2002.
Wilson, Alexander. *The Culture of Nature: North American Landscape from Disney to the
    Exxon Valdez.* Toronto: Between the Lines, 1991.
Yogis, John A. *Canadian Law Dictionary.* 1983. Reprint, New York: Barron's Educational
    Series, 2003.
Yuval-Davis, Nira. *Gender and Nation.* London: Sage, 1997.

Index

The letter *f* following a page number denotes a figure.

virgin forest, 64-65; wilderness, 24. *See also* Bear Island case; cautions

land ownership: British imperial perspective, 46; Constitution Act of 1867, 103; Ontario's case for, 103; race, 110, 115-16, 121; Royal Proclamation of 1763, 106-7, 109-10; Treaty of Paris (1763), 103. *See also* land rights

land rights: creation of Temagami Forest Reserve (TFR), 46-47, 52; forest conservationist discourse, 45; race, 11; removal of First Nations from "wilderness," 14; removal of title, 52; Supreme Court ruling (1991), 7. *See also* Aboriginal rights; land ownership; n'Daki Menan; Teme-Augama Anishnabai

land use: Austin Bay timber, 82-83; Bear Island rent request, 75, 80, 81, 82, 85; cautions, 93; development of Temagami, 28-29; fire protection, 49; forest reserves, 41; Forest Reserves Act (1898), 47-48; land stewardship, 31; land-use decisions, 76-77, 80; leasing to cottagers, 77-79; Maple Mountain resort, 93, 96; Ontario management plan, 126-27; power generation, 62; Teme-Augama Anishnabai philosophy on, 29-30, 31, 140*n*92; threats to timber resources, 48-49; use of land as proof of ownership, 103; verbal agreement on land use, 88; Wendaban Stewardship Authority (WSA), 140*n*91. *See also* cottagers; logging; mining; resource development; tourism

Lands and Forests, Department of: Bear Island, 87; Bear Island rent request, 80; name changes of, 153*n*7; preservation of landscape, 79, 84, 87; proposal for joint management of Temagami Forest Reserve (TFR), 88-90; on timber sales, 76-77. *See also* Crown Lands; Ministry of Natural Resources; Ontario

landscape painting, 22, 23, 75-76, 137*nn*62, 64, 138*n*69

language: First Nations, 5; race, 18; sustainable development, 140*n*92; of Teme-Augama Anishnabai, 100. *See also* discourse; naming

Lanoie, J.P., 86

Laronde, Mary, 26, 31, 140*n*91

Lawrence, Bonita, 24

Layoun, Mary, 19

legal discourse: as cultural process, 95; power of, 96

legal system. *See* Canadian legal system

legislation: Constitution Act, 1867, 37-38, 103; *Crown Timber Act*, 103; *Fire Act* (1878), 43; on immigration, 76; impact of forest conservation movement, 43; Indian Act, 102, 106, 131*n*1; *Mining Act*, 103, 110-11; *Public Lands Act*, 114. *See also* Forest Reserves Act

linguistics. *See* language

Linné, Carl, 12

Lismer, Arthur, 137*n*62

logging: encroachment on n'Daki Menan, 73; environmentalist efforts, 16-17; felling timber, 48; pulpwood licenses, 47, 48; Temagami Association, 79, 84-85, 154*n*22; in Temagami Forest Reserve (TFR), 76-77, 79-80; Teme-Augama Anishnabai concerns, 36-37, 47, 77; Teme-Augama Anishnabai road block, 122; tourism, 152*n*76. *See also* land use

logging (clear cutting): author's experience of, 6-7; no-cut shorelines, 62, 79, 85, 154*n*22, 155*n*52; skyline reserve, 79; tourist expectations, 62

Loo, Tina, 150*n*35

Macdonald, Craig: creation of map by, 30, 159*n*37; as non-Native witness, 104, 119, 120; testimony in Bear Island case, 100, 104, 139-40*n*84. *See also* maps

MacDonald, D.F., 38-39, 143*n*30

MacDonald, J.E.H., 137*n*62

Mackey, Eva, 20, 22

magazines. *See* newspapers and magazines

Mahoney, Patrick, 98, 159*n*29

Making Native Space (Harris), 17

Manitoulin Island event, 113

Maple Mountain, 93, 96, 152*n*76

maps: of n'Daki Menan, 100, 159*n*37; potential settlement land for reserve, 128f; Temagami Forest Reserve (TFR)

Printed and bound in Canada by Friesens

Set in Garamond by Artegraphica Design Co. Ltd.

Copy Editor: Deborah Kerr

Proofreader: Tara Tovell

Cartographer: Rajiv Rawat

Indexer: Natalie Boon